Cold War Analytical Structures and the Post Post-War World

PRAEGER SERIES IN POLITICAL COMMUNICATION
Robert E. Denton, Jr., *General Editor*

COLD WAR ANALYTICAL STRUCTURES AND THE POST POST-WAR WORLD

A Critique of Deterrence Theory

CORI ELIZABETH DAUBER

Praeger Series in Political Communication

Westport, Connecticut
London

Copyright Acknowledgments

The author and publisher gratefully acknowledge permission to quote the following:

Extracts from Stephen J. Cimbala, ed., *Strategic War Termination*, copyright © 1986 by Stephen J. Cimbala, Praeger Publishers, an imprint of Greenwood Publishing Group, Inc., Westport, CT. Reprinted with permission.

Extracts reprinted from a book by Stephen J. Cimbala and Joseph D. Douglass, Jr., eds., *Ending a Nuclear War: Are the Superpowers Prepared?* Published and permission by Pergamon-Brassey's International Defense Publishers, Inc. © 1988.

Extracts reprinted from *Gorbachev and His Generals: The Reform of Soviet Military Doctrine*, William Green and Theodore Karasik, eds., 1990, by permission of Westview Press, Boulder, Colorado.

Library of Congress Cataloging-in-Publication Data

Dauber, Cori Elizabeth.
    Cold war analytical structures and the post post-war world : a
critique of deterrence theory / Cori Elizabeth Dauber.
        p.   cm. — (Praeger series in political communication ; ISSN
1062–5623)
    Includes bibliographical references and index.
    ISBN: 0–275–94419–0
    1. Deterrence (Strategy) 2. Nuclear warfare. I. Title.
II. Series.
    U162.6.D38   1993
    355.02′17—dc20   92–28475

British Library Cataloguing in Publication Data is available.

Library of Congress Catalog Card Number: 92–28475
ISBN: 0–275–94419–0
ISSN: 1062–5623

First published in 1993

Praeger Publishers, 88 Post Road West, Westport, CT 06881
An imprint of Greenwood Publishing Group, Inc.

Printed in the United States of America

The paper used in this book complies with the Permanent
Paper Standard issued by the National Information Standards
Organization (Z39.48—1984).

10 9 8 7 6 5 4 3 2 1

For May Rocklin and Pauline Rocklin Dauber

Contents

About the Series

Those of us from the discipline of communication studies have long believed that communication is prior to all other fields of inquiry. In several other forums I have argued that the essence of politics is "talk" or human interaction.[1] Such interaction may be formal or informal, verbal or nonverbal, public or private, but it is always persuasive, forcing us consciously to interpret, to evaluate, and to act. Communication is the vehicle for human action.

From this perspective, it is not surprising that Aristotle recognized the natural kinship of politics and communication in his writings *Politics* and *Rhetoric*. In the former, he establishes that humans are "political beings [who] alone of the animals [are] furnished with the faculty of language."[2] And in the latter, he begins his systematic analysis of discourse by proclaiming that "rhetorical study, in its strict sense, is concerned with the modes of persuasion."[3] Thus, it was recognized more than 2,300 years ago that politics and communication go hand in hand because they are essential parts of human nature.

Back in 1981, Dan Nimmo and Keith Sanders proclaimed that political communication was an emerging field.[4] Although its origin, as noted, dates back centuries, a "self-consciously cross-disciplinary" focus began in the late 1950s. Thousands of books and articles later, colleges and universities offer a variety of graduate and undergraduate coursework in the area in such diverse departments as communication, mass communication, journalism, political science, and sociology.[5] In Nimmo and Sanders' early assessment, the "key areas of inquiry" included rhetorical analysis, propaganda analysis, attitude change studies, voting studies, government and the news media, functional and systems analyses, technological changes, media technologies, campaign techniques, and research techniques.[6] In a survey of the state of the field in 1983, the same authors and Lynda Kaid found additional, more specific areas of concern, such as the presidency, political polls, public opinion, debates, and advertising, to name a few.[7] Since the first study, they also noted a shift away from the rather strict behavioral approach.

Today, Dan Nimmo and David Swanson assert that "political communication has developed some identity as a more or less distinct domain of scholarly work."[8] The scope and concerns of the area have further expanded to include critical theories and cultural studies. While there is no precise definition, method, or disciplinary home of the area of inquiry, its primary domain is the role, processes, and effects of communication within the context of politics broadly defined.

In 1985, the editors of *Political Communication Yearbook; 1984* noted that "more things are happening in the study, teaching, and practice of political communication than can be captured within the space limitations of the relatively few publications available."[9] In addition, they argued that the backgrounds of "those involved in the field [are] so varied and pluralist in outlook and approach, ... it [is] a mistake to adhere slavisly to any set format in shaping the content."[10] And more recently, Swanson and Nimmo called for "ways of overcoming the unhappy consequences of fragmentation within a framework that respects, encourages, and benefits from diverse scholarly commitments, agendas, and approaches."[11]

In 1988, in agreement with these assessments of the area and with gentle encouragement, Praeger established the series entitled "Praeger Series in Political Communication." The series is open to all qualitative and quantitative methodologies as well as contemporary and historical studies. The key to characterizing the studies in the series is the focus on communication variables or activities within a political context or dimension. Scholars from the disciplines of communication, history, political science, and sociology have participated in the series.

Cori Dauber provides a fascinating and unique analysis of deterrence theories by applying methods of criticism from the study of rhetoric and argument. By focusing on the texts of the debate between two schools of thought, "Mutual Assured Destruction" and "warfighting," Professor Dauber explores the nature and development of deterrence theory. In essence, deterrence theories are best understood as "theories of state-to-state persuasion."

This book makes several important contributions to the study of political communication and to nuclear strategic doctrine. From a communication perspective, this study demonstrates the role and importance of symbolic structures in impacting national policies and actions. In addition to providing insight into the continuing debate over strategic defense issues, this study provides a new approach to the study of public policy. Finally, in this period of euphoria over our perceived victory of the Cold War and the emerging New World Order, now is the time to understand that era so we do not repeat the mistakes of the past.

I am, without shame or modesty, a fan of the series. The joy of serving as its editor is in participating in the dialogue of the field of political communication and in reading the contributors' works. I invite you to join me.

Robert E. Denton, Jr.

NOTES

1. See Robert E. Denton, Jr., *The Symbolic Dimensions of the American Presidency* (Prospect Heights, Il.: Waveland Press, 1982); Robert E. Denton, Jr., and Gary Woodward, *Political Communication in America* (New York: Praeger, 1985; 2nd Ed., 1990); Robert E. Denton, Jr., and Dan Hahn, *Presidential Communication* (New York: Praeger, 1986); and Robert E. Denton, Jr., *The Primetime Presidency of Ronald Reagan* (New York: Praeger, 1988).

2. Aristotle, *The Politics of Aristotle,* trans. Ernest Barker (New York: Oxford University Press, 1970), p. 5.

3. Aristotle, *Rhetoric,* trans. Rhys Roberts (New York: The Modern Library, 1954), p. 22.

4. Dan Nimmo and Keith Sanders, "Introduction: The Emergence of Political Communication as a Field," in *Handbook of Political Communication,* Dan Nimmo and Keith Sanders, eds. (Beverly Hills, Calif.: Sage, 1981), pp. 11–36.

5. Ibid., p. 15.

6. Ibid., pp. 17–27.

7. Keith Sanders, Lynda Kaid, and Dan Nimmo, eds. *Political Communication Yearbook: 1984* (Carbondale, Il.: Southern Illinois University Press: 1985), pp. 283–308.

8. Dan Nimmo and David Swanson, "The Field of Political Communication: Beyond the Voter Persuasion Paradigm," in *New Directions in Political Communication,* David Swanson and Dan Nimmo, eds. (Beverly Hills, Calif.: Sage, 1990), p. 8.

9. Sanders, Kaid, and Nimmo, p. xiv.

10. Ibid.

11. Nimmo and Swanson, p. 11.

Preface

This book was written over a period of several years. As the Cold War began to sputter to a close, I initially considered rewriting it as a historical study of the last few years of that period. However, as time went on, I realized that, in fact, the constructs I had examined in the original study were not only still operative, but were still dictating policy even after the dissolution of the Soviet Union and the perception of the Communist threat. Thus, although the first five chapters discuss specifics of a defense debate that is all but over, I believe this book is directly relevant to the way American defense policy will be structured in a post–Cold War world.

The debate over deterrence theory in the West has been determined to a large extent by the presence of nuclear weapons. The first five chapters examine the way that debate was played out in the mid–1980s, the last years in which the need to deter the nuclear arsenal of the Soviet Union served as the guiding light and primary purpose of the deterrence debate. Although the issues dealt with, such as whether or not to procure increasingly accurate Intercontinental Ballistic Missiles (ICBMs) have been rendered moot by the passage of time, this analysis still is worth while. For the full development of the argument that deterrence theory is a theory of persuasion is necessary for the argument made in Chapter 6 to make sense. It is in that chapter that the implications of the way this debate developed are fully examined. What becomes clear is that the assumptions of deterrence theory so constrained the debate over defense policy that other alternatives have been essentially squeezed out. The terms of debate were dictated by the single case of nuclear deterrence. As a result, our perspective on defense needs in a world without a Soviet Union is being determined by the same terms of debate. My goal is to examine those terms, so that the way they establish boundaries that may or may not be useful can be better understood.

I am immensely grateful for the help and advice of Charles Kauffman, David Zarefsky, and G. Thomas Goodnight of Northwestern University. Dr. Goodnight, and indeed the entire Goodnight family, went way beyond the call in bringing this project to fruition, opening their home to me and making sure I was fed on more occasions that I can count.

I have been involved in intercollegiate debate throughout the time I worked on this project, and for their support and encouragement I am grateful to the members and assistant coaches of the Northwestern Debate Society 1986–1987, the William Pitt Debating Union 1987–1990, and the UNC Debate Team 1990–1992, particularly Julie Arthur, Ben Attias, Scott Mayberry, Doni Reiter, Tom Goldstein, and Joy Rhyne.

When this book was almost completed, I had to stop work on it for prolonged periods because of a bad back. My colleagues at the University of North Carolina were tremendously supportive and helpful, and I would like to thank them, especially Dr. V. William Balthrop, who took over classes, graded papers, and did everything else I should have been doing until I was back on my feet. The people at Praeger, particularly Anne Kiefer, were incredibly patient and understanding, waiting more than a year for the completed manuscript.

Finally, my counterpart at Northwestern University, Scott Deatherage, has been an enormous help and has probably done more of the administrative work for this project than I have.

Chapter One

Introduction

For more than twenty years an intense debate has been waged in the West over the nature of deterrence and the requirements imposed on Western, particularly American, force structures by deterrence. Despite the commitment and intellectual rigor brought to the discussion by participants, and despite the truly stunning amount of material produced[1] there was still little hope of resolution in sight when the collapse of the Soviet Union permitted scholars to reconsider the entire debate. This is the case despite the recognition by numerous critics that deterrence theory was, by the mid–1980s, in a state of crisis. As one author noted:

The established framework of theories and policies about peace and security in the nuclear age has come under increasing challenge. This is a time for judgment. It is sometimes said that an age passes when its basic illusions crack. . . . Since the late 1970s, the golden age of nuclear deterrence, spawned by the ideas and technology of the cold war, has seemed to be cracking.[2]

By the mid–1980s, laypersons and experts alike throughout the Western alliance were increasingly dissatisfied with a structure that appeared to be bankrupting economies while offering little more than a perpetual risk of nuclear holocaust. What little consensus there was, was threatened by critiques of the entire deterrence enterprise and by simplistic attempts at offering escape, through calls for disarmament from the left, and grandiose proposals for eliminating the very need for deterrence via the erection of comprehensive defenses from the right.[3] This crisis was only exacerbated by the coming to power of a Soviet leader able to convince Western publics that there was in fact no threat left to counter.

This book provides a new way of examining the debate over nuclear force postures and strategic doctrine. While this new perspective cannot answer all questions, it can offer insights not otherwise available into the causes which underlie the crisis in deterrence theory, and suggestions for more appropriate and productive directions in future research.

One might well ask at this point why such an undertaking is worthwhile in an era of glasnost and democratization, where even the most hardened hawk is inclined to agree that the Cold War is over. Is not nuclear strategic doctrine in the U.S.-Soviet context little more than fodder for historians? I would argue that, to the contrary, now is precisely the time to take stock of the deterrence project in its entirety. This is the case for two reasons.

First, as both sides seek to disengage, to gradually build down their arsenals, there is widespread recognition that quantitative reductions, whether negotiated or unilaterally undertaken, must at all times be guided by criteria for establishing *stability*. Because of the way deterrence works, in other words, there is widespread acknowledgment that fewer weapons do not necessarily mean a safer world, even without an ongoing ideological dispute. The characteristics and structure of forces remaining must be assessed at qualitative as well as quantitative levels. But the only conceptual tools available to us for defining stability, and thus for determining appropriate guidelines for new, smaller forces, are the same conceptual tools that produced the original arsenals now slated for reduction: in short, deterrence theory manifested as nuclear strategic doctrine. The structure of the "New World Order" will therefore be born out of Cold War ways of thinking, for nothing new has developed to take their place. There is no other way of thinking about stability. Nuclear strategic doctrine is as much a part of our world today—and as worthy of study—as it was in the early years of the Reagan Administration.[4]

Even if one were to argue that the end of the Soviet Union meant that the relationship between the United States and the Commonwealth of Independent States had moved beyond deterrence,[5] there are other potential aggressors in the world, and other challenges to Western interests. Because there is no way to *prove* what "won" the Cold War, all sides in the deterrence debate will claim credit for victory. That, in turn, creates room for the claim to be made that the experience of the Cold War validates the applicability of various perspectives,[6] initiating a new debate which has the potential to last for years to come. Because all sides will draw the lessons from the Cold War most consistent with their own positions, we find ourselves today at a crossroads, when the debates of the last twenty years can be examined with a certain critical distance, even as they are becoming vitally important in new contexts.

ARGUMENT STUDIES

The analysis in this book, made possible through the application of contemporary understandings of argument to the existing debate over deterrence, is unique. It is also particularly appropriate for several reasons.

First, as a scholarly endeavour, the study of argument seeks to explore and understand the way reason giving is used to persuade.[7] Because persuasion often depends on the giving of reasons, on argument, the two are tightly linked. Human communication depends on the manipulation of symbols in order to produce meaning.[8] And symbols, even when they are nonverbal, are the means employed by advocates in order to make and defend arguments. In fact, many symbols compress arguments, but the entire argument remains, even if expressed implicitly.[9] Because deterrence theorists are seeking ways in which an opponent can be convinced—persuaded—to behave in certain ways (generally negative ways, i.e. to avoid certain activities) it is my argument that deterrence theories are at essence, and are best understood as, theories of state-to-state persuasion.[10] An analytic perspective firmly grounded in this understanding of argument and persuasion is therefore helpful.

The starting point for the various schools of thought engaged in the deterrence debate is textual analysis. Since the question of what would be a credible deterrent to the Soviets precedes all other discussion (since it was the Soviets who were the target audience for our persuasion and not ourselves, as most practicioners of strategic theory recognized at least implicitly), strategic theorists had to begin by determining their position on the nature of Soviet military doctrine and political culture. "The importance and difficulty of determining the other side's intentions raise a prescriptive dilemma, since the policy appropriate for dealing with a state with one kind of intentions may be harmful in dealing with one that seeks different goals."[11] Determinations are made by what is essentially a critical reading of Soviet texts on defense issues. All other forms of data are interpreted through the lens provided by textual analysis. Large areas of ambiguity—beginning with the fairly basic problem of determining which texts were "authentic" representations of the Soviet position—permitted the on-going debate as to the nature of the Soviet audience and the best means of persuasion to continue without resolution.

The purpose of the audience analysis, which is the goal of the critical study of texts, was in each instance to discover how to persuade the Soviets to behave in some ways and not in others. The whole point in creating a "credible" deterrent is to create a force structure that sends the proper message to the Soviets. The nuclear arsenal itself, supported by declaratory and other policies, is a medium for sending persuasive messages about the United States' capabilities and intentions. But theorists did not agree about what message would best serve U.S. interests.[12] This disagreement, however, does not change the fact that "every perceptual rationale for a given nuclear programme involves the claim that if the programme is abandoned, some outside audience may perceive the strategic situation in a way detrimental to Western security. The first test of any such perceptual appeal must therefore be to ask if this claim is correct."[13] My argument is that at base, all deterrence arguments are grounded in "perceptual appeals" in a context in which there is no way to determine if the claim is correct or not. As nuclear strategic doctrines develop, they incorporate competing theories of persuasion.

Second, the debate over deterrence theory has centered on a debate between two schools of thought, Mutual Assured Destruction (or MAD), and warfighting (sometimes called the countervailing strategy or counterforce dominance).[14] These schools each involve highly developed, rigorous, internally consistent, and utterly exclusive theoretical structures.[15] These nuclear strategic doctrines dominated the technical literature. MAD advocated an extremely narrow mission for the American nuclear arsenal. Nuclear weapons were to be used solely to deter the use of nuclear weapons against American territory. The key assumption for advocates of MAD is that when both sides know that either side can absorb a nuclear attack on its territory and still retain the capacity to inflict unacceptable damage on an aggressor, neither side will have an incentive to launch, even in a crisis. This condition is referred as "Crisis Stability."

Advocates of "warfighting" held significantly different assumptions. To these theorists, nuclear weapons could be used to deter a broad range of actions on the part of the Soviet Union. Whether or not a protracted nuclear war can be fought, the only way to deter the Soviets was to convince them that the United States believed so and had such a capacity. Clear military superiority at every stage of the "escalation ladder" is essential to avoid situations where military force must actually be used.[16]

Both are best understood as *argument* structures for several reasons. They postulate means for maximizing the collective good.[17] They are empirically unverifiable,[18] thus completely textual, dependent upon arguing in an inferential fashion from data to claim.[19] After all, anything "[a]nd everything about nuclear war is subject to argument because there is no way that any proposition can be demonstrated to be correct."[20] Deterrence theory functions as argument, making an argument-centered approach *to* deterrence theory again of special benefit. As one author noted, "one can only obtain proof in the negative."[21] Understandings of argument structure, the use of evidence, and the development of standards for both evidentiary and argumentative validity are all therefore of use.[22] This study, in other words, seeks to apply methods of criticism drawn from the study of rhetoric and argument to the texts generated in support of MAD and warfighting in order to articulate and explore several arguments about the nature of deterrence theory as it is developed in the dispute between those two theories or schools of thought. The first argument is that theories of deterrence share similar assumptions about the structure of communication. Theories of persuasion, implicit in theoretical texts, will be explicated by laying out the assumptions concerning the Soviet Union, the nature of nuclear war, and the communicative functions of nuclear weapons. To do this requires textual analysis, but that is only a first step. By raising these assumptions to the level of explicit discussion, the strategic debate itself may be opened up to alternative methods of analyzing possible configurations of communication.

This metacritical examination of what are proposed as persuasive structures permits analysis of the second proposition: that deterrence theory depends on discerning and articulating what military forces will persuade the Soviets in various situations in such a fashion that a univocal view of communication is perpetuated. In other words, the vision of deterrence theory is one where the United States communicates, and the Soviet Union interprets. Both MAD and warfighting therefore were based on a mechanistic view of the Soviet Union, built on the assumption that both verbal and nonverbal symbols can be effectively manipulated. Each theory adopts what scholars in rhetoric refer to as a "Sender-Message-Receiver" model of communication. This model is one that, within the communication discipline, has been abandoned, since it permits no room for feedback or for similar communicative attempts on the part of the other, in this case the Soviet Union. Soviet actions were therefore always seen as being "genuine" (in other words meant to create some real military advantage) and never as communicative. The Soviet Union was therefore denied a truly authentic voice.

These arguments matter because of the problem of objectivity. For scholars working with the persuasive uses of symbols, it is a fundamental tenet that our experiencing of reality is always mediated through a symbol structure (generally linguistic) which has its own logic. While clearly there exists an objective physical reality "out there," our apprehension of it is always shaded by the symbols through which we understand it. In this sense our understanding of the world and the people in it is *always* subjective: it cannot really be otherwise.[23] This study is designed in part to examine the way the symbolic structures of deterrence theories effected our interpretation of the Soviets (interpretation itself being a term which implies subjectivity). And it is in part meant to examine the ways those structures worked to preclude a more open and less stereotyped vision of the Soviets. Therefore, I would not take the position that if there were an objective "real" Soviet Union we could ever have come to fully know it. What we could and can do is come to better understand our own cultural constructs and perspectives in order to better control and shape those which do not serve us well.[24] This claim is in and of itself not unique.[25] Nevertheless, this is the first time that an exploration of the issue has been grounded firmly and explicitly within the perspective of argument and rhetoric. As I will argue, this permits assessments not otherwise possible. As one author noted, "neither they [statesmen] nor scholars have fully explicated the dilemmas and understood the extent to which our conceptions of the role of nuclear weapons in world politics change the world—and, indeed, create it— as much as they mirror it. Many of our standard analytical tools do not serve us well here."[26]

Finally, although the purpose of this study is to generate insight into the on-going debate over defense posture and sizing, it can, if successful, serve also to demonstrate the benefits of an argument-centered approach to the study of public policy. If this study proves useful, then there is no reason why similar approaches cannot be attempted vis-à-vis policy literatures dealing with a broad array of contemporary problems.

LITERATURE REVIEW AND METHODOLOGY

As extensive as the existing literature is, this study both complements and contributes to it. It fills a gap that has not as yet been met. What is available tends to fall into one of several categories. On the one hand, there are studies which primarily attempt to "objectively" lay out the claims and conclusions of the various schools of thought,[27] focusing primarily on the differences dividing MAD and warfighting in order to permit an explanatory focus.[28] The focus on substantive policy differences has of necessity drawn these authors away from the kind of structural analysis I am engaging in, since it is my goal to focus precisely on the ways in which MAD and warfighting, while *substantively* distinct— in fact exclusive—are *structurally* identical.

On the other hand there is the policy literature itself, in which the advocates of the two schools of thought employ argument structures as grounding from within which particular policy outcomes (primarily weapons systems) can be defended or indicted. It is this literature in which the debate is played out, and which is the subject of this study. This literature embodies a number of underlying assumptions held in common by advocates of MAD and warfighting, and which serve as the basis for this study. But because the assumptions are implicit, they remain unquestioned. Specific debates between MAD and warfighting theorists presume the truth of these assumptions and begin from that point. The assumptions therefore remain unexamined.

Initially, all deterrence theorists believe peace is preferable to war. The entire point of the deterrence project was to maintain a stable peace between the United States and the Soviet Union. Even those who believe nuclear wars can be fought and won prefer peace. This assumption is so obvious, it hardly bears mentioning, but to the extent this assumption served—and serves—as a guiding constraint, it serves as the basis from which other assumptions flow for theorists of both schools.

The second assumption was that the United States needed to exert influence upon the Soviets. The need to avoid war provided an over-arching constraint. That constraint required that the United States not provoke the Soviets and that the Soviets in some way be prevented from taking actions provocative to the United States. The assumption was that this requires the exertion of influence; that American and Soviet interests were so inimical that if the Soviets were to pursue their interests without interference, competition and ultimately provocation, would have been inevitable.

However, the third assumption was that reasoning with the Soviets could not serve this need. Both sides shared an interest in avoiding conflict, but there was something of a tragedy of the commons at work. The Soviets wished both to avoid conflict and to maximize their own goals throughout the world. It was, therefore, considered insufficient to simply "ask nicely" that the Soviets refrain from behavior threatening to us unless we were willing to abandon the pursuit of all policies except the avoidance of war. Threats of some sort were necessary if we sought to avoid conflict while retaining sufficient freedom to play a role in global affairs.

Discourse, in other words, would fail as a mechanism for influencing the Soviets. It was not that the Soviets were irrational per se, but rather that merely asking for, or reasoning through to, some kind of mutual accommodation in the same fashion as the give and take that occurs between members of an alliance was out of the question. The question then became, how are we to communicate our threats? Language will not work. Obviously, language alone is never enough. Whatever the context, threats depend upon the demonstrable ability to carry them out.[29] The threat of military action requires that the nation making the threat possess armed forces. But this assumption goes beyond that. A complex relationship such as that between the United States and the Soviet Union requires the communication of complex threats. More is needed than the simple message that under some conditions the United States will resort to force. The message needs to be communicable in a fashion that permits nuance. For those additional layers of nuance, of complexity, a mechanism other than language must be found. Because of the competing interests, their history, each nation's ability to destroy the other, the relationship is characterized by distrust. National survival is at stake. Neither side can trust declarations of the other about what actions will be taken under what considerations. Decisions of such con-sequence must be based on something more.

None of this is controversial. My argument is that the final assumption was that the specifics of the force structure could be manipulated in order to send refined messages of threat. All the assumptions I have articulated lead to the conclusion that deterrence theory, MAD or warfighting, functions as theory of persuasion. The weapons themselves (or at least their particular characteristics) play the role of medium for the message. I base this conclusion on an analysis of the policy literature in which deterrence theory is debated and discussed. In that literature, weapons are evaluated based on their ability to influence Soviet decision making. Operational characteristics are relevant, not because we intended to use the weapons, but because the characteristics could be used to convey a message about what we *would* do, based on what we *could* do.[30] The "key to existential deterrence" after all "is ambiguity."[31]

In later chapters I will first articulate this position in greater detail, indicating the way MAD and warfighting have developed structurally. I will then explore the way arguments generated by MAD and warfighting in support of various weapons systems fit this pattern, serving as the bases for proposals for message construction, and explore the implications of this perspective for the future development of deterrence theory.

In recent years a third category of literature has appeared and proliferated. This category is closest to the present study and complementary to it. This is an extensive body of literature which critiques the deterrence enterprise in its entirety, without slipping into the role of actually advocating either MAD or warfighting, and without making the mistake of ignoring the differences that divide the two. While useful and often insightful, this body of research does not eliminate the need for the current study. For while this book in many ways complements the work that has already been done, its primary aim is to uncover and ultimately take issue with basic assumptions which underlie the entire deterrence project. In their attempt to "reform" deterrence theory, the social scientists who have heretofore examined it have adopted several of these assumptions as their own. But it is my position that it is exactly these assumptions which in a sense "build in" the flaws which mar deterrence theory as currently conceptualized. Critics from history, sociology, or psychology, seeking to correct the mistakes made by deterrence theory "on the margins" therefore build the same flaws into their own perspective and ultimately fail to uncover that which, in my view, freezes deterrence theory into its present counterproductive and irresolvable form.

This study proceeds from the assumption that symbol structures possess embedded logics that, while implicit, serve as critical motivating factors for those employing the symbol systems. Rhetorical criticism, by permitting focus on the embedded logics, can provide important insights into persuasive and argumentative structures. This study, therefore, analyzes those texts in which advocates use the relevant symbol systems to generate arguments for particular policy options. In this case, the focus is on texts where arguments are used to support or indict military deployments that have been generated from within the relevant symbol structures—MAD and warfighting.

Given the amount of literature that discusses military deployments a number of choices have been exercised in structuring the body of literature to be considered. Initially, the study has been limited to texts that are technical in nature.[32] It is in the texts intended for a technically sophisticated audience, presumably already familiar with the symbol systems in question, that the intricacies of those systems are most readily apparent. Authors in such situations are more likely to offer the complete range of arguments made available to them by the overarching structures of assumptions from within which they are writing. They are more likely to describe in greater detail the interactions between arguments. And, critically, the authors are able to write with less attention to the constraints imposed by outside audiences. The focus of such texts is therefore almost exclusively on arguments concerning deterrence theory. Perspectives imposed by concerns for public acceptability are substantially underemphasized. Since such perspectives are outside the scope of this study, their exclusion permits a tighter focus on the arguments that are relevant.

For similar reasons the study excludes texts that are explanatory. Textbooks and the like, which attempt to simplify in order to clarify, are texts in which authors strive to present material in "objective" fashion. The purpose of the study is better served by a focus on instances where authors consciously *advocate*. It is in those circumstances that authors are most likely to present positions in all their complexity and, critically, to provide their indictments and critiques of alternative positions. It is in the indictment of alternatives that advocates often lay out the most fundamental assumptions of their own positions.

The study also excludes documents in which authors articulate and defend official government policy. Again, the number of constraints operating on such authors above and beyond the logics of the available symbol systems are substantial, and beyond the scope of this study. It is more likely that such constraints will create a need for authors in an official capacity to offer justifications for policy that are both more and less than those made available by the symbol structures. Additionally, both MAD and warfighting are *normative* positions: discussions of what American force structures should be. The actual arsenal, and the declaratory policy that explains its configuration, reflects the sensibilities of both MAD *and* warfighting in a conglomerate of options.[33]

Finally, the texts to be included in the study have been limited by date. The study focuses almost exclusively on texts published during the 1980s, for a number of reasons. It was during that period that warfighting became a perspective as fully articulated and robust as MAD.[34] It was also during that period that extensive numbers of publications appeared that attempted to justify various force deployments from within a warfighting perspective explicitly, rather than trying to justify "counterforce" weapons on the grounds that they would not destroy MAD.[35] And it was during this period that large numbers of forces became technologically feasible that, if deployed, would clearly move the United States' military capabilities closer to the vision offered by warfighting. Each option—the MX missile, the Trident submarine with the D-5 warhead, the B-1 and B-2 bombers, cruise missiles—had to be debated. Since each promised to erode MAD and further warfighting each was discussed from the perspectives this study seeks to critique, and thus offers texts likely to lay out the assumptions of those perspectives. The few exceptions included are texts published in the late 1970s that have proven important within the symbolic structures dominant today. In each instance the relevance of the older text is proven by the continued references to it made by authors publishing during the mid- to late 1980s. Texts generated in the later part of the decade are dealt with separately in Chapter 6, in order to permit a clear focus on the ways the debate has changed—and not changed—since the "end" of the Cold War.

This study also makes extensive use of literature dealing less with normative standards for nuclear deterrence and more with specific descriptive analyses of Soviet military doctrine. While it may be argued that such texts are generated by a separate group of scholars and ought be considered as distinct, I do not believe it is possible to consider contemporary deterrence theory without considering these texts. This is the case for several reasons. One consistently made critique of deterrence theory has been since it argued in an abstract fashion (emphasizing the effect of nuclear weapons on international relations and arguing deductively from assumptions made on that score) that it existed in a vacuum, with no real relationship to either international politics or the findings of area-studies specialists on the Soviet Union. This argument certainly must be given substantial weight, especially when one looks to the origins of deterrence theory in the arcana of mathematical game theory. It might, therefore, seem a questionable decision to include in the body of literature examined here several works that might more easily be described as stemming from the study of Soviet military doctrine rather than from deterrence theory per se.

There are several reasons why the inclusion of such texts in this data base is not merely legitimate but necessary. Initially it is critical to understand that while both MAD and warfighting may have been generated from mathematical abstractions, their adherents have been involved in prolonged debate for the hearts and minds of policymakers.[36] No nation can build a force structure dictated both by MAD and by war-fighting, since their prescriptions are completely exclusive.[37] It has, therefore, been absolutely essential that advocates of MAD and war-fighting forcefully maintain in their presentations in defense of particular policies that their positions are suited specifically to deterring the Soviets (since that was the case American policymakers have been concerned with) or, at a minimum, that their position was better suited to deterring the Soviets than the alternative. Whether these doctrines were developed in a political or conceptual vacuum, they have been *defended* on the basis of their suitability given detailed and consistent portrayals of the Soviets, conceived as the target audience for force structures designed as per-suasive gestures.[38]

To that end, they have made long use of the work of area specialists. Whether or not authors publishing research on Soviet military doctrine ever intended their work to become grist for the deterrence theorist's mill, it is clear that it has. Specialists in Soviet military policy may believe the bodies of literature to be discrete, but in fact they are not, at least not from the perspective of the deterrence theorist seeking to bolster claims about the superiority of their own doctrinal position.[39]

Finally, even if one believes that the two bodies of literature are dis-crete, the same is *not* true of the authors producing them. Many of the most vigorous participants in the debates over force structure and de-terrence have presented their positions on the Soviets and many senior scholars in Soviet studies have dabbled in deterrence theory. To the extent that the work of these authors are to be studied as a corpus, both sets of literature would need to be included.

Furthermore, while analysis of Soviet military doctrine could have occurred without reference to normative positions on deterrence theory, the reverse is not true.[40] Thus as the debate over deterrence theory became more robust, more arguments in that literature referred to the actual nature of the Soviets and their beliefs as justification for various positions. The deterrence debate in this sense became far less abstract, and came to rely far more heavily on the findings of Western analysts of the Soviet military. To the extent this process took place, such analysis became additional grounding for argument and entered the debate as evidence, whether the original authors intended for that to happen or not. Often what is of concern here is not the actual work of these analysts but the way that work is cited and "bootlegged" into the deterrence debate.

What happened in the mid–1970s was that these two worlds converged for the first time. They did not, however, enter into the symbiotic relationship that might have produced the necessary insights into how differences in Soviet and U.S. doctrine and strategy actually might affect the requirements for a viable

Western deterrent posture. On the contrary, while there clearly was a sharp growth in the analysis of Soviet military thought, most of this was used by the two sets of protagonists in the U.S. strategic debate in an attempt to prove the validity of the positions that each already advocated concerning the basic requirements of Western strategy under conditions of parity. The analysis of Soviet strategic doctrine, rather than informing and disciplining the consideration of U.S. strategic choices, became one more tool in that highly politicized debate. This, in turn, influenced the nature and quality of the analysis of the Soviet military, ultimately politicizing the debate here as well.[41]

Whether these authors would even agree with the way their work is used is not the point. In fact, once strategic theorists "discovered" the analysis of Soviet military doctrine "[p]eople found in the data that which they expected to find, or wanted to find, which was, in turn, used to support policy positions which they already basically endorsed."[42] It is the use that was made of such work by deterrence theorists that becomes interesting here.[43]

OUTLINE OF STUDY

The study is designed to examine the propositions outlined above. Because the material at hand is fairly complex, a systematic approach is necessary involving the development of a method that can be employed in succeeding chapters to consider the distinct schools of deterrence theory. Two chapters will be devoted to explicit textual analysis of MAD and warfighting. For each doctrine, several representative authors will be chosen and their work examined. Assimiliating the writings of each school into a cohesive whole, textual analysis is undertaken to make explicit the basic premises of the following ideas: assumptions about the Soviet Union, about nuclear war, and about the use of force structures and nuclear arsenals in persuasion. To investigate the first category, assumptions about the Soviet Union, is to ask questions about whether the advocates considered the Soviets to be aggressive or defensive, motivated by national interest or ideology, and whether the Soviets viewed nuclear war as a legitimate tool of policy. Analysis of the second set of assumptions is designed to specify considerations of the utility of nuclear weapons and the risks involved in making certain threats about their use. Views of the Soviet Union and the utility of nuclear weapons will then be examined in light of the way these advocates argued for structuring forces to affect Soviet behavior.

Finally, the way these doctrines were applied will be considered through an analysis of arguments concerning the defense of NATO. MAD and warfighting are theories that were designed to articulate normative guidelines for military forces designed to deter the Soviet Union from attacking the United States directly. Yet there are other actions the

United States wished to deter the Soviets from taking, such as attacking Western Europe. Deterrence below the strategic level stretches the doctrines and it is where the doctrines are stretched in this fashion that interesting tensions are most likely to surface.

The argument unfolds as follows: Chapter 2 considers the doctrine of MAD. Advocates of this policy asserted that the use of nuclear weapons could not be controlled, and the effects of an all-out nuclear war would be disastrous. They viewed the Soviets as rational and pragmatic, more concerned with the interests of the state than with the ideologically motivated destruction of capitalism. They believed the Soviets did what was best for the Soviets: thus, they felt the Soviet government could be counted on to cooperate with the United States in avoiding nuclear war. Because the Soviets understood the demands of deterrence, they could be trusted in the maintenance of a stable system. However, because they were extremely defensive in nature, there was great danger in pushing them into increasingly qualitative arms races. Improvements in the speed, accuracy, and delivery capabilities of nuclear weapons were viewed with deep suspicion and often opposed because of their destabilizing potential. They would have created a high risk situation in a crisis, where the Soviets might have perceived their only choice as being between striking first or striking second. Although United States' arsenals and force structures can communicate in an active sense, Soviet deployments only communicated in a passive sense. In other words, the Soviets were believed to structure their forces based on their perception of military need, not in order to send messages in a direct manner. We can therefore interpret the state of their belief from those structures, but that was not the clearly defined intent of those structures, as is the case for the United States.

The third chapter examines warfighting, or the countervailing strategy. This doctrine involves perhaps the most detailed, though straightforward, theory of persuasion. Warfighting advocates believed that the Soviets were aggressive and ideological (i.e. not rational actors) and in particular were expansionist. The Soviet Union, it was held, could only be controlled by the communication of will and capability at every potential level of aggression. Thus it had to be made clear, through force structures deployed by the United States, that America not only had military superiority but that she would use nuclear weapons, denying the Soviets what they valued most—their own political control over their people. Additionally, protection of the American population ("damage limitation") was necessary, not because it would actually work, but because it indicated a level of seriousness that would have precluded the need to ever use nuclear weapons. Like its sister theory, warfighting assumes that communication flowed from the United States to the Soviet Union, but in a number of different forms, since the essential messages had to be repeated over and over again at every level of military force. The Soviets did not communicate their intentions even passively—those were already known. All that we could learn from their force structures was the level of forces necessary quantitatively at each step of potential engagement in order to deter.

Chapter 4 provides a case study of the way deterrence theories were applied. Both MAD and warfighting authors conceded that the United States needed to "extend" deterrence in order to protect Western Europe from Soviet aggression. Despite the importance of these countries to the United States, however, the "loss" of Europe would not be an issue of immediate national survival in the way a Soviet nuclear attack on American territory would be. The application of nuclear deterrence theory to the defense of NATO is therefore less than perfect. Because the theories had to be stretched in order to apply in this instance, an examination of MAD and warfighting arguments about European deterrence serves to reveal internal tensions in the doctrines themselves.

Chapter 5 draws two sets of conclusions. First, the initial research hypotheses are considered in light of the findings articulated in the previous chapters. In particular the limits to a mechanist view of communication with the Soviets will be established. Second, some conclusions will be advanced regarding communicative aspects of foreign policy activity where the nation is regarded as the speaker. The implicit models of communication in use in the doctrines will be critiqued against a possible alternative. Models now in use assume perfect interpretation of the way signals are intended by completely predictable actors who are unaffected by prior encounters with one another. The model of communication that I am assuming is obviously basic, but serves as a starting point from within which to view the strategic doctrines, as it would be somewhat fruitless to critique the model they provide without some ideas as to what "better" communication would involve. A view of communication that is unidirectional cannot account for the possibility of shared learning from cooperative conduct.

Chapter 6 reconsiders the findings of the study in light of the dramatic changes which occurred in U.S.-Soviet relationships immediately prior to the collapse of the Union. In particular, the effort of strategic theorists to account for, and deal with, the "New Political Thinking" will be assessed. The argument will be made that, since those assessments are driven by the Cold War analytical structures of MAD and warfighting, change cannot be accommodated by these theorists. In particular, I will examine discussions of conventional warfighting strategies, the Intermediate Nuclear Forces (INF) Treaty, and the potential for deep cuts in strategic arsenals.

NOTES

1. The number of journals and publishing houses devoted to the issue is staggering enough, without even beginning to count individual pieces of works.

2. Ken Booth, "Nuclear Deterrence and 'WW III': How Will History Judge?" in Roman Kolkowicz, ed., *The Logic of Nuclear Terror* (Boston: Allen and Unwin, 1987), 251.

3. As Colin Grey has noted, "Nuclear threats . . . cannot be exorcised magically by disarmament treaties or defensive systems . . . neither will be able to bear the traffic of physically or functionally repealing the nuclear age." Colin Gray, "Nuclear Strategy: What is True, What is False, What is Arguable," *Comparative Strategy* 9, no. 1 (1990): 16.

4. As one author noted in a recent work, "Under the circumstances, a book analyzing war scenarios might seem anachronistic. . . . To my mind, the book could not be more timely or essential. Those who would resist progress in arms control . . . are likely to dismiss proposals for deep reductions, arguing that the recent upheavals in Eastern Europe and the apparent demise of Soviet control are—like Gorbachev's revolution itself—'reversible.' " Joshua Epstein, *Conventional Force Reductions: A Dynamic Analysis* (Washington, D.C.: The Brookings Institution, 1990), 3. In other words, the Cold War frames of reference are still operative.

5. Which is certainly not the case, if only because the "maintenance of a stable, deterring nuclear balance *vis-à-vis* the Soviet Union must remain paramount—only Soviet nuclear forces threaten our very existence." Donald Rice, "The Manned Bomber and Strategic Deterrence," *International Security* 15, no. 1 (Summer 1990): 101. Replace "Soviet Union" with "Russia" and the claim remains true today.

6. Already there are questions as to whether somebody "lost" Kuwait by carelessly signaling that it was not a vital strategic interest for the United States. The entire discussion, along with the repeated references to Munich, makes clear that what is being applied in this instance is the "appeasement theory of war" which I discuss in Chapter 3.

7. Goodnight discusses "the practice of making some kind of reasoned decisions in the face of uncertainty." See G. Thomas Goodnight, "Generational Argument," in Frans van Eemeren et al., eds. *Argumentation: Across the Lines of Discipline: Proceedings of the Conference on Argumentation 1986* (Providence: Foris Publications, 1987), 131.

8. To be clear, this study comes out of a broad theoretical posture regarding the importance and role of symbols called Symbolic Interactionism. An excellent introductory piece which lays out the assumptions, not just of Symbolic Interactionism (or SI) but of the various competing schools within that perspective, is Stephen Littlejohn, "Symbolic Interactionism as an Approach to the Study of Human Communication," *Quarterly Journal of Speech* 63, no. 1 (February 1977): 85–174. For a more detailed articulation, see Peter Berger and Thomas Luckmann, *The Social Construction of Reality* (New York: Anchor Books/Doubleday, 1967).

9. It is for this reason that such emphasis is placed within Symbolic Inter-

actionism on the importance of *naming*, for a name or a label can compress an entire argument, but in a fashion that makes it extremely difficult to access and therefore to counter. Consider, for example, that if the word "boy" is defined as being a minor child, that word becomes associated with characteristics such as irresponsibility, immaturity, vulnerability. It implies the relationship between the namer and the named as one of protection and caring, since that is an appropriate relationship for an adult to have towards a child. Those characteristics carry over when the label "boy" is then attached to adult males of a particular race, and the compressed argument is unstated but still complete: even adults of that race are incapable of caring for themselves; our appropriate relationship to them is one of guardianship. For additional examples, see Charles Kauffman, "Names and Weapons," *Communication Monographs* 56, no. 3 (September 1989): 273–285.

10. "To a considerable extent, this [something matters because we believe the Soviets think it matters] is what many people have in mind when they say that a military posture is politically important although it lacks military utility." Robert Jervis, *The Meaning of Nuclear Revolution* (Ithaca, N.Y.: Cornell University Press, 1989), 196.

11. Robert Jervis, "Introduction: Approach and Assumptions," in Robert Jervis, et al., eds., *Psychology and Deterrence* (Baltimore: Johns Hopkins University Press, 1985).

12. In each instance, in other words, there will be disagreement over the persuasiveness or credibility of a particular message, not over what message is sent by a given deployment. "Weapons programmes, of course, rarely stand alone, but are set within specific strategic doctrines which may themselves be justified partly on perceptual grounds. . . . After all, what forces one needs to carry out a given mission is essentially a military question, and perceptual arguments revolve more around the doctrinal issue of which missions one should be able to fulfil (sic)." Philip Sabin, "Shadow or Substance? Perceptions and Symbolism in Nuclear Force Planning," *Adelphi Papers* #222 (London: International Institute for Strategic Studies, Summer 1987), 7.

13. Sabin, "Shadow or Substance," 24.

14. Other authors have described far larger categories, but since there is cohesion at the level of the assumptions I am interested in exploring, two categories seemed to provide enough simplicity to permit a coherent analysis without sacrificing the flexibility necessary to preserve a sense of difference between authors in the same category. For an example of an analysis employing a far larger range of categories see Stephen Cimbala, *Rethinking Nuclear Strategy* (Wilmington: Scholarly Resources, 1988).

15. That the schools of thought are mutually exclusive as developed is clear. That they are of necessity incommensurable is not as clear. See Gregory Flynn, "Doctrine, Images, and the East-West Relationship." in Flynn, ed., *Soviet Military Doctrine and Western Policy* (New York: Routledge, 1989), 13, where he argues that the debates themselves, as they became increasingly polarized, tended to "create the illusion of mutually exclusive choices. During the 1970s, the middle ground . . . all but disappeared." Nonetheless, the contemporary debate is in many ways still "a dialgoue of the deaf." Roman Kolkowicz, "Intellectuals and

the Nuclear Deterrence System," in Kolkowicz, ed., *The Logic of Nuclear Terror*, 31.

16. This is clear just from an examination of the journals in which discussion of the pertinent issues takes place. See for example, William Arkin, *Research Guide to Current Military and Strategic Affairs* (Washington, D.C.: Institute for Policy Studies, 1981), 197–227.

17. In fact one author defined nuclear strategy as "a species of public policy, which means choosing of a collective good from among a number of alternatives." Cimbala, *Rethinking Strategy*, ix. Compare that to the definition of argument in the public sphere provided by Goodnight: "Rhetorical argument [is] the study of practical reason as it engages discourse communities confronted by choice in history." "Generational Argument," 129.

18. "Deterrence theory cannot tell us which view will prevail or which is correct." Jervis, "Approach and Assumptions," 9. To some extent the inability of proving or disproving competing theories forces advocates to take certain assumptions on faith, which produces "a quasi-religous debate about the future profile the West should take toward the East." Flynn, "Doctrine, Images and the East-West Relationship," 8.

19. "What is central is that different kinds of behavior yield predictions of future actions through quite different chains of inference." Robert Jervis, *The Logic of Images in International Relations* (New York: Columbia University Press, 1989 ed., originally published 1970), Preface to the 1989 edition, xvii. There is no more fundamental characteristic of argument as distinct from say, formal logic, or even ordinary persuasive utterences, than this notion of an inferential leap.

20. Gray, "What Is True, What Is False," 15.

21. Flynn, "Doctrine, Images and the East-West Relationship," 9.

22. Admittedly, despite the fact that a study of this nature has never been done, there is an understanding of deterrence as argument within the existing literature. Consider the statement that "the argument for this sort of control [the escalation ladder] rests on a metaphor, not evidence. . . . But there is no way to determine which picture [ladder or slippery slope] is more accurate, in part because how escalation would occur will be influenced by decision makers' expectations, which in turn are influenced by the terms and analogies they employ." Jervis, *The Meaning of Revolution*, 184. Said another author "ultimately doctrine [is] in the end analysis, a matter of belief systems." Flynn, "Doctrine, Images and the East-West Relationship," 6. Similarly, a "lack of experience with nuclear wars, which means that the beliefs on which we operate must remain speculative. Nuclear strategy must remain hypothetical." Jervis, *Meaning of Revolution*, 182.

23. We do not, in other words, see things as we would in a state of nature, since the symbol systems we employ inevitably color the way we see the world. Is a tree evidence of the beauty of God's plan? Of the desperate need for environmental policy? A resource to be used? A barrier to be walked around? What is critical is the distinction between the word, which is a symbol, and which is what we deal with whenever we speak or think, and the thing. The word may refer to the thing, but they are by no means the same, something obvious when you think about it but rarely thought about as we go through the daily round.

Thus while the effort to rename the MX the "Peacekeeper" or the Strategic Defense Initiative "Star Wars" would be less effective precisely because they are so obvious, names such as "Tomahawk" or "Wild Weasel"—or "Queer" in reference to homosexuals—are less obvious and therefore more insidious. Consider, for example, that a husband at home with the kids is likely to call his activities "babysitting," so that no matter how equally divided the household tasks are, the implication remains that such work is appropriately the wife's— he is going above and beyond the call.

24. It is clear that this has been recognized at least to an extent as a phenomenon in strategic studies, although it is not as clear that the implications are understood in full. See for example, Flynn, "Doctrine, Images," where he argues that an individual participant's position tends to determine the way they see events (p. 7). That is also my argument in "Validity Standards and the Debate Over Nuclear Strategic Doctrine," *Defense Analysis* 5, no. 2 (1989): 115–128.

25. Part of my claim will be that those scholars who do recognize the importance of symbols hedge, which has important ramifications for the development of their arguments. For example the claim that "beliefs can *strongly shape* reality," does not go far enough. Jervis, *Meaning of Revolution*, 176, my emphasis. See also, Flynn, "Doctrine, Images," 7.

26. Jervis, *Meaning of Revolution*, 175.

27. I do not mean the quotation marks to imply any kind of inadequacy on the part of these authors. Rather, they signal my own discipline's acknowledgment of the impossibility of objectivity in any use of discourse, whether scholarly in origins or not.

28. See for example William Baugh, *The Politics of Nuclear Balance* (New York: Longman, Inc., 1984) or Bruce Russett, *The Prisoners of Insecurity* (New York: Freeman, 1983).

29. In fact, the very structure of the system itself, designed to get around problems with discourse in this particular case, serves to perpetuate the dysfunction of language. As one author noted "for a state to admit that it is behaving as it is in order to bolster its reputation should be self-defeating: there is no reason for others to see the behavior as typical of what the state will do in the future." Jervis, *Meaning of Revolution*, 194.

30. "Technical criteria such as accuracy and survivability matter little in their own right given the inescapable destructiveness of nuclear war; they are important because of how they affect Soviet calculations in peacetime, whether about the risks of aggression or about the desirability of an arms-control deal." Sabin, *Shadow or Substance*, 21.

31. Gray, "What Is True, What Is False," 31.

32. I make a distinction between *technical* argument forms, where standards for argument are pre-agreed upon by members of a specific (generally professional community) and *public* argument forms, where standards must transcend those of any given community, but are themselves subject to discussion, and (hopefully) centered around discussions of the "collective good." See G. Thomas Goodnight, "The Personal, Technical, and Public Spheres of Argument: A Speculative Inquiry Into the Art of Public Deliberation," *Journal of the American Forensic Association* 18 (Spring 1982): 214–227.

33. See Desmond Ball, "The Development of the SIOP, 1960–1983," in Ball

and Jeffrey Richelson, eds., *Strategic Nuclear Targeting* (Ithaca, N.Y.: Cornell University Press, 1986), 57–83.

34. While it is generally acknowledged that American forces have never reflected a purely MAD configuration (with presidents dating back at least to Kennedy consistently striving for more flexible targeting options), declaratory policy has consistently emphasized MAD over warfighting. The technical literature followed that emphasis in phrasing, if not in options argued for.

35. One author noted, although dating the shift to the late 1970s, that from the 1950s the debate was over competing visions of absolute truth. Flynn, "Doctrine, Images," 2. But he points out that from the 1970s on, two important conditions changed: first, the Soviets finally obtained parity in strategic forces, and second, on-going negotiations made it clear that the Soviets conceptualized strategic doctrine differently, which made it essential then for deterrence theorists to seek out the work of area specialists (1).

36. "The policy-making process subjects Western analysts to powerful pressures. Unlike answers concerning the quantity and quality of Soviet military equipment, which can be deduced from satellite photos, the data needed to formulate reliable assessments of Soviet intentions or military thinking are not available." Peter Vigor, "Western Perceptions of Soviet Strategic Thought and Doctrine," in Flynn, ed., *Soviet Military Doctrine and Western Policy*, 31. It is arguably the case that the effort to persuade policymakers has not been all that successful, as argued in John Lewis Gaddis, "Expanding the Data Base: Historians, Political Scientists, and the Enrichment of Security Studies," *International Security* 12, no. 1 (Summer 1897): especially 4. Nonetheless, that is a concern for scholars in this area of work.

37. At least in the pure form. Obviously the SIOP (Single Integrated Operating Plan) can reflect or include targeting options drawn from an infinite number of perspectives. But the force posture will in that case never be a perfect example of either school; thus the debate will continue.

38. One interesting clue lies in the footnotes used by various authors. Those interested in the specific details of Soviet doctrine cite Soviet sources almost exclusively, while those interested in employing that work in order to support their own strategic conclusions regarding force posture, tend to cite secondary Western sources, and to cite them as conclusive.

39. I should point out that, while this legitimizes my own reference to the work of Soviet specialists in a work ostensibly designed to explain the foibles of deterrence theorists, it does not undermine my own original criticism. Deterrence theory was formulated and developed in a political vacuum. References to research on the Soviet Union, and the emphasis on Soviets as audience, do not change that because of the way such references are used as evidence. As I will argue in more detail in Chapters 2 and 3, the theories dictate a certain view of the Soviets. Deterrence theorists then point to research supporting that view as confirmation. For them, then, the nature of the Soviet Union does not lead to the development of a deterrence theory. They do not *start* with the research on the Soviet Union, they end there, selecting as evidence that which supports an already available deductively arrived at conclusion. Hence both the complaint that deterrence thory is overly abstract and my claim that the study of Soviet military doctrine ought be included in the present study are true.

40. "Deterrence is about the discouragement of inimical action by a person or persons who must make the best decisions they are able in favour of the interests of an actual historical entity. The logic of deterrence can be explained with reference to 'Country A' or 'Country B,' but the always unique circumstances for the practice of deterrence deny it the character of a branch of an applied science of strategy." Gray, "What Is True, What Is False," 10.

41. Flynn, "Doctrine, Images," 3. He argues that prior to that point Soviet "military thought and doctrine" was studied intensively in the United States, but that this took place "in total isolation from the parallel debates that were taking place over Western strategy" 3.

42. Flynn, "Doctrine, Images," 19. This is also the position I take in "Validity Standards."

43. Flynn argues that the process I am describing caused the "politicization" of the debate over Soviet military doctrine, in the sense that that work was used to support whatever position the quoting author wished to support. See Flynn, "Doctrine, Image," especially 3.

Chapter Two

Mutual Assured Destruction as Theory of Persuasion

Advocates of MAD believe that given the current—and forseeable—lack of adequate defenses for a civilian population, the consequences of a full-scale nuclear war would be so great that no legitimate policy goal would be furthered by the military use of these weapons.[1] Additionally they argue that discussion of, and planning for, smaller, controlled nuclear exchanges is useless. The risk that any use of nuclear weapons would escalate quickly and uncontrollably is so high that it should be assumed a certainty, if not in intent then in outcome. "Indeed, much of deterrence rests on the fact that both sides know that events are not entirely under their control, and that war could occur even though neither side sought it."[2]

The only legitimate use of American nuclear weapons, therefore, is the deterrence of nuclear attacks on the American homeland, and in the 1980s this primarily meant Soviet attacks. The purpose of these weapons was to convince the Soviet government that the consequences of attacking with nuclear weapons would be so devastating to the Soviet Union—whatever the effect on the United States—that, for the Soviets, too, no conceivable policy aim would be served by the use of nuclear weapons.[3] The ultimate goal for a sustainable deterrence system for these authors is *Crisis Stability*.[4]

RHETORICAL ANALYSIS

A textual analysis of the literature supporting MAD makes apparent a set of underlying assumptions held in common by these authors. Beginning with a core set of beliefs about the physical constraints imposed on strategists by nuclear weapons, and about the Soviet government, these authors then move to construct a strategic theory that functions as a theory of persuasion.

Assumptions about Nuclear War

The starting place for the analytic developed by MAD advocates is the belief that, at the current time and for the long-term foreseeable future, there is no defense against nuclear weapons.[5] There are no plausible steps that can be taken to defend a civilian population, an industrial or agricultural base. In short, after a nuclear attack, the nation that had absorbed that attack would at minimum quickly regress to a pre-technological age, if one were willing to postulate its survival as a political, social, or even biological entity.[6] Independent of the unavoidable deaths of hundred of millions of people in the near short term after an attack, industrial, agricultural, medical, communications and transportation systems would collapse immediately. The shocks attendant to the near instantaneous, and possibly simultaneous, destruction of all urban centers combined with the long-term radioactive contamination of large sections of the nation would be unprecedented.

An understanding of the consequences of full-scale thermonuclear war is clearly central to MAD theorists. It is that understanding that leads to the prioritization of goals: Preventing nuclear war takes precedence over almost every other policy concern. Analyses of potential levels of destruction after hypothetical uses of portions of the nuclear arsenals, on the other hand, are not relevant. This conclusion stems from the second assumption made about nuclear weapons: Use cannot be controlled. Furthermore, "what might be destroyed is so infinitely precious that even a slight increase in the possibility of nuclear war can never be other than of compelling importance."[7] This is judged to be the case for several reasons.

First, and most simply, scenarios and plans developed by rational people in peacetime will not be followed given the special psychological pressures on leaders during a nuclear war.[8] The strains on decision makers will be so great, and so unique, that no one can predict the feelings and reactions of the individuals in positions of responsibility during a war. This is perceived as a particularly strong indictment of scenarios for prolonged nuclear warfighting. Leaders, from the perspective of the MAD theorists, are likely to respond to any form of nuclear attack, sooner or later, with all-out "spasm" launches against an opponent's homeland.

The U.S. targeting list in the early to mid–1980s reportedly included upwards of 500,000 targets in the Soviet Union, divided into four categories.[9] There was, however, significant overlap between target categories.[10] This overlap, combined with the fact that the Soviets did not really attempt to separate strategic targets from population centers (the phenomenon of "co-location") made discriminating attacks extremely difficult.[11] Thus, for example, an attack intended to strike only military targets would have resulted in the inadvertent (or "collateral") deaths of 50 million–100 million Soviet citizens, only 20 million less than would result from an attack directly targeted against population centers.[12] MAD authors therefore concluded that "much of the discrimination that has been programmed into U.S. nuclear war plans in recent years is probably significant only to U.S. target planners themselves."[13] In other words, the Soviets would simply be unable to distinguish subtle distinctions in types of attack once the weapons had landed.[14] Additionally, even if the Soviets did not respond to an American attack in a "spasm" mode, the United States would have been just as unable to make fine distinctions in its interpretation of the Soviet attack pattern. If for no other reason, this would be the result of the degradation of warning and attack assessment capabilities that could conceivably occur as soon as the first detonation.[15]

Finally, even a limited attack on either side would so badly damage command, control and communications (C3) facilities, as to make controlled responses highly unlikely.[16] Even if the president and his or her advisers, and the Soviet premier and his advisers, had been able to follow precise, pre-planned options of strike and counterstrike, there is a near insurmountable problem in controlling the actions of those who directly control the nuclear weapons. The example most often used to disprove the belief in operational control is the ballistic missile submarine (SSBN). A United States *Trident* or *Poseidon* submarine patrolled with sufficient armament to destroy, if its crew chose, virtually every major city in the Soviet Union.[17]

Whatever agreements on termination were being negotiated between Washington and Moscow, a single submarine crew out of contact, deciding that the war was still going on, could attack the largest cities in the Soviet Union. This one action would essentially destroy the Soviet Union by any relevant criteria. Depending on what stage of a war this occurred during, the status of Soviet warning radars and surviving forces, it could easily cause the immediate launch of Soviet weapons sufficient to destroy the United States.

Additionally, physical constraints imposed by the use of nuclear weapons make the control of those weapons impossible. The smallest nuclear weapons are powerful enough to create enormous zones of destruction. The physical vulnerability of command centers, warning radars, computers, and human lines of authority means that there is a high probability that sequenced, precise orders could be neither relayed nor received nor, if received, carried out.[18] Given all of these constraints, the MAD analyst concludes that any use of nuclear weapons would inevitably—and probably quickly—escalate into all-out war. For these analysts then, the most important "firebreak" is the one between non-nuclear and nuclear weapons.[19]

Assumptions about the Soviet Union

Whatever one believes about the ability of societies to survive various forms of nuclear attack, it is quite clear that it is preferable to avoid nuclear conflict. Obviously the easiest way to avoid nuclear war with the Soviet Union would have been to surrender. The more difficult question was how to avoid nuclear war, while protecting American sovereignty and that of its allies, while pursuing American policy goals as vigorously as possible.

This set of goals requires a strategy of deterrence; assuming that the United States would not initiate a nuclear war, it somehow had to persuade the Soviet Union to likewise refrain from actually using its arsenal. If American policy was to present a persuasive message to the Soviets, then the construction of that message had to begin with the development of an accurate picture of the audience. Advocates of MAD have been frequently accused by advocates of alternative theories of "mirror-imaging," this is, of simply projecting their own world views and assumptions onto the Soviets.[20]

While that may well be true of the way these authors interpret evidence, and while, like the advocates of warfighting, they may simply be finding what they are looking for, they did support their claims about the Soviet Union with as much evidence as warfighting authors used. They understood that "[i]n the most elemental sense, deterrence depends on perceptions."[21] The goal, therefore, was to influence and structure, through our actions, the perceptions of the Soviets. This in turn required an accurate perception of Soviet attitudes and goals (a correct audience analysis), in order to ensure that the message was properly "encoded."

The appropriate way to determine Soviet attitudes is to begin with a thorough analysis of Soviet texts. The importance placed on this method is indicated in an exchange between Colin Gray, one of the most prominent advocates of warfighting, and Raymond Garthoff, an advocate of MAD. In an article largely devoted to attacking the MAD portrait of the Soviet leadership's positions on nuclear doctrine, Gray noted that:

Recently, Raymond Garthoff claimed . . . to have literary and oral evidence of Soviet endorsement of the idea of mutual assured destruction—derived both from the content of some articles in the restricted Soviet journal *Military Thought* from the late 1960s and from the classified record of SALT I. Unfortunately for

Ambassador Garthoff's case, precisely the reverse interpretation of his argument can be read from issues of *Military Thought* of a later vintage than those from which he quoted, while the SALT I record is sufficiently rich and diverse as to lend itself to any number of interpretations.[22]

Garthoff responded to this attack by asking:

What later issues of the journal? And what evidence in the SALT I record contravenes the concrete statements and facts I advanced? Such comments do not constitute rebuttal, nor do they contribute to a dialogue. As a matter of fact, I have . . . presented a post-SALT I vintage reaffirmation from *Military Thought*, when that later issue became available for reference; I have also read all available issues, and I have found none which reverse or contravene those I cited.[23]

In fact, it is his position that "it simply will not wash to allege that there is uncited evidence which 'can be read' to undercut authoritative evidence precisely quoted and referenced."[24] Gray's position will be explored in detail in the next chapter, but it is, I think, telling that in his answer to the Garthoff response he notes that he has several "reasons for disliking argument by quotation."[25] In direct contrast to the MAD analyst's emphasis on developing a textually centered method he states that "The only reliable check on whose quotation offering . . . [is] likely to be correct, is to refer to the real world of defense programs."[26]

The MAD advocate's reasoning in defense of this method is somewhat circular. Textual analysis led these authors to make two general assumptions: first, that Soviet leaders are defensive, not aggressive, and second, that Soviet leaders are not ideologically motivated. These textually generated assumptions in turn led the MAD author to make attributions that explained Soviet deployments as reactions to American ones. That interpretation in turn is what justified a position based entirely on Soviet texts, while almost entirely ignoring their actual force structures. In this way, the MAD advocate constructed a "real" Soviet leadership whose responses to hypothetical American actions can then be predicted.

The assumption that the Soviet Union is motivated by paranoid defensiveness is argued in this literature to be a phenomenon as much Russian as Soviet. Russia, with no natural borders, has been invaded over and over. Invaders and occupiers have been thrown off, but at tremendous cost. Thus "[t]he Bolshevik's initial feeling of vulnerability fitted easily into the centuries old Russian experience of foreign intervention."[27] In fact, "Brezhnev and Andropov were brought up in a climate in which the world beyond the Soviet borders was seen more as a threat than a promise."[28] The Soviet Union has itself been invaded several times. It is assumed by the Soviet leadership, as that leadership is constructed by the MAD authors, that the capitalists would, if they could, invade if only to destroy a political system that threatens them.[29] It is only the military power that the Soviet government controls that deters the West from taking such action.[30] In the Soviet Union, at least, the 1917 invasion and occupation of Soviet territory by the West has not been forgotten.[31]

From this frame of reference, various actions which appear as aggressive are explained as genuinely defensive in motivation. It is argued for instance that the occupation and communization of Eastern Europe and the Baltic states was not an expansionist attempt to gain territory, but, rather an attempt to protect Soviet borders with a ring of "buffer" states.[32] Attackers had come from that direction before. Even if those states were tied to the Soviet Union through force, drawing off military power that could otherwise be used against the West, they still provided protection against potential invaders. A similar interpretation explains the Soviet invasion of Afghanistan.

Great importance is placed on the fact that at the time of the 1979 invasion, Afghanistan had been Communist for several years.[33] Warfighting authors have seen the invasion as an attempt to secure a launching point for a future attack on the Middle East.[34] The MAD advocate argues that if that was the motivation for the invasion, the Soviets could have moved much earlier. It was, from their perspective, fear that the fragile Afghani government would soon collapse, leaving an anti-Communist replacement on the border of the Soviets' most untrustworthy republics, that forced Soviet action.[35]

In order to support their interpretation of Soviet motives generally, MAD authors have had to pay a great deal of attention to one specific historical event: the loss of 20 million Soviet citizens and thousands of villages in the German occupation of World War II. The fact that 20 million died is, of course, a matter of historical fact. What has generated significant debate in the literature is the question of what interpretation the Soviets themselves have placed on this fact. Deterrence, the construction of a persuasive message, depends on accurately determining what an opponent values. As one author has pointed out, "[o]ne could not have coerced Pol Pot by threatening to destroy his cities."[36] Developing an effective American deterrent requires a strategy "aimed at what the Soviets think is important to them, not just to what we might think would be important to them."[37] Advocates of warfighting have argued that, in fact, the Soviets do not value their population per se. Partial proof for this proposition is argued to be the fact that the Soviet leadership recognizes that the state emerged from the war and its losses stronger than it had been before.[38]

MAD advocates have therefore been placed in the position of having to defend the sincerity of the Soviet Union's sense of loss in order to win the debate over whether the Soviets placed value on their population. They must discredit the position that the Soviet leadership would willingly risk that population if its own continued safety and political power would be ensured. Typical are the arguments advanced by Fred Kaplan:

First, the Soviets did not enter World War II knowing that twenty million Russians would die in battle. Second, the deaths and all the assorted injuries were spread out over four years, not thirty minutes or so, as would be the case in a nuclear castastrophe. Third, the Soviet decision to go to war was an act of self-defense in the face of impending Nazi conquest—not, as would be the case in the launching or provocation of nuclear war, a display of suicidal adventurism. Fourth, the Soviets were able to save much of their industrial base by transporting it eastward . . . in a nuclear war, for which there would be little warning and during which targets all across the country could be blasted, they would have no such assurances in advance.[39]

The belief that the Soviet leadership cares about the population it rules is seen as support for both of the basic assumptions about the Soviet leadership held by MAD authors. It explains their defensiveness in as much as the Soviets did not wish to risk the loss of so many people again. And it explains their non-ideological character as well: The security of the Soviet population remained the highest priority of the Soviet leadership.

Ideological differences are believed to be central to the Soviet perception of Western aggression. In other words, the MAD authors believe that the Soviets saw the West as aggressive because of the ideological differences in the systems. Yet they are believed to have been non-ideological in their own decision-making processes.[40] Over the years, the Soviet Union is argued to have become a "status-quo" power. As such it was believed susceptible to all the motivations of a "Great Power." Certainly it would not have rejected the prospect of spontaneous global revolution. But for the most part it remained content to retain what it had, while making use of any available opportunities to gradually expand its power and influence.

According to the MAD interpretation, the Soviet government is seen to be fundamentally conservative in its approach to foreign policy. It acted prudently, out of an unwillingness to take risks without a high likelihood of very great benefits.[41] Certainly, the Soviet Union was opportunistic, taking advantage whenever it could of chances to expand its power globally. But there was no such thing as the "Grand Strategy" some warfighters have proposed.[42]

This became most apparent in Soviet relations with Third World revolutionary movements or governments. Soviet public rhetoric (as opposed to internally circulated texts) was always supportive. There are a number of possible reasons for that, not the least of which is the domestic political constraints imposed on leadership rhetoric. Because of these potential external causes of the rhetoric, an appropriate analysis of Soviet strategy in these instances requires an analysis of Soviet actions. When this approach is taken by the MAD advocate they conclude that for the Soviet leadership the highest priority was the Soviet Union.

If in a particular instance the Soviets could aid a Communist insurgency or government without risking unacceptable levels of provocation (levels where the West would have been forced to respond) it would do so. But if such support was judged to be too likely to produce direct conflict, or even uncomfortable levels of tension, support was mainly rhetorical. Little aid or personnel was forthcoming. Whereas an analysis assuming that the Soviets were primarily motivated by ideology would predict otherwise, the interests of the Soviet Union actually took priority.[43] The determinative factor in Soviet decisions regarding levels of support was always the level of risk a given venture would entail for Soviet—not Marxist—interests.

These general assumptions underly more specific ones made about Soviet military theory. The Soviets are, in this literature, presumed to be rational, and to function within the constraints of Great Power realities. They could therefore be expected to understand contemporary military reality. That reality, according to the MAD advocate, is that at its most fundamental level, the nature of war has been completely changed by the development of nuclear weapons. Because the mutual vulnerability of each superpower to the other is unalterable, all classical military theories have become obsolete.

Warfighting is indicated as "conventionalization": the attempt to treat nuclear weapons as though they were conventional, applying the same strategies and concepts that applied in the pre-nuclear age.[44] This concept of ultimate change, and the argument that the Soviets participated in that understanding, is central to the MAD position. Warfighters, as I will argue, made the claim that Soviet texts make clear that they believed a nuclear war could be won: They must, it is argued, have assumed that it can be fought like any other type of war. MAD authors admitted that the goal of Soviet doctrine was to "win" but argued that this was not inconsistent with the concept of mutual vulnerability. Holloway argues, for example:

The Soviet leaders have been forced to recognize that their relationship with the United States is in reality one of mutual vulnerability to devastating nuclear strikes, and that there is no immediate prospect of escaping from this relationship. Within the constraints of this mutual vulnerability they have tried to prepare for nuclear war, and they would try to win such a war if it came to that. But there is little evidence to suggest that they think victory in a global nuclear war would be anything other than catastrophic.[45]

In fact, "The nuclear war the Russians are thinking of is one without restraint."[46]

The MAD position was that the fact that the Soviets did not prefer mutual vulnerability was irrelevant. The important fact was that they recognized this to be an unanswerable condition of the age, as was the lack of a viable alternative.[47] If there is confusion, it may be a result of different Soviet labels. In other words, the warfighters have not given Soviet texts a careful enough reading. "Parity is now the official Soviet description of the Soviet-American strategic relationship . . . the relationship [is] normally described in the West as 'mutual assured destruction' or 'mutual deterrence.' "[48] The interpretation is defended through textual analysis because, unlike the situation with the Soviet's Third World relations, "genuine" documents are available. That is to say that although the MAD analyst accepts the fact that some literature on Soviet strategic thought may be disingenuous, he or she also believes that appropriate distinctions can be made.

These analysts additionally believe that documents which authentically represent Soviet thought are available to the Western scholar. The level of argument used to defend the categorization of any given text as authentic or disingenuous is almost universally poor. It is assumed that there is an identifiable "Soviet" position that can be discussed, although several of the MAD authors perceive a great deal more internal debate than do the warfighting authors.[49]

It is taken as a given that Soviet thought can be divided between the "military-technical" and the political so that:

The political aspect of doctrine stresses the possibility, and the importance of preventing, a world war between capitalism and socialism. The military-technical aspect of doctrine attends to the question of fighting such a war "if the imperialists should unleash it" (to use the standard Soviet qualification.) In Soviet thinking, deterrence is a political rather than a military concept and has received relatively little attention in military writings, which are concerned primarily with the preparation for war and the conduct of war; there is no Soviet equivalent to the theory of deterrence developed in the United States.[50]

Holloway, for example, concludes that force planning and foreign policy will be based on an acceptance of mutual vulnerability, since the party/political element is always dominant. "The prevention of war is seen as the responsibility of the Party leadership, not of the military. . . ."[51] So although Holloway believes that there is significant internal debate on these issues, his posture towards the texts still leaves him a discernible position that can be studied.[52] This is only one example of the way MAD authors resolve the need to isolate a particular position to study, but it is an extremely common one.[53]

Generally, the basis for establishing a particular text as authentic is little more than the fact that it meets the author's initial assumptions. This is true both for arguments about particular texts and about the Soviet position as a whole. So, for example, Kaplan simply asserts that because "*Military Thought (Voyennay Mysl')* is circulated confidentially and exclusively within the Soviet military; it is not meant for a civilian or a Western audience; one should not mistake its articles for those in some Soviet publications designed to propagandize the West."[54] Holloway dispenses with Sokolovski's *Military Strategy*, a key source for advocates of warfighting, by stating that "[parity] has made aspects of Sokolovski's *Military Strategy* outdated."[55] Other authors make equally sweeping statements about Soviet literature as a whole. Thus, these writings "for decades [have] dismissed the possibility of limited nuclear war and stressed massive comprehensive attack at the outset."[56] Jervis flatly states that "flexibility, nuclear counterforce, and 'implementable' options which are thought to be militarily effective are not linked to Soviet doctrine."[57] He also attempts to use warfighter's indictments against them, arguing that concepts such as intra-war deterrence are nothing if not the result of Western analysts mirror-imaging their own abstractions onto the Soviets.[58]

Arguments over the proper interpretation of Soviet texts are especially important because MAD authors de-emphasize Soviet force deployments as an alternative method for discerning the specifics of Soviet strategy. Social scientists have noted instances where individuals interacting together in a given situation will offer radically different explanations for events, particularly in terms of identifying causes and effects. The individuals involved have *punctuated* the event differently. "Ordering sequences in one way or another creates what, without undue exaggeration, may be called different realities."[59] This theory becomes relevant when MAD advocates are confronted with empirical evidence that seems to contradict their position; for example, Soviet weapons deployments that signal counterforce intentions.

Such evidence is discounted because the deployment is interpreted with a punctuation different from that provided by an author advocating warfighting. While warfighters argue that counterforce deployments provide evidence corroborating their interpretation of Soviet strategic thought, MAD authors essentially reject their validity *as* evidence. This is because they believe deployment signalling a warfighting posture is reactive, punctuating it as effect not cause. Rather than reflecting Soviet strategy, Soviet deployments actually constituted a reaction to perceptions of American strategy. Whether or not the Soviets really believed the United States to have been the initiating actor, that is certainly what MAD authors *believe* the Soviets believed. Gervasi claims that "it was America which took almost every new step in the arms race first, and thereby gave the Soviet Union the opportunity to claim, each time, that it was forced to respond."[60] Laird and Herspring agree that the "Soviet Union, of course, holds the United States responsible for 'causing' the technological arms race."[61]

Further, it is argued that the Soviets desired respect as a world power. Strategic parity (the rough equivalence of nuclear forces) in their eyes should have earned them that respect when they attained it in the mid–1970s.[62] Independent of any substantive benefits the Soviets gained from the SALT II accords, these agreements mattered to the Soviets because they provided official recognition that parity existed.[63] From the Soviet perspective, they were humiliated by the United States in the Cuban Missile Crisis precisely because they had not yet attained parity.[64] Therefore, even though their strategic doctrine makes minimal requirements on their forces (a survivable second strike capability) they do not wish to be put in a position of inferiority again, for fear the United States could gain political leverage in a crisis. Whatever systems the United States deploys, the Soviet Union will develop equivalents to protect parity whether they see a need for a given system or not.[65]

This view permits the MAD analyst to retain the focus on textually based interpretations of Soviet intent. Physical evidence—such as Soviet deployments—does not reflect any essential elements of Soviet strategic thought. All that can really be read into Soviet actions is their perception of American strategy, and their determination to counter it. Thus warfighting is discounted for several reasons. Warfighters read aggressive intent into Soviet deployments, ignoring the factors that generate deployments aside from Soviet strategy. Besides attempting to discern the Soviet position from the types of weapons deployed, they also focus too much attention on the number of weapons built.

Given the asymmetries between American and Soviet forces, MAD advocates argue that strict numerical comparisons ("beancounting") are inappropriate for several reasons. At the most basic level these comparisons are irrelevant because once each side has a secure second-strike force, relative strengths bring no advantage.[66] Force asymmetries also mean that the basis of comparison is subjective, reflecting the position of the counter. "Because they are presented in numbers or ratios, the assessments look 'hard' and reliable. Yet that is not necessarily so. The assessment is no 'harder' than the assumptions on which it is based."[67] And finally, domestic political factors tend to distort evaluations of Soviet force levels upwards and of American levels downwards.[68]

The second reason competing analyses are rejected is that when warfighters use Soviet texts to support their position, they do not properly interpret those texts. In some instances, they have not correctly categorized the text (for example, Sokolovski). Further, the warfighter does not take interpretive difficulties into account.[69]

Ultimately, though, the problem is that the method of analysis is itself deeply flawed. Because warfighters draw conclusions primarily from physical evidence (deployments) and only secondarily from texts, using them to support conclusions already drawn, the texts are decontextualized.

At their bluntest, MAD authors will simply take the position that "analysts, such as Pipes, Nitze and others, have seriously misread or distorted" Soviet texts.[70] Several types of errors are identified. For example, Soviet literature discussing "protracted" nuclear war is interpreted as actually referring to nuclear wars which culminate and end a long-term conventional conflict.[71] It is further argued that warfighting authors quote indiscriminately from different periods of Soviet history which are irrelevant by the time they are used.[72] Contextual readings of Soviet texts are said to in fact offer the opposite conclusions.[73]

This is particularly interesting in light of the debate that occurred in the literature over the meaning of the Soviet use of Clausewitz. Warfighters argued that the regular use of Clausewitz as a source in Soviet texts implied that the Soviets do not see any difference between fighting conventional and nuclear battles. MAD authors instead argued that the Soviet reliance on Clausewitzian perspectives proved their point: That using nuclear weapons requires finding a policy benefit that justified the risk and that there is no such benefit. Kaplan argues that the warfighting position "reveal[s] a misunderstanding of both Clausewitz and of Soviet military doctrine."[74] Argues another author, "even if the Soviets do believe that war is a continuation of politics (and who could doubt it?), that bears no resemblance to a belief that nuclear war is a rationally derived policy option."[75] These authors, then, develop a portrait of a "real" Soviet leadership through their analysis of texts. They defend that analysis against both other readings and alternative forms of evidence. This portrait, combined with their understanding of the physical constraints imposed by nuclear weapons, allows them to conceive of an audience for a specific message, and an understanding of what that message must accomplish. The medium for their message is the deployment and structure of American nuclear forces.

FORCE STRUCTURE AS PERSUASION

Nuclear weapons, for the MAD advocate, have no real operational utility. Because the use of nuclear weapons could not be controlled, a nuclear war would inevitably produce intolerable levels of damage, if not extinction. The consequences would be so great that it is literally impossible to conceive of a potential gain great enough to justify use of nuclear weapons by either side. However, this does not lead the MAD advocate to take a position suggesting unilateral disarmament. Nuclear weapons have no operational value but this does not make them non-essential. Their utility is not military but political.

The United States benefits from possession of a nuclear arsenal in that the existence of such weapons deters other nations—at the time primarily the Soviet Union—from using nuclear weapons against the American homeland. Because their purpose is to convince another actor to refrain from certain actions, the political use of the weapons depends on persuasion. If the preceeding analysis of the MAD advocate's perspective on the Soviets is seen as a form of audience analysis, their perspective on various weapons systems is the equivalent of message construction.

For various reasons, policy declarations of a discursive nature are inadequate persuasive tools. The amount of "noise" generated by public debate in a free society makes it doubtful the Soviets would ever have been able to distinguish between statements that came from academics or low-level officials with little real influence, from those that described policy perspectives at the highest levels, and between propaganda and sincere intent.

Domestic and allied political concerns were obviously of somewhat greater importance to American policymakers than to their Soviet counterparts. The Soviets, speculated the MAD advocate, would have had to be aware of this constraint on American rhetors. Being aware of it, they would give little credence to American statements. They could never be sure what elements of Declaratory Policy were directed at them and which to Congress, the political right, the American peace movement, or the various governments and public constituencies of the alliance.

Moreover, even if the Soviets could clearly determine which statements were directed at them, they were still unlikely to take them seriously. As an essentially conservative elite group, feeling great responsibility towards the population they protected, one could hardly expect Soviet leaders to base their national defense on the conciliatory statements of their most powerful competitor. As the late Herbert Scoville, Jr., pointed out, "[w]hen national survival is at stake, we do not put our trust on statements by Soviet leaders. Can we expect them to react differently?"[76]

For all these reasons the MAD authors did not seek reliance on mere verbal declarations to ensure stability. They did not reject, for example, conferences, summits, and other types of direct meetings with Soviet delegations. In fact quite the opposite is true. But such meetings served a very different purpose. They sought to control the competitive relationship between the countries, and to do so in such a way as to lay the groundwork for a future relationship based on trust. In the atmosphere of the mid–1980s, the maintenance of a stable strategic relationship could not rest solely, or even primarily, on such unpredictable ventures.

Leaders can lie about their intentions. Or they may have only the best intentions and still succumb to pressure in a crisis. In an age of sophisticated satellite capabilities (National Technical Means of verification, or NTMs), they cannot, however, lie about their capabilities, at least not for long. "In the confrontation between NATO and the Warsaw Pact now, there is so much suspicion that declarations of peaceful intentions— which are often made—are ineffective. Capabilities are the dominant signals."[77] Because we know that the Soviets will know what we deploy and where, and base their interpretations on it, we can use those deployments to structure their interpretations: in short, to effectively communicate intent. Thus, "whether consciously intended or not, any military formation sends out political as well as military signals."[78] The weapons themselves, then, serve as a common, understandable, and credible form of symbolic language. These theorists "assume that adversaries, who usually speak different languages, nevertheless share common symbols that facilitate communication."[79] That it is weapons characteristics that provide these common symbols is made clear by Scoville:

Particularly in the case of MX *our actions must speak louder to the Soviets than words.* A countersilo capability is effective only if it is used in a first strike. Silo-busting warheads used in retaliation will crush only silos, not missiles. The Soviets will have emptied some of their silos in the first strike, and they will surely empty the rest when they detect our retaliation underway.[80] [My emphasis]

I will explore Scoville's specific rationale below. What is relevant here is his belief that the type of weapon deployed by the United States, and its characteristics, sends a clear, detailed and understandable message.

An examination of the arguments made by MAD advocates in support of certain weapons and force characteristics as opposed to others demonstrates an implicit theory of persuasion. At each level, the position centers on a discussion of how the Soviets would respond to a given deployment. The fundamental nature of this aspect of the position makes sense. If deterrence theory is in fact functioning as a theory of persuasion, all that really matters about any given deployment is whether it will effectively communicate the appropriate message.

Force Levels

All sides in the doctrinal debate agree that the forces of the two superpowers are asymmetrical. That is, because of different technical backgrounds and organizational structures, the strategic arsenals of the two superpowers developed very differently. For example, the United States generally builds smaller weapons than the Soviets and bases far fewer of its warheads on land-based missiles. Because of these and other asymmetries it is impossible to determine relative strength through a simple comparison of numbers: The numbers represent very different things. This intrinsic ambiguity means that the relative status of the two forces is open to debate even today.

The concept of parity (rough equivalence) is of great importance to MAD authors. This was argued to be the status of the forces from, at the latest, the 1970s. The size and number of Soviet weapons was believed compensated for by the greater accuracy and reliability of American weapons.[81] Gervasi, for example, argues that the larger size of Soviet missiles can be explained through a technical inferiority on the Soviet's part. They must be larger because of the heavier fuel used,[82] because superior American capabilities in miniaturization have permitted smaller guidance systems,[83] and, finally, because larger size "was simply an attempt to compensate for their inferior accuracy."[84]

This position separates the MAD author from the warfighter on two counts. First, as I will argue in Chapter 3, warfighters did not necessarily believe parity was an accurate description of the status quo. Second, for the MAD advocate, unlike the warfighter, parity is an actively desirable state. MAD requires a finite number of missiles. If both sides can absorb ("ride-out") an attack and still respond in kind, then the situation is stable. Once each side has developed sufficient missiles to secure that necessary survivable second-strike force, no more missiles are needed. Equivalence implies stability.

Once the Soviets caught up with the United States from their early 1960s position of inferiority, then the appropriate response was to maintain that condition. The attainment of equivalence meant a great deal to the Soviet Union: An insecure state, historically ambivalent about the way its culture compared to that of the West, finally had to be granted the status it craved.[85] The Soviets, humiliated by Kennedy in Cuba, will not permit themselves to fall behind again.

Independent of potentially destabilizing ramifications of an American attempt to regain superiority, MAD authors consistently rejected such attempts on the grounds that such an effort would ultimately prove useless. Because the Soviets were determined to match us deployment for deployment, the arms race that would be initiated would be endless.[86] Further, because stable deterrence, based on mutual vulnerability, demands only a finite arsenal, there is no real gain to be had from continued stockpiling. "Superiority without the ability to protect one's civilization does not give either side much leverage. Drawing even with the Soviets—assuming that they are indeed ahead of us—would not alter the vulnerability of American cities, and it is this which inhibits the United

States."[87] Most important, though, is that the attempt to either gain or retain strategic superiority would itself be destabilizing.

The maintenance of strategic equivalence communicates to the Soviets a true commitment to strategic stability. The message reinforces the concept that nuclear weapons are only useful as a deterrent to other nuclear weapons. In a situation where both nations are roughly equivalent, any gain to one at the expense of the other should come without recourse to nuclear weapons.

The opposite reaction to the Soviet achievement of equivalence conveys the opposite message. Rather than a genuine commitment to stability, it would communicate to the Soviets a United States intention to regain (or retain) a real strategic advantage that could be used against the Soviet Union. Use is, in this context, still a political and communicative term, not an operational one. If one side did gain clear superiority it would conceivably be able to use that advantage as a threat, forcing the other to back down in a crisis (as in 1962) or in response to provocative action. It is just that scenario that motivated the Soviets to make their initial commitment to gaining, and keeping, parity. "The Soviet Union has built up powerful nuclear forces not only in preparation for a possible nuclear war, but also to deprive the United States of any political advantage that superiority might bring."[88] Such an attempt on the part of the United States would convince the Soviet leadership that our goal is not stability, but a usable political advantage. The only response available to them would be to counter our deployments in order to "keep up."

Force Structures

Just as relevant as the number of weapons deployed is the way that they are deployed; that is, the basing mode. Both American and Soviet forces are deployed in a triad structure. In other words, any given warhead can be placed on three kinds of missiles: land-based on ICBMs, seabased on SSBNs, or airbased on strategic bombers, and both countries use all three types of missiles.[89] The triad is considered important because it gives a nation's nuclear forces redundancy. Even if two "legs" of the triad are destroyed in an enemy attack, there is no way all three legs can be destroyed, and any single leg is sufficient for the necessary devastating retaliatory strike.

Although ICBMs are in some ways the most reliable weapons, they are also the most vulnerable. MAD authors place great emphasis on the fact that despite such vulnerability, if there is enough warning time for bombers to become airborne and for submarines to be flushed out of port, a preemptive strike on the United States would always fail. And in fact, the warning time necessary was fairly low. At the time, the navy was keeping over twenty submarines on-station at all times (more than 4,000 warheads) while another sixteen (3,000 warheads) were always on alert.[90] Congressional estimates indicated that even a short range attack from off America's coast would provide time for 73 percent of the bombers to become airborne.[91]

The ICBMs on the other hand, are vulnerable because they are deployed in fixed, and therefore easily located, sites. Even though silos are "superhardened" to withstand significant amounts of blast pressure, it is far less likely that they would survive an attack. Nonetheless, despite their vulnerability, the ICBMs do serve an important communicative purpose.

Whereas the submarines and bombers communicate the futility of a nuclear attack on the United States, because the second strike capacity would always survive, the ICBMs make clear the danger of such an attack. The silos are based on the continental United States.[92] An attack on them would be essential if any enemy sought a disarming preemptive strike. Yet no matter how accurate the incoming missiles, it would be impossible to attack them without causing tens of millions of American deaths from fallout ("collateral damage").[93] There is, in other words, no way to attack the U.S. strategic arsenal that would not serve to commit an American president to immediate retaliation against the Soviet homeland. The triad structure therefore, guarantees redundancy (ability to retaliate), and homeland location (motivation to retaliate). This structuring of forces served to communicate to the Soviets that, even in a crisis, there was nothing to be gained from launching first. The order in which the forces are used is ultimately irrelevant. The outcome for both sides would be much the same.

Warfighters proposed the development of a new generation of highly accurate ICBMs. MAD authors argued that these weapons were destabilizing for reasons explored in the next section. But they also argued that there was no reason for these deployments. The warfighters argued for force modernization on the grounds that American ICBMs are now vulnerable. This, they claimed, was dangerous because it tempted the Soviets to launch an attack on them. Without extremely accurate weapons, the only military response available to us would be an attack on Soviet cities. They would then respond by destroying our cities. After the Soviet first strike, then, an American president would be self-deterred from any military response. Aside from their arguments against specific deployments, MAD authors have spent much effort in responding to this scenario.

Essentially, their position is that the risk of failure at a logistical level, and the uncertainty about an American response at a political level, made this scenario completely unattractive to the Soviets. There was fundamentally "no rational motivation for Moscow to launch. . . . The exchanges would likely escalate to total nuclear war, in which case both sides would be devasted."[94] In fact, they would not even be sure of their ability to destroy the ICBMs. Technical uncertainties in the first attempt at a large, coordinated use of nuclear missiles could easily preclude an attack from going as planned.[95] And whatever the capacity of the weapons "[a]ll of our Minutemen can be launched after an impending attack is confirmed, but long before it could hit them."[96] And most importantly, they cannot be certain the United States would not promptly retaliate without the ICBMs, leaving the Soviets to "face wave after wave of certain retaliation from our bombers and missiles at sea."[97]

Force Characteristics

Within the overall triad structure, weapons can be developed with a wide variety of specific characteristics. Three types of characteristics are especially relevant to the MAD position: size, accuracy and survivability. The MAD advocate evaluates weapons deployments based on the effect those deployments are believed to have on Crisis Stability. Each individual characteristic is seen by the MAD advocate as having the potential to structure Soviet (and any other potential enemy's) interpretations and send a message. The message can be either constructive (stabilizing) or destructive (destabilizing). MAD advocates in almost every instance favor large weapons. It is not that they argue for weapons as large as is technically feasible, for "[a]lthough it is often true that the greater the power to harm others, the greater the power to affect their behavior, the relationship is not linear; past a certain point the ability to destroy may not be useful."[98] Rather, they vehemently oppose the development and deployment of extremely small weapons. The United States has deployed nuclear weapons so small they can be used in a "battlefield capacity" as depth charges, mines, or artillery shells.[99] The MAD advocate rejects all these weapons for the same reason: a "small" weapon does not give the appearance of threatening apocalyptic levels of destruction. Instead, they suggest that the side deploying them sees at least a potential for operational use of nuclear weapons in a controlled, isolated battlefield setting.

The size of these weapons makes them appear "thinkable." Since deterrence in large part comes from all sides being persuaded that the use of nuclear weapons could lead to suicidal destruction, thinkability can undermine the entire structure of deterrence.[100] For these authors, the most important "firebreak" is between conventional and nuclear war. Anything which blurs the distinction between the two types of weapons weakens the firebreak and lowers the "nuclear threshold," the point at which use of nuclear weapons can be expected. This, in turn, is dangerous because any use of those weapons carries an unacceptably high risk of all-out nuclear war. Crisis Stability assumes that the only time nuclear weapons would be used would be in an all-out strategic war.[101] It is the fact that these weapons cannot be used for military gain that keeps both sides from using them.

Smaller weapons, however, would not be particularly useful in a strategic war. With greater firepower than any pre-nuclear weapon, they still offer insignificant yield when compared to the "city-busting" intercontinental missiles.[102] The deployment of such weapons on the U.S. side suggests a strategic doctrine that postulates some operational role for nuclear weapons. Battlefield, tactical, or theater nuclear weapons lead the Soviets to interpret American doctrine in this way. When that message is sent, given the priority the Soviets place on parity, they will counterdeploy their own versions of these weapons (as did, indeed, happen). They would not be able to ignore a system that, with imbalance, might give the United States a political edge.

The inevitable result is that both sides deploy small nuclear weapons. This is a far more unstable, dangerous situation than would exist without such weapons. Each side is left with the impression that, in a purely conventional, regional conflict, the other side might use nuclear weapons to secure advantage or in an attempt to salvage a losing operation. Crisis Stability is then undermined, because a situation exists where there is a definite advantage to using the weapons first.

Either side may use them to effect the outcome of a conventional conflict, or simply because they fear that the other side is about to do so. Once this cycle has started, MAD authors postulate a rapid, cyclical escalation, leading inevitably to strategic war. Alternatively, as each side reaches higher and higher levels of alert, either or both could decide that full-scale nuclear war is inevitable. They could then themselves initiate homeland attacks in the belief that they would suffer less from the retaliation than from a first strike.

Nevertheless, the only result of all the refinements the superpowers have made and continue to make in their nuclear arsenals is that once they believe war is bound to occur, both nations have an increasing incentive to strike first. This is not because either nation thinks it can avoid damage from a retaliatory attack if it strikes first. It is because both nations hope to prevent the much greater devastation each has now given the other good reason to expect from being struck first. It is not because either nation hopes to win a nuclear war. It is because neither nation believes it could otherwise survive one.[103]

The second relevant characteristic of a given weapon is its accuracy. This is generally measured by CEP, or Circular Error Probable. This measures the radius from the target in which at least 50 percent of a given weapon type will fall.[104] For the MAD advocate the smaller the

CEP and the more accurate the weapon, the less desirable it is. In a situation of Crisis Stability, fairly inaccurate weapons are needed. Since MAD assumes that weapons use is deterred by making it clear that if the weapons are used, they will be used against population centers and industrial targets, large and inaccurate weapons are more than adequate. MAD "requires powerful city-killing weapons with no very stringent demands in terms of accuracy."[105] The "zones of destruction" created by a large weapon are such that, if it were off target by several miles it would make very little difference. Extremely accurate weapons, able to come within yards of a specific target, are therefore unnecessary.

When the United States does deploy accurate weapons, the Soviets will have to interpret such a move. Their reasoning, as postulated by MAD authors, would be as follows: Since accurate weapons are not necessary for targeting cities, the United States is either going to great trouble and expense for no reason (an unlikely proposition) or has other targets in mind, targets for which accuracy matters. The only possible target set requiring accurate weapons is military facilities; submarine ports, airforce bases, and most particularly the super-hardened ICBM silos. After all, "[j]ust about any warhead of adequate range and reliability can knock out some section of a city. But it takes special features to destroy targets that are hardened to resist strong blast, such as missile silos."[106] If, then, accuracy leads the Soviets to conclude that their ICBMs are being targeted, it is no longer clear that there is no advantage to being the first to use nuclear weapons.

Accurate weapons obviously exacerbate greatly the intrinsic vulnerability of nonmobile silos. (The fear that the Soviets have or are obtaining accurate weapons generates the fear that American silos are becoming vulnerable, as discussed above.) This would be particularly threatening to the Soviets. The vast bulk of America's strategic warheads are survivably based on bombers or submarines. For various reasons, though, close to 70 percent of Soviet warheads are land based.[107]

It will be quite clear to the Soviets (whatever American intentions) that an accurate counterforce capability is an integral part of a disarming first strike ability. As Scoville indicated, the reasoning for this is simple. Weapons targeted against missile silos must be used in a preemptive attack. "It simmers down to the fact that the only plausible reason for developing a counterforce capability is to acquire the capacity to launch an unanswerable first strike against the Soviet Union."[108] Such weapons are useless in a second, retaliatory strike because they would hit only empty silos. If in a crisis the Soviets felt war was inevitable they would then have every incentive to strike first. Attacking first would not prevent an American retaliation, but it could lessen the effect while ensuring that the post-war status of the superpowers would be approximately equal. "Russia is more likely to be pushed into striking by the fear of what will happen if she does not than pulled to war by the attraction of positive gains. The most potent fear, of course, is that the war will start no matter what the Soviet Union does."[109]

This entire line of argument indicates how much the MAD position rests on assumptions of persuasiveness. The argument against the fear of American ICBM vulnerability essentially rests on the belief that the Soviets have no motivation to attack. It is not argued that, given the ability, an American president is likely to attack the Soviets. Rather, the fear is that sending an inappropriate message will persuade the Soviets that what is in their best interest is an action we hope to discourage.

The danger is particularly high in a crisis because of the nature of both sides' alert systems. In a tense situation, the actions that the United States would take to protect its forces in case of a Soviet launch are the same that would be taken preparatory to an attack. Sound military reasoning may generate pressure for politically ambiguous activities: flushing alert submarines from port, launching strategic bombers, opening silo doors, all moves designed to protect weapons systems, and also all moves taken prior to use of the weapons. A Soviet leadership already convinced that the United States plans a first strike would not be predisposed to interpret such activities in the most favorable light.[110]

The final weapon characteristic of concern to MAD advocates is survivability. For purposes of properly structuring Soviet views of American doctrine, these authors believe it is generally better to procure and deploy weapons with the best possible chance of surviving a Soviet preemptive strike. This is more than operationally intelligent strategy. Survivable weapons are believed to send a clear and stabilizing message to the Soviet leaders.

If the United States based its war plans on the constraints of Crisis Stability, it would work under the assumption that weapons are to be used only in a second strike, as retaliation. It would then need weapons that would remain operational after absorbing a Soviet attack. There is no plausible explanation the Soviets could put forward to explain our deployment of vulnerable weapons that would be consistent with the constraints of Crisis Stability. Vulnerable weapons (new weapons, not those such as second generation ICBMs that became vulnerable after deployment) are only worth developing and deploying if the nation deploying them considers vulnerability irrelevant. And a weapon's vulnerability is only of no concern if the ability to survive an attack does not matter—in other words, when the weapon is intended to be used in a first strike. Once willingness to initiate nuclear war is conveyed to the Soviets, independent of what actual American intentions may be, the same dangers are introduced into the system as with small or accurate weapons.

Command and Control

Command, control, and communication (C3) presents a delicate issue for the MAD advocate. A certain amount of sophistication is necessary if American C3 systems are to communicate the appropriate message. On the other hand, it is very easy to create a system too sophisticated, that will send the exact opposite of the desired message. It is a very fine line.

The C3 system intended to permit the president and others with legal authority to launch nuclear strikes (the NCA or National Command Authority) must have a minimum level of "robustness." It must be survivable enough to ride-out a Soviet attack close to intact. Otherwise, our commitment to launching the promised retaliatory attack would be called into question. Our ability to operationalize and coordinate such an attack would be unclear. Deterrence then might be undermined not because the Soviets did not believe an American retaliation would be devastating but because they did not believe our ability to carry it out was credible.

A robust C3 must be able to support several specific operations. Someone with the authority to launch weapons must survive the initial attack. Those individuals directly responsible for implementing launch orders must survive. The two groups must be able to communicate with each other, so that launch orders can be sent. Launch crews must be able to receive, confirm, and respond to those orders.

If it does not appear to the Soviets that our C3 capability is adequate to support these operations and guarantee a second strike, and if it appears to them that it also does not appear adequate to us, they again must construct a plausible rationale for our behavior. Because even a weak C3 structure could certainly operate well prior to an attack, a non-survivable C3 structure sends a destabilizing message. If the United States planned to rely on purely second strike abilities it would have to be an American priority to construct a command system that would meet the needs of that policy. If we both lack the appropriate C3 abilities and are unconcerned with that lack, it would only be because the system was not actually designed to function in a post-strike environment. A weak C3 can too easily be interpreted by the Soviets as proof of an American first strike policy. They would believe that the system was not survivable simply because it was not intended to be.[111]

For this reason, MAD advocates will generally support basic improvements in the system. For example, they would support various upgrades in the airborne command posts used by the services.[112] Hardening relevant phone lines, protecting groundlinks for U.S. satellites, and generally building more redundancy into C3 systems are all supported.[113]

From the MAD perspective it is possible to go too far. A C3 system needs to be secure enough to ride out an attack and last long enough to coordinate a single, devastating retaliatory launch against the Soviet Union. Once that has been accomplished additional capabilities and layers of sophistication can send an inappropriate message. A massive retaliatory strike is a "blunt instrument." Subtle gradations over a prolonged period of time are irrelevant and unnecessary. All that is needed is the ability to send a single "go code." A nondegradable C3 system—or the attempt to construct one—communicates more.

The survivable ability to send graduated, specific instructions to nuclear forces in a post-strike environment is believed by the MAD advocate to communicate a destabilizing interest in developing a prolonged warfighting capability. "The primary systems requirement for a protracted nuclear war strategy is a C3 system capable of surviving and enduring for the notional period of such a war—say 60 days."[114] It is for this reason that MAD advocates do not support most of the proposed C3 upgrades of the Reagan Administration. They are believed to go too far.

Both the weapons and C3I programs of the Reagan Administration can be understood as a continuation of America's effort to align its nuclear posture with the requirements of flexible response. In terms of C3I the stated goal is to create a system that allows for central, flexible direction of strategic forces throughout a protracted nuclear conflict. To this end, the administration has said it would increase C3I endurance and provide for its reconstruction to ensure continuing positive control over the forces for six months.[115]

It is only a strategy of prolonged warfighting that requires that the NCA communicate with its forces, not once, but over a period of days, weeks, or months. Any indication that this is American strategy again undermines Crisis Stability.

It suggests a belief in the operational value of nuclear weapons: that they can be used like any other weapons in wars rationally conducted along the lines of classical military strategy. It, in short, communicates a lack of faith in the primary tenet of MAD: that nuclear weapons have fundamentally altered warfare. It is a "conventionalization" of nuclear weapons: "the attitude that classical theories of military operations can be applied to the conduct of prolonged nuclear war."[116] If that becomes the Soviet perception of American doctrine then, again, they could easily convince themselves that there is a benefit to first use in a crisis.

Therefore, while upgrades such as better equipment for airborne command posts will be supported, MAD authors reject proposals for fundamental restructuring of the C3 system. The Ground Warning Emergency Network (GWEN), a series of radio towers interconnected across the United States is, for example, rejected as destabilizing and ineffective.[117]

CRITIQUE

As the above analysis indicates MAD authors neither support nor reject weapons systems in an automatic or unreasoned fashion. Rather, their opinions on procurement decisions all stem from the application of a sophisticated theoretical construct, even if that construct is based on a methodological analysis which is fundamentally circular. What makes MAD particularly rhetorical is that it is in essence a purely argumentative structure, defining a view of persuasion. Based on assumptions that, though empirical, cannot be falsified or proven with certainty, the entire structure is designed to maximize deterrence by minimizing motives for nuclear war.

The claims of the MAD authors cannot be proven either in the abstract or in relation to competing claims from alternative positions. This is the case for two reasons. First, although the nature of the Soviet audience can be argued, certain knowledge of motives cannot be obtained. MAD authors base their portrait of the Soviets on findings gleaned from Soviet texts. They believe these texts adequate to inform a "reading" of Soviet actions. The texts become legitimate representations of motives through the construction of an interpretive framework, but that framework provides the basis for argument, not final proof. This is especially true since it is only the framework that permits the MAD analyst to reject competing forms of evidence. The framework subsumes evidentiary counterclaims rather than refuting them. The Soviet Union was, after all, a society closed to us and in the final analysis the Soviet leadership viewed its relationship to the United States as, at best, competitive. Perfect information beyond argument was unobtainable. Identical evidence is available to analysts of different schools of thought. It is because certainty is impossible that competing conclusions can be drawn, and reliance on argument became necessary.

Second, because the Soviets were not about to step in and correct our decisionmaking processes if our assumptions were wrong, the interpretive framework can only be defended through argument. There was not, and never could have been, definitive evidence certifying the MAD position as true or false. The only event that would have supplied empirical data of this kind is the one all sides sought to prevent, and an act whose consummation would in all likelihood have made the outcome of the dispute irrelevant. "As defense analyst Pierre Sprey says, 'Strategic analysis is a dream world. It is the realm of data-free analysis.' "[118] It is "a system of abstract logic, all of whose principal postulates have been derived deductively."[119]

Because MAD is itself an argumentative structure, historical acts cannot falsify conclusions. Rather, rationales for action are provided which permit interpretation of Soviet acts in a manner consistent with the theoretical structure. In this way historical events become "textualized," and can be critiqued from within the assumptions of the analytic structure. Analysis of Soviet texts provides the basis for defending that structure. The structure is, in turn, used to place the now textualized acts in the proper context for analysis. In its development of a position on the meaning and purpose of deterrence and its search for the appropriate deterrence posture, MAD is fundamentally a theory of communication. It details both the ways in which we can communicate with the Soviets and the proper way to approach those signs of Soviet doctrine unintentionally "left behind." The theory requires a search for textual artifacts and delineates a method for applying the framework asserted to be embedded in the texts to the acts. Only this process assures motives will be "properly" read.

Therefore, the Soviet occupations and military actions in Eastern Europe and Afghanistan are not used as proof for the theory's portrait. Instead, the portrait is created and then used to generate a series of arguments explaining the actions as consistent with the theory. In this way, the disconfirming power of historical events is denied. Afghanistan does not prove the Soviet's defensive and non-ideological nature, it leads the MAD advocate to construct explanatory claims as to why the invasion of Afghanistan does not prove the opposite. The projected Soviet characteristics can be used to explain that they are paranoid enough to have been motivated to undertake drastic action at the mere potential of a hostile government on their Southern border. The theory *explains* the evidence rather than the evidence *proving* the theory. Because MAD is a theory about how to interpret texts and then acts, there is no confirming or disconfirming evidence. Once the analyst develops the portrait of the Soviets, the position becomes self-sealing. It does not seek to explain Soviet actions as much as it looks to subsume them into its explanatory framework.

Critics who generate attacks on the MAD position from within alternative analytic frameworks gain little ground. As I will argue in the next chapter, warfighters make the same types of assumptions: They simply make different substantive claims. What would be more productive is a critique of MAD from the structural perspective, an analysis of the way MAD functions rather than of what it says. Since MAD is a theory of persuasion it is appropriate that its assumptions concerning how communication works be opened to analysis and subject to critique.

The most basic assumption driving MAD is that American decisions regarding procurement and deployment of strategic forces can be used as a form of communication. Our actions "signal" our intentions in a nonverbal, but easily understandable, way. Once it has been determined what message will persuade the Soviets to refrain from various activities we can work backwards from that point. It is possible to construct and deploy a strategic force structure that articulates the right message to the Soviets. The weapons, their number, their characteristics, taken together create a nondiscursive symbolic message that can generate the Soviet interpretations we desire.

From the point of view of the rhetorical critic, this approach makes some sense. Critics recognize that symbols do not need to be discursive to effectively and persuasively communicate.[120] And if that is truly reflective of communication between individual rhetors and their audiences, there is no reason to believe it would not be the case between governments composed of individual human beings. It is important to note that this assumption is so deeply embedded in the theory as a whole that it is not explicitly considered. MAD authors discuss signalling, but that is an entirely different construct.

The term "signalling" refers to certain actions that can be used within the context of preexisting force structures to send a specific message in a specific situation. For example, raising the alert levels of American nuclear forces can be used to "signal" resolve during a regional crisis. Beyond the communicative resources of the overall force structure, the manipulation of elements of that force structure can lend specificity to a message conveyed, making it temporally and spatially precise. My argument is that the basis of the way procurement decisions are supported and opposed is the predicted communicative impact of the decision. Signalling theory assumes that form of communication is already in place. Yet the basis of the more general argument—the idea that force structures can communicate nondiscursively—is so fundamental as to almost completely avoid discussion.

Any given procurement decision may be disputed on other grounds, for example, cost or efficiency. But these are not arguments grounded in strategic theory. They are additive. Arguments about the costs and benefits of a given procurement decision's effect on strategic stability are always based on the way a given weapon will affect Soviet perceptions: that is, its persuasive potential.

Additional proof for this perspective comes from the avoidance of any discussion of what would happen if deterrence fails. As I will argue, warfighters use the same approach for arguments over the comparative quality of the doctrines. MAD authors argue that warfighting increases the likelihood of a deterrence failure, and that failure would be disastrous. The disastrous consequences of nuclear war are discussed, but only insofar as they are relevant to the determination of the constraints on deterrence. The question of what would happen if deterrence failed is not considered, because it is not judged relevant. The only point of the theoretical exercise is to develop a set of conditions under which the opposing parties can be persuaded to avoid that situation.

At a superficial level, force structures can be defended for two reasons:

"perceptual" benefits of a political nature, vis-à-vis the Soviets, and purely military benefits. But this distinction ultimately collapses of its own weight. Since no one actively desires a nuclear war, military capability is not judged good per se, at least at the nuclear level. It is only a benefit or detriment in so far as it influences Soviet perceptions and, hence, decision making.

The problem with MAD as theory of persuasion is that it is mechanistic in its interpretation and application of human communication processes. The basis for the American force structure is held to be (and therefore in the final analysis is) the attempt to consciously exercise control over Soviet interpretations of American goals and intentions: It sends a message. Credibility in large measure refers to a rhetor's ability to convince an audience of his or her sincerity. It is no mistake that the label has been borrowed by strategic theorists and applied almost obsessively.

It is assumed that the Soviets will be able to clearly interpret our decisions. There may be debate between strategic theorists over what message would be appropriate, as the next chapter will show. But there is no real questioning of the essential premise: We effect Soviet interpretations, and because we can, within constraints, prejudge the way they will interpret certain moves, we can do so consciously. There may be debate over whether, say, large ICBMs send a message that is appropriate; there is no debate over what message is sent. Stasis rests on the issue of which portrait of the Soviet leadership is the appropriate one.

Additionally, there is agreement that the Soviets communicate with us, although there is dispute over whether they do so through texts (as MAD authors hold) or through deployments (as warfighters argue). However, although strategic doctrine is designed to permit U.S. policymakers to communicate forcefully and intentionally with their Soviet counterparts, the Soviets themselves were not believed to be engaging in the same sort of behavior. In fact, those MAD analysts who argued that the Soviet goal is to avoid war but to use an all out effort to win if war is begun prove this point. The Soviets do not deploy weapons to persuade, but to provide themselves with operational military capabilities. The military/political distinction is judged appropriate in the Soviet case. It is assumed that from the Soviet perspective military deployments are purely functional—that is, meant to support a military effort. True, procurement decisions are believed to carry usable information, in the sense that any individual's actions will tell an educated analyst something about that person. For the MAD theorist, the United States communicates (or at least intends to) in a direct, thoughtful way with force composition and deployment. The Soviet Union does not. Since it has forces and they cannot be hidden, information is unavoidably gained by the discerning analyst. We deploy to communicate such a message as will yield war avoidance. They deploy in order to be able to "win" (although what that means is not clear) should their other efforts at war avoidance fail. For the Soviets, preparation involves an analysis of what would be militarily useful in a nuclear war. For the United States, preparation involves an analysis of what would be necessary to persuade an opponent that our preparation undermines any motive to initiate nuclear exchanges.

Thus, while Soviet actions can be communicative, the forces that provide the context for these actions are not. Just as the United States may "signal" in a crisis, the Soviets will also engage in specific manipulations of military forces in order to send a message. But whereas American deployment choices at the nuclear level are guided by arguments over the way those choices will be interpreted in the Soviet Union, Soviet choices are held to be guided by far less sophisticated criteria. They are based solely on calculations of Soviet needs at an operational level, with no concern for the communicative potential for such choices. Their military deployments are not signals, intentionally constructed nondiscursive messages, but evidence. These "evidentiary signals" can be interpreted from within the framework of the MAD analyst. That is, although the MAD analyst does not see such choices as intentionally communicative, they can still be "properly" interpreted in light of the portrait of the Soviets already developed from the prior textual analysis. Such decisions do need to be explained as being consistent with that portrait: they are purposeful reflections of centralized decision making. The "bureaucratic push" model of decision making is not generally applied to the Soviet Union. The MAD model of communication, then, is mechanistic in that the United States sends, the Soviet Union receives. The Soviets do not communicate back except insofar as they cannot in all instances hide their reactions (the "feedback loop").

The perception that the Soviets do not attempt manipulation of military force deployments to communicate colors interpretation of Soviet texts. After all, the key determinant of whether a text is relevant in the construction of an audience analysis is whether or not it is genuine. And the only way to prove that a text is genuine is to prove that it was not intended for Western audiences. A statement meant for the West—an intended communication—is almost automatically disregarded as propagandistic, hence unimportant. Such statements are not completely irrelevant. Great weight, for example, is placed on Nikita Khrushchev's statements that war was not "fatalistically inevitable" and on Brezhnev's that a nuclear war must never be fought.[121] But they are still tainted in that the validity of such statements cannot be assumed. Internal documents, or rather documents argued to be internal, are always given presumption as being more reflective of Soviet thought. So in neither the initial textual analysis nor in the subsequent analysis of Soviet actions, is the Soviet leadership ever given a legitimate voice. That the leadership might have been developing force structures based on their own portrait United States, in an attempt to structure our interpretations, is never given consideration.[122]

CONCLUSION

It would be a mistake to characterize these authors as relentlessly rejecting all military expenditures under all circumstances. They do support various proposals, while rejecting a large number, but in all instances their judgments are dictated by a complicated theoretical structure. The ultimate question that must be answered about any weapons system is the effect it will have on the overall endeavor of structuring Soviet interpretations.

While this structure is sophisticated, it suffers from two flaws. It is obviously intended as a theory of persuasion in-the-particular-case. Yet its audience analysis is based on a circular methodology that permits the analyst to support all conclusions in a nonfalsifiable way. Second, at the other end of the process, where the prospective audience is presumably responding to initial messages in an on-going cycle, there is no room in the model for reciprocal communicative efforts. No attempt is made to explore evidence from a point of view that would admit that the reactions might be communicative efforts. This makes the theory mechanistic, and adds to the unreliability of the method employed for the audience analysis. Of course, since deterrence depends on directing the appropriate message to an audience, such a flaw is a considerable problem in developing an effective persuasive posture.

NOTES

1. Thus MAD theorists believe that the mutual vulnerability of the superpowers as civilizations is an unavoidable condition of the nuclear age. Aside from the specifics of the debate over President Reagan's proposed Strategic Defense Initiative, the condition of vulnerability will remain until well into the twenty-first century. See Robert Jervis, *The Illogic of American Nuclear Strategy* (Ithaca, N.Y.: Cornell University Press, 1984), 42; Tom Gervasi, *The Myth of Soviet Military Superiority* (New York: Harper and Row, 1986), 15; David Holloway, *The Soviet Union and the Arms Race*, 2nd ed. (New Haven: Yale University Press, 1984), 50; Robert Jervis, "Strategic Theory: What's New and What's True," Unpublished manuscript, Center for the Study of War and Peace, Columbia University, New York, April 1986, 14, 47. Because of this, the justification for strategic nuclear weapons is to deter the use of an opponent's nuclear weapons. See, for example, Jervis, *The Illogic*, 24–25 and McGeorge Bundy, "The Unimpressive Record of Atomic Diplomacy," in Gwyn Prins, ed., *The Nuclear Crisis Reader* (New York: Vintage Books, September 1984), especially 47–49. Bundy

explicitly argues (42) "one way of reducing the hazards of the nuclear age is to understand more clearly the sharp limits on their usefulness for anything but the avoidance of nuclear war." See also Robert MacNamara, *Blundering Into Disaster: Surviving the First Century of the Nuclear Age* (New York: Pantheon Books, 1986), 30. "Thus, strategic nuclear weapons have lost whatever military utility may once have been attributed to them. Their sole purpose at present, is to deter the other side's first use of its strategic forces."

2. Robert Jervis, "Deterrence Theory Revisited," *World Politics* 31, no. 2 (January 1979): 300. He also argues; "But in fact statesmen cannot dismiss the dangers that what starts out as controlled violence [even at the conventional level] could lead to all-out war." Jervis, "What's New," 16. See also MacNamara, *Blundering*, 35. MAD authors also argue that the uncertainties intrinsic to the use of nuclear weapons make precise, graduated war plans impossible to implement. See Desmond Ball, *Can Nuclear War Be Controlled?*, Adelphi Paper, no. 169 (London: Institute for Strategic Studies, Autumn 1981), 30; Desmond Ball, *Targeting for Strategic Deterrence*, Adelphi Paper, no. 185 (London: Institute for Strategic Studies, Summer 1985), 41; and Bruce Blair, *Strategic Command and Control: Redefining the Nuclear Threat* (Washington, D.C.: The Brookings Institution, 1985), 217.

3. In other words, as I will argue, the actual numbers of a weapons system are less important to the evaluation of these authors than the specific weapons characteristics. See Jervis, "What's New," 20.

4. As one author said, "In order to be effective as a deterrent, U.S. retaliatory forces must be able to survive the worst conceivable enemy attack, *and still* cause massive destruction in the Soviet Union." Robert Aldridge, *The Counterforce Syndrome: A Guide to U.S. Nuclear Weapons and Strategic Doctrine* (Washington, D.C.: Institute for Policy Studies, 1979), 1. (Emphasis in original.)

5. See note 1 for a discussion of "active defense." Civil Defense ("passive defense") is also rejected as impossible by these authors. See Jennifer Leaning and Langley Keys, eds., *The Counterfeit Ark: Crisis Relocation for Nuclear War* (Cambridge: Ballinger Publishing Co., 1984).

6. This is primarily the case because of the Electromagnetic Pulse (EMP), an effect of high altitude nuclear detonations. Although EMP does not affect buildings or people, even a few weapons exploded over the United States could destroy all microchips and transmissions in most of the United States and in parts of Canada and Mexico. See Paul Bracken, *The Command and Control of Nuclear Forces* (New Haven: Yale University Press, 1983), 112 and 235. For a description of other effects of nuclear war see Ruth Adams and Susan Cullen, eds., *The Final Epidemic: Physicians and Scientists on Nuclear War* (Chicago: Educational Foundation for Nuclear Science, 1981). While there has been a significant debate over effects of more limited war scenarios (see Brad Sparks, "The Scandal of Nuclear Winter," *National Review* 37, no. 22 (November 15, 1985): 28–38), particularly the question of what number of weapons of what size are necessary to produce a given impact, there has not been equivalent debate over the effects of total war.

7. Ken Booth, "Nuclear Deterrence and 'World War III': How Will History Judge?" in Roman Kolkowicz, ed., *The Logic of Nuclear Terror* (Boston: Allen and Unwin, 1987), 251.

8. See, for example, Blair, *Strategic Command*, 213 and 233.

9. Ball, Adelphi Paper no. 185, 25–26.

10. Jervis, "What's New," 7.

11. Ball, Adelphi Paper no. 185, 28 and 31.

12. Ball, Adelphi Paper no. 185, 34.

13. Ball, Adelphi Paper no. 169, 30.

14. Ball, Adelphi Paper no. 185, 27 and 32.

15. Blair, *Strategic Command*, 266.

16. Ball, Adelphi Paper no. 169, 35 and Jervis, "What's New," 42.

17. At least 160 cities per Poseidon could be targeted. Aldridge, *Counterforce Syndrome*, 10.

18. Even if command and control facilities were not specifically targeted, the EMP effect would still effectively destroy the system. See Blair, *Strategic Command*, 228, and Bracken, *Command and Control*.

19. Jervis, "What's New," 16, and Blair, *Strategic Command*, 219. It should be noted that the firebreak, a clearly defined pause between escalatory steps, created in part by the way the forces are structured, is a fairly rhetorical construct because it involves structuring perceptions in such a way as to make certain decisions appear more important than others.

20. See Chapter 3.

21. Jervis, "Deterrence and Perception," *International Security* 7, no. 3 (Winter 1982–1983): 3.

22. Colin Gray, "Strategic Forces and Salt: A Question of Strategy," *Comparative Strategy* 2, no. 2 (1980): 117.

23. Raymond Garthoff, "Letter to the Editor," *Comparative Strategy* 2, no. 4 (1980): 365. (Emphasis in original.)

24. Garthoff, "Letter," 366.

25. Colin Gray, "Letter to the Editor," *Comparative Strategy* 2, no. 4 (1980): 366.

26. Gray, "Letter," 367.

27. Jonathon Steele, *Soviet Power: The Kremlin's Foreign Policy—Brezhnev to Chernenko* (New York: Simon and Schuster, 1983), 15.

28. Steele, *Soviet Power*, 15.

29. Holloway, *The Soviet Union*, 16 and 28.

30. Holloway notes in *The Soviet Union*, 33: "No contradiction is seen between the prevention of war and the preparation for war; war can be prevented only if the Soviet Union prepares to wage it." See also, Steele, *Soviet Power*, 17.

31. Steele notes (*Soviet Power*, 16) "Whatever exaggeration or distortion there may be in this analysis, it is part of Soviet historiography and the received perception of Soviet leaders."

32. For example, "throughout its history, whether Russian or Soviet, the nation has been unprepared for those invasions. Its armed forces have had to fall back and defend on their own territory, and the people suffered for years before the invaders were driven from the land. As a consequence, between wars, the nation adopted a policy of continental expansion ... to create buffer states around the Russian homeland." William Manthorpe, Jr., "A Background for Understanding Soviet Strategy," in Philip Gillette and Willard Frank, Jr.,

eds., *The Sources of Soviet Naval Conduct* (Lexington, Mass.: Lexington Books, 1990), 5.

33. Holloway, *The Soviet Union*, 96.

34. See Chapter 3.

35. Holloway, *The Soviet Union*, 97.

36. Jervis, "Deterrence and Perception," 5.

37. Harold Brown, quoted in Jervis, "Deterrence and Perception," 6.

38. I will develop this position in more detail in Chapter 3. However, the classic statement of this argument comes from Colin Gray, who says: "[i]t is a sobering thought that the loss of 30 or 40 million people might well be compatible with a context defined by the Soviet leadership as victory." "What Deters? The Ability to Wage Nuclear War," in John Reichart and Steven Sturm, eds., *American Defense Policy*, 5th ed. (Baltimore: Johns Hopkins University Press, 1982), 179.

39. Fred Kaplan, *Dubious Spector: A Skeptical Look at the Soviet Threat*, 4th ed. (Washington, D.C.: Institute for Policy Studies, 1984), 22.

40. See Jervis, *The Illogic*, 108, and Holloway, *The Soviet Union*, 98.

41. Mandelbaum has argued that this is in large part a function of nuclear weapons, that the weapons themselves instill a sense of conservatism. See Michael Mandelbaum, *The Nuclear Revolution: International Politics Before and After Hiroshima* (Cambridge: Cambridge University Press, 1981), 177–206. See also Bundy, "Unimpressive Record."

42. See for example, Edward Luttwak, *The Grand Strategy of the Soviet Union* (New York: St. Martin's Press, 1983).

43. Steele, *Soviet Power*, 32.

44. Jervis, *The Illogic*, 57. Although it is primarily Jervis who uses this label, he cites it as coming originally from Hans Morgenthau. "What's New," 15.

45. Holloway, *The Soviet Union*, 179.

46. Jervis, *The Illogic*, 106.

47. Holloway, *The Soviet Union*, 52. See also Robin Laird and Dale Herspring, *The Soviet Union and the Strategic Arms Race* (Boulder: Westview Press, 1984), 5, and Jervis, *The Illogic*, 30.

48. Holloway, *The Soviet Union*, 49. See also, David Holloway, "Soviet Policy and the Arms Race," in Prins, ed., *Nuclear Crisis Reader*, 113.

49. Although this process became admittedly more difficult as glasnost progressed, and increasing numbers of "institutniki" or civilian analysts similar to think tankers in the United States entered the fray.

50. Holloway, *The Soviet Union*, 32–33.

51. Holloway, *The Soviet Union*, 56.

52. Holloway, *The Soviet Union*, 164–168.

53. Ann Sloan, "Soviet Positions on Strategic Arms Control and Arms Policy: A Perspective Outside the Military Establishment," in Roman Kolkowicz and Ellen Mickiewicz, eds., *The Soviet Calculus of Nuclear War* (Lexington, Mass.: Lexington Books, 1986), 120.

54. Kaplan, *Dubious Spector*, 19.

55. Holloway, *The Soviet Union*, 55.

56. Blair, *Strategic Command*, 218.

57. Jervis, *The Illogic*, 104.

58. Jervis, *The Illogic*, 106.

59. Paul Watzlawick, *How Real Is Real?* (New York: Vintage Books, February 1977), 62.

60. Gervasi, *The Myth*, 32.

61. Laird and Herspring, *The Soviet Union*, 96.

62. Holloway, *The Soviet Union*, 101 and 180, and Laird and Herspring, *The Soviet Union*, 6.

63. Holloway, *The Soviet Union*, 46.

64. Laird, "Preface," in Laird and Herspring, *The Soviet Union*, xiii.

65. See, for example, Robbin Laird and Dale Herspring, "The Soviet Union and Strategic Arms," in Laird and Eric Hoffman, eds., *Soviet Foreign Policy in a Changing World* (New York: Aldine, 1986).

66. Jervis, *The Illogic*, 60.

67. Robert Neild, "What Political Signals Should Our Armed Forces Send?" in Prins, ed., *Nuclear Crisis Reader*, 212.

68. This is the thesis of both Kaplan, *Dubious Spector*, and Gervasi, *The Myth*.

69. The body of literature discussing these difficulties is almost entirely generated by MAD authors (see Chapter 1.)

70. Kaplan, *Dubious Spector*, 15. Others speak of the "distorting selectivity" of Pipes' work. See R. R. Baker, "Book Reviews," *Defense Analysis* 5, no. 2 (June 1989): 168.

71. Laird and Herspring, *The Soviet Union*, 25.

72. It is argued that many documents of the late 1950s and early 1960s which seem to address strategic warfighting actually refer to the Soviets' relationship with China. Kaplan, *Dubious Spector*, 18. The date of other documents leads these authors to argue that they actually discuss Soviet perceptions of American strategy. See Gervasi, *The Myth*, 233.

73. See Ball, Adelphi Paper no. 169, 30–35; Blair, *Strategic Command*, 218, and Laird and Herspring, *The Soviet Union*, 66–67.

74. Kaplan, *Dubious Spector*, 15.

75. Baker, "Book Reviews," 168.

76. Herbert Scoville, Jr., *MX: Prescription for Disaster*, 4th ed. (Cambridge, Mass.: The MIT Press, January 1982), 140.

77. Neild, "What Signals," 212. For a description of NTMs and their uses see Michael Krepon, *Arms Control: Verification and Compliance*, Foreign Policy Headline Series no. 270 (New York: September/October 1984). See also Gervasi, *The Myth*, 91.

78. Neild, "What Signals," 210.

79. Richard Ned Lebow, "Deterrence Reconsidered: The Challenge of Recent Research," *Survival* 27, no. 1 (1985): 21.

80. Scoville, *MX*, 140.

81. The balance results from assymetries in basing mode, accuracy, reliability, and size (in megatonnage,) For specific comparative information about the two arsenals see John Collins, *U.S.-Soviet Military Balance 1980–1985* (Washington, D.C.: Pergamon-Brassey's International Defense Publishers, 1985).

82. Gervasi, *The Myth*, 87.

83. Gervasi, *The Myth*, 86–87.

84. Gervasi, *The Myth*, 95.

85. Manthorpe argues that the combination of access to Western technology

and social isolation "has given the Soviets feelings of superiority and pride—and also inferiority and embarrassment." "Background for Understanding," 4.

86. This is a result of ARP, the Action-Reaction Phenomenon. For an overview to the theoretical literature on ARP, see William Baugh, *The Politics of Nuclear Balance: Ambiguity and Continuity in Strategic Policies* (New York: Longman, Inc., 1984), 95–97. For a specific application to the U.S.-Soviet strategic relationship see Holloway, *The Soviet Union*, 178.

87. Jervis, *The Illogic*, 44.

88. Holloway, *The Soviet Union*, 179.

89. For a description of the way weapons on both sides are fit into the triad structure see Nigel Flynn, *The Nuclear Duel* (New York: Arco, 1985).

90. Gervasi, *The Myth*, 10.

91. Gervasi, *The Myth*, 11.

92. For a state by state listing of nuclear weapons facilities and strategic sites see "U.S. Nuclear Infrastructure," in William Arkin and Richard Fieldhouse, *Nuclear Battlefields* (Cambridge, Mass.: Ballinger, 1985), 171–250.

93. For an extended discussion of the impacts associated with various scenarios, see William Daugherty, Barbara Levi, and Frank von Hippel, "The Consequences of 'Limited' Nuclear Attacks on the United States," *International Security* 19, no. 4 (Spring 1986): 3–45.

94. Aldridge, *Counterforce Syndrome*, 8.

95. Gervasi, *The Myth*, 10, and Kaplan, *Dubious Spector*.

96. Gervasi, *The Myth*, 10.

97. Gervasi, *The Myth*, 10.

98. Jervis, *The Illogic*, 23.

99. For a description of these weapons see Thomas Cochran, William Arkin, and Milton Hoenig, *Nuclear Weapons Data Book*, Volume 1: *U.S. Nuclear Forces and Capabilities* (Cambridge, Mass.: Ballinger Publishing Co., 1984). The following sections are especially relevant: "Surface Combatant Ships," 255–263, "Nuclear Artillery," 300–309, and "Atomic Demolition Munitions and Earth Penetration Weapons," 311. See also "Nuclear Battlefield Weapons," in Christopher Chant and Ian Hogg, *Nuclear War in the 1980s?* (New York: Harper and Row, 1983), 74–75.

100. This imperative led to the argument that even if a war could be controlled, losses would be unacceptable. See William Daugherty et al., "The Consequences of 'Limited' Nuclear Attacks on the United States," *International Security* 10, no. 4 (Spring 1986): 3–45.

101. "Strategic" in this usage means that nuclear strikes would be aimed at each side's homeland, rather than being used in a spatially restricted manner, on a given "battlefield" or regional "theater."

102. For precise data on the yield of given weapons see Arkin et al., *Data Book*.

103. Gervasi, *The Myth*, 35.

104. For the precise formula used to determine CEP see Kaplan, *Dubious Spector*, 31. Limitations are noted, 42.

105. Allan Krass and Dan Smith, "Fallacies in Deterrence and Warfighting Strategies," Paul Joseph and Simon Rosenblum, eds., *Search for Sanity* (Boston: South End Press, 1984), 22.

106. Kaplan, *Dubious Spector*, 28.

107. Kaplan, *Dubious Spector*, 56.

108. Aldridge, *Counterforce Syndrome*, 8.

109. Jervis, "What's New," 52.

110. "Actions taken for purely military considerations may, under some circumstances, contradict or exceed the political signal that is desired. Conversely, the political restraints placed upon operational preparations in a crisis may, under other circumstances, unintentionally reduce force readiness." Scott Sagan, "Nuclear Alerts and Crisis Management," *International Security* 9, no. 4 (1985): 99. See also Alexander George, "Crisis Management: The Interaction of Political and Military Considerations," *Survival* 26, no. 5 (1984): 223–224; Gervasi, *The Myth*, 37; and Jervis, "What's New," 21.

111. That there were weaknesses was clear. For example, the system was constructed on the assumption that after a Soviet attack only the various airborne systems would survive. (Ball, Adelphi Paper no. 169, 15.) Yet despite missile flight times of fifteen to thirty minutes these specially outfitted communications planes took almost an hour to come fully on line until well into the 1980s. (Blair, *Strategic Command*, 230.) At least one crucial line, the Navy's TACAMO (Take Command and Move Out) planes, meant to control the ballistic missiles submarines, could not be refueled in flight. They would not, therefore, have stayed on line for more than ten and a half hours. (Ball, Adelphi Paper no. 169, 17.)

112. Besides TACAMO, the Strategic Air Command uses the "Looking Glass" planes, which were on twenty-four hour alert in the air from the 1960s through 1990, to coordinate the bombers and NEACP (National Emergency Airborne Command Post) which would presumably have provided overall coordination. For a description see Chant and Hogg, *Nuclear War*, 38–39.

113. See for example, Ashton Carter, "Assessing Command System Vulnerability," in Carter, Steinbruner and Zracket, eds., *Managing Nuclear Operations*, especially 605–610.

114. Ball, Adelphi Paper no. 185, 36.

115. Blair, *Strategic Command*, 212–213.

116. Jervis, *The Illogic*, 56–64.

117. See Arkin et al., *Nuclear Battlefields*, 31–32.

118. Quoted in Kaplan, *Dubious Spector*, 41.

119. Lebow, "Deterrence Reconsidered," 20. In fact "One cannot even say that these questions have objective answers that could be determined by the course of an actual war, because the way such a war would be fought and its outcome would depend in part on beliefs." Jervis, *The Illogic*, 38.

120. See, for example, Stephen Littlejohn, "Symbolic Interactionism as an Approach to the Study of Human Communication," *Quarterly Journal of Speech* 63, no. 1 (1977): 84–91.

121. See the first chapter of Laird and Herspring, *The Soviet Union*.

122. It is true that the Soviets are seen to have manipulated their force structures in order to persuade the West in certain instances, but these are instances of deception, where Soviet forces were made to appear far greater numerically than they actually were.

Chapter Three

Warfighting as Theory of Persuasion

This chapter examines the assumptions and structure of warfighting from a rhetorical perspective. Although warfighting advocates may not have believed it possible to fight a nuclear war, they do hold that American force structures should be constructed on the assumption that it is. Based on textual analyses of the works of these authors, I will explicate the assumptions (concerning the Soviet Union and nuclear war) from which such a position was constructed. From that analysis, I will examine the way warfighting was conceived and structured as a theory of persuasion which was intended to provide an alternative to MAD. Finally, I will offer a critique of warfighting, along the lines of the previous chapter. Two basic versions of this doctrine can be identified. Both versions advocate preparation for waging selected types of nuclear combat. Both hold that the best deterrent posture is the operational capacity to successfully wage nuclear war. The most persuasive message that can be sent to the Soviet leadership is not that their society will be punished for aggressive behavior, but that their military (and therefore political) goals will be denied to them.

What is essential, then, is the operational capacity to effectively wage war at the nuclear level. Stability is assured through the clear possession of a number of options, and the ability to dominate each level of war implied by those options. *Escalation Dominance*, clear superiority at every potential level of violence, is the best way to ensure deterrence of the Soviets or any other potential enemy. Such dominance creates a situation where the potential opponent knows they cannot win a war, even if they were willing to accept the risks associated with various escalatory moves. To ensure the credibility of American options, it is also necessary for the United States to possess *Damage Limitation*. This is the capacity to, at least in some measure, restrict or control the amount of damage opposing, in this case generally Soviet, forces can impose on the American homeland. Without such an ability, warfighters were afraid that the Soviets would become more willing to take risks, deciding that we would be unwilling to exercise in a war the options we had prepared in peace. Such a judgment could have led to a failure of deterrence, as the Soviets came to believe we would deny to ourselves the military actions necessary to defeat them in the field.

Disagreement between warfighters centers more on tactics than strategy. The question revolves around the issue of defining the "successful" prosecution of a nuclear war. Is defeating the Soviet Union sufficient, or is there some goal we can define as American "victory"? If there is a substantive difference between a Soviet defeat and an American victory, is one set of capabilities more persuasive that the other? This debate in turn focuses on the subsidiary question of what target set, or sets, must be threatened in order to convince the Soviets that they will "lose," whatever that might mean in Soviet terms.

In spite of espousing concern over strategy and tactics for an actual nuclear war, warfighting advocates freely admitted that their scenarios could not actually be implemented and that, in particular, disputes over targeting sets were academic. Once a war had actually begun, the ability to determine which target set had been destroyed would have been nonexistent. Thus, although the substantive assumptions of warfighting differ dramatically from those of MAD, they are constructed within a conceptual framework that is almost identical. Deterrence remains the goal for these advocates, but they hold that the way to assure stability is to multiply, not limit, strategic options.

TEXTUAL ANALYSIS

As with MAD advocates, warfighting authors developed a coherent set of criteria with which to evaluate policy decisions concerning the U.S.-Soviet strategic relationship. And, as with MAD authors, this theoretical structure rests on basic, underlying assumptions that can be discerned from a close textual analysis of documents.

Assumptions about the Soviet Union

I here reverse the order of analysis from Chapter 2 because the advocates reverse their priorities. Whereas MAD advocates view nuclear was as the ultimate failure and collapse of policy, warfighters (while not understating the physical devastation a war would bring) feared the Soviets more. Thus where MAD advocates saw war-avoidance as an ultimate constraint on policy choices, warfighters were willing to tolerate higher levels of risk so long as their ultimate policy requirement—effective constraint on the Soviets—was met.

These assumptions about the Soviet Union fit into the conceptual framework of the appeasement theory of war, which is essentially a rewriting of the containment theory of the 1950s. Some nations are aggressor states. They seek to make the most of all opportunities for expansion of their control and dominance over weaker states. Victim states have two options for dealing with aggressors. They can respond quickly and forcibly to every attempt at expansion, or they can attempt to satisfy the aggressor through small concessions, thus appeasing it. The root assumption of this philosophy is that "the use of force or the threat of force against other state's rights, is the supreme issue in international relationships."[1]

If appeasement is the chosen option, war will almost inevitably result. This is the case because the aggressor calculates the likelihood of success based on two factors: a victim's capability to resist (which is tangible) and its will to resist (which is not). Appeasement misleads an aggressor into miscalculating the victim's will. It will continue to make demands believing itself to be free of the need to counter the victim's capability. This continues until the aggressor goes too far, forcing the victim to react, leading to armed hostilities. Even though the actions leading to war are initiated by the aggressor state, the war itself is the fault of the victim, or appeaser. If the aggressor had initially been led to "believe that adopting one alternative probably will provoke war, they are less inclined to choose it."[2]

The fact that war might ultimately become nuclear war does not alter this structure of relations. The "larger and more dangerous the threatened war appears to them, the less attractive the alternative that leads to it, and the more likely they are to forego or compromise their objectives to avoid it."[3] Although an elegant theory, this view is hard to apply in practice. Will (credibility or resolve) is intangible. Conceivably it can be demonstrated through military procurements. The weapons systems alone may be inadequate (since capability without will is meaningless); but timely procurement helps signal intent to deploy and to use force under certain conditions. This still leaves the problem, as Gray explains, that literally "[e]verything the United States does or does not do has meaning in perceptions of will and determination . . . as often as not, the real stake for the United States is its reputation, which may be viewed as credibility capital in the bank."[4] This is in fact particularly true for nuclear acquisitions. "[S]trategic nuclear capabilities—specifically changes in relative strategic capabilities—are interpreted by officials in both the United States and the U.S.S.R. (and in third nations as well) as indicators of the two great powers' standing with important political consequences."[5] Such a view creates a perpetual need for more weapons. The weapons per se are less important in relative or absolute terms, than is our willingness to continually obtain more of them. In fact refusal to do so, in every important circumstance, is likened "to the non-resistance of the British and French to Hitler's expansionism in the 1930s."[6]

There is, of course, no question to these authors as to which roles the United States and the Soviet Union assumed under this schema. The aggressive nature of the Soviets was held to be "self-evident."[7] Some warfighters concede that Soviet expansionist tendencies may have been a result of defensiveness, and a desire for security. This desire, however, was so all-encompassing that, at least in Luttwak's view, it "offers no certain security for any country less remote than New Zealand (and considering potential rivalry over the Antarctic, even that is not a safe presumption)."[8] The Soviets desired perfect security, apparently not realizing or not caring that this may be a zero-sum commodity. The fact that expansion is defensively motivated should be of little concern to the West since it is still offensive in design.[9]

Others claim that Soviet expansion was a necessary, historically consistent outgrowth of the inevitable instability of empire. Thus, Colin Gray argues that "[t]he Soviet desire for hegemony will not disappear by the year 2000, because that outward thrust is inherent in the character of the insecure empire of Moscow. In Soviet terms, hegemony means security."[10] This form of expansion may still be defensive, each acquisition of territory intended as a "buffer" to protect older acquisitions. Nevertheless, it is still the case that defensively motivated aggression is still aggression.[11] This must be a particular cause for worry to the United States since it is the existence of the United States that, in large part, motivates Soviet defensiveness.

The concept of a bipolar world is "central to Soviet thinking."[12] In fact, "there is no defense perimeter behind which Soviet leaders would feel truly secure."[13] It may be that Soviet nuclear policy does frame security as a zero-sum situation.[14] Thus, Gray is convinced that,

because of its domestic political system its historical experience, and its culture, the Soviet Union regards the United States as a permanent enemy (permanent, that is, pending removal of the United States from a position where it can do harm to Soviet interests). In the Soviets' eyes, our very existence as the one country capable of organizing and enforcing an effective resistance to Soviet imperial ambitions is our wrongdoing.[15]

In this conception, "the United States is the Soviet Union's mortal foe because of its very existence as the preeminent center of countervailing power, which the Soviet Union does not control."[16]

The Soviet Union's near-pathological inability to accept outside centers of power and influence is frighteningly exacerbated when joined as it was with almost Messianic revolutionary fervor. This is "a state ideology that has universalistic, messianic pretensions."[17] In fact, Simes concluded that "[n]o conceivable economic benefits would be accepted by either the elite or the majority of the Soviet people as adequate compensation for the abandonment of the much cherished dream of Soviet imperial greatness."[18] Whereas MAD postulates Soviet leadership defensively seeking a finite protective buffer for non-ideological reasons, warfighters see an ever expanding, ideologically driven state. They point to Marxism-Leninism, the state "religion," as clearly presenting an ultimate goal towards which the Soviet leadership was obligated to work: global domination. The fact that Marxism-Leninism holds capitalist collapse to be inevitable was no cause for consolation. Soviet leaders had no latitude to choose stagnation even for a time. They were driven always forward to gain more territory and more influence.

The drive for hegemony manifested itself in several ways. One was the attempt to support revolutionary movements in the Third World. This not only met the Soviet Union's ideological obligation to spread its system, it served as a key tool in the struggle with Western capitalism. The only support the Soviets were able to lend was military aid.[19] This helped them create instability in areas on which the West depends for various minerals and resources that the Soviet Union did not need; thus these activities served as a form of "economic warfare."[20] In short, the Soviet Union "would fill any local vacuum as a sneak thief in a hotel tries every door."[21]

The Soviets' aggressive nature was also signalled by its careful management of direct relations with Western states. Since they were by definition enemies, both ideologically and in the threat they posed to Soviet hegemony, the Western states ultimately would have to be faced and defeated. Though a tenet of Marxism-Leninism, there is nothing which says that a Communist victory must be accomplished in the most costly and painful manner possible.[22] They would have much preferred to be the beneficiary of Western weakness, lack of resolve and (Soviet inspired) instability—in sum "to win without war, if possible."[23] Much attention is drawn by warfighting authors to the subterfuge of peaceful coexistence, which they claim meant for the Soviets a constant state of war just below the level of open hostilities.[24] The Soviets sought to avoid open conflict until such a time as they were ready for it. If war could not be avoided, they had every intention of approaching it from conditions as favorable as possible.

According to warfighting authors, for the Soviets aggression always underlies strategy and its appropriate moment is determined through a formula called the *correlation of forces*.[25] The correlation of forces balances and compares the strength of the two sides not just in military hardware but in a number of less easily quantified bases for comparison. Thus economic strength, strategy, resolve, quality of leadership, and the willingness of the population to sacrifice for the war aims of the state are all factored in. Moreover, the Soviets would not, if at all possible, initiate hostilities if they believed the correlation of forces to favor the opponent.[26]

These general assumptions about the perspectives and attitudes of the Soviet leadership lead in turn to a set of more specific beliefs held by the warfighters regarding Soviet military doctrine. As with MAD authors, warfighters look to specific forms of evidence in order to determine an authentic Soviet position on strategic doctrine, and that determination is developed through a circular reasoning process. They do not believe complex analyses of hypothetical Soviet motivations should overcome firm physical evidence. This is because the "only reliable check on whose quotation offering or general appraisals of policy inclinations are likely to be correct, is to refer to the real world of defense programs."[27] The assumption is that these physical forms of evidence do, in fact, reflect operational policy. It is "wartime and postwar objectives that drive Soviet military force design,"[28] and not any attempt to communicate with or respond to Western governments.

Physical, or empirical, indicators form a fairly large evidence category. A great deal of information is available about Soviet military forces and their capabilities.[29] Warfighters, then, looked to numbers of deployed Soviet weapons systems, their characteristics (speed, accuracy, size, survivability, and range), and their location (since where a weapon is deployed can determine estimates about its mission in combination with information about its range). These data were accumulated and assessed to depict the end product of Soviet strategic and procurement decisions. Actual decision-making processes and motivations for deployments were for the most part ignored.[30]

This emphasis on judging intentions by assessing the empirical capabilities of weapons systems is certainly understandable. One might even argue that motivations become irrelevant when developing strategies based on assessments of capability.[31] What is interesting is the claim that "Soviet words alone, no matter how carefully translated, cannot suffice as a source of understanding Soviet programs or Soviet actions,"[32] coupled with a consistent reference to various supporting Soviet statements of doctrine, as evidenced in the above citation.[33] Soviet writings were employed in order to prove the primacy of empirical forms of evidence and the untrustworthiness of doctrinal texts.

Once texts are introduced, criteria must be developed for determining the status or truth value of any given text. Public statements intended for broad distribution are assumed to be propagandistic and disingenuous.[34] Nevertheless, some Soviet publications were held to be credible. As with MAD authors little argument is presented to validate any given document.[35] The difference seems to be that MAD authors began with a textual analysis in order to uncover motivations or approaches that could explain force structures. Warfighters agreed that "Soviet long-range objectives—that is Soviet-defined Soviet interests—can be identified,"[36] but they appear to have reversed the process. They looked first to physical evidence, then selected as authentic those texts confirming expansionist Soviet motivations. MAD proponents constructed a framework for analysis that permitted the rejection of contradictory physical evidence. The physical evidence, however, can be easily argued to support the warfighters' portrait of the Soviet leadership. Warfighters then are faced with making distinctions between documents supporting their view, as developed from empirical evidence, while rejecting texts contradicting that perspective. Thus deployments are elevated to a primary form of evidence, whereas texts can be either confirmatory (in which case they are authentic) or contradictory (in which case they are propagandistic).

Warfighters are less likely to argue as MAD authors do that the opposition has incorrectly interpreted the correct texts. Rather, they will argue that the texts selected by MAD authors, since they are not confirmed by the empirical evidence, are illegitimate. Thus Caravelli, for example, makes the argument that "the characteristics and size of Soviet forces provide a telling indicator of the methods to be employed in the initial stage of a war. Military writings in the 1969–1979 period offer *further substantiation*"[37] [my emphasis].

Methods for determining which texts are "authentic" are not always this straightforward. For example, Miller examines trends in the body of literature as a whole in order to determine claims about the validity or inaccuracy of given statements about Soviet doctrine. He concludes that "[i]f in fact, there is looming convergence between the Soviet and Western strategic philosophy, one would expect to see Soviet doctrine in a state of ferment, much like . . . the mid-to-late 1950s."[38] (The author, of course, did not find any such ferment.)

This still leaves the problem of constructing a rationale for rejecting contradictory Soviet statements published in journals that the warfighters find generally acceptable. This problem is resolved by the argument that some Soviet authors publishing in Soviet military journals comprise "a discredited minority,"[39] with no impact on procurement policies or force structures. (Why they were permitted to continue to publish in centrally controlled publications is left unexplained.)

Even if there was some debate in Soviet publications, it is believed to have been academic or theoretical, with no relevance to determination of force acquisitions.[40] Gray, for instance, concedes the existence of internal debate, but rejects its importance for interpreting the Soviet position.

Clearly, some considerable violence is done to the variety of Soviet opinions by indulging in such gross simplifications as "the Soviet Union" or "the Soviets" as if attitudes, opinions and policy preferences were monolithic. Of course, they are not monolithic. However, Western Soviet watchers have a poor track record in identifying and tracing internal Soviet debates and, as one would expect, people tend to find that for which they search—they expect to find hawks, doves, and owls, and that is what they find.[41]

Thus the supremacy of physical evidence is further supported by the inability to make concrete, defendable conclusions from mere texts. It is ultimately "not surprising that Soviet military programs should show close congruence with the formal precepts of Soviet military doctrine."[42] This is the case since any given precept is not considered an aspect of formal Soviet doctrine unless it is proven legitimate by its congruence *with* Soviet military programs.

This approach to evidence is used to support the view that Soviet strategic doctrine was simple and clear: Nuclear war can be prepared for, fought, and in a meaningful sense won—or lost. The MAD perspective is flawed because for it to be reliable, a belief in the unwinnability of nuclear war must be mutual. The internal consistency or elegance of strategic theory is irrelevant if it can not serve its purpose: to persuade the Soviets to avoid those actions we desire them to avoid. A view of deterrence is workable only if it appeals to Soviet attitudes and values concerning war. The vulnerability sought by MAD is magnified in specific cases of power confrontation. Crisis Stability cannot be achieved in a non-MAD world.

Prior to developing a specific portrait of the Soviet doctrinal position, warfighters discussed what they felt the Soviets did not believe: the validity of Crisis Stability, as articulated by the MAD position. Thus "while MAD may work when there is no threat of possible war, or when one has dominant superiority, its credibility in a real confrontation is believed to have been undermined . . . if for no other reason than that the Soviets simply do not subscribe to this point of view."[43] What is more, it was incorrect to assume that the Soviet position would shift closer to the preferred Western view, for "over the last two decades . . . there has not been the slightest hint that Soviet doctrine is moving toward Western concepts of deterrence or strategic stability,"[44] despite Western hopes that the Soviets would eventually accept the MAD perspective. The Soviets are unwilling to trust "any autonomous and allegedly self-sustaining 'system' over and above their own efforts" at developing a force structure.[45] This position, of course, ultimately depends on the assessments of the empirical evidence (deployments, etc.), and the assumption that they accurately reflect Soviet doctrinal preferences as opposed to being a response to American deployments. Put simply, "the Soviet strategic posture does not lend itself to interpretation in the light of some variant of mutual assured destruction."[46] In fact, the Soviets were "working energetically to undermine what we understand to be the requirements of stability."[47]

A Soviet concept of equal security is admitted, but this is sharply differentiated from Crisis Stability. The Soviets are thought to believe that they should be compensated for geographical disadvantages and for the fact that they must also counter the French, British, and Chinese nuclear forces. This theory calls for a "condition where Moscow can wage war with equal success on all fronts simultaneously," which is obviously not conducive to strategic equality between the United States and the Soviet Union.[48] None of this should be taken to indicate that the Soviets did not recognize the existing mutual nature of deterrence. Rather, the point is that far from being a desired state, rough equivalence was to them a "frustrating obstacle" to the goal of security through dominance.[49] A stable deterrent system, therefore, should be of little comfort. It is clear that "the Soviet leadership has signalled its unambiguous commitment to the accretion of a comprehensive warfighting capability."[50] This doctrinal position must be countered, for the strength of a deterrent posture can only be assessed relative to the attitudes and beliefs of the state to be deterred. Lambeth makes clear that the starting point for doctrine, if it is to be sound, must be an analysis of the relevant audience, in this instance the Soviet Union. "The imperative thus facing the United States in the immediate years ahead is to begin forging a new approach to stability that appeals primarily to Soviet strategic sensitivities and insecurities, rather than to the dubious prospect of eventual Soviet empathy with the preferred goals and concepts of the West."[51]

The hypothesized Soviet rejection of MAD is "proven" by reactions to U.S. policy during the period when the MAD doctrine was dominant.[52] In general, according to Miller, "the Soviet attitude is that competent, responsible governments do not voluntarily entrust the fate of the nation to the enemy's rationality and self-restraint."[53] Soviet leaders are thus portrayed as dumbfounded by Western conceptions of Crisis Stability.[54] They are therefore not only contemptous but suspicious, viewing the U.S. strategic posture as "the epitome of strategic folly."[55]

Students of Clausewitz, the Soviets believed a nuclear war to be as susceptible to classical military strategy as any other war.[56] The Soviets therefore "are firm adherents of the Clausewitzian principle that... purely military considerations must not be allowed to transcend the governing political objectives."[57] Significantly, this would result in a consistency between objectives before, during, and after another war,[58] and not, as MAD authors would argue, a rejection of war as an instrument of policy.

Nuclear war, then, can be manipulated to achieve policy goals. As a result of this perceived Soviet belief in the utility of nuclear war as a means of accomplishing policy goals these authors define "the fundamental tenet of Soviet military doctrine: that the security interests of the state demand nothing less than the acquisition and maintenance of a credible warfighting, warwinning capability."[59] Once the Soviets are portrayed as believing in nuclear war as a potentially effective instrument of policy, the question then becomes one of determining possible Soviet objectives in such a war. If the war per se is not feared by the Soviets it then becomes necessary to determine under what conditions the Soviets would wage war and for what objectives. Only with this knowledge can an appropriate and persuasive deterrent posture be established. Such objectives can be determined through an understanding of Soviet strategy.

For the warfighter, interpretation of Soviet strategy flows from a basic premise: "The most important aspect of Soviet strategy is that it is designed to achieve victory."[60] This premise is particularly salient to warfighters' concerns because these authors believe that in the crucial Soviet estimate of the correlation of forces, which is what these authors seek to manipulate, strategy itself is an important variable. This method of balancing inputs into the equation means that to the Soviets "[a] superior strategy and military policy . . . can be sufficient to achieve victory, even against an opponent whose individual weapons systems may possess greater technical properties."[61] It is conceivable then, to the warfighter, that the Soviets may see themselves as weaker militarily and still predict victory as a likely outcome in a war.

In part because of ideological predispositions,[62] the Soviets believed the "the Soviet Union could take the prescribed measures to survive such a [nuclear] conflict and emerge as a functional society."[63] Unlike American strategists, therefore, the prospect of the inevitable devastation to be wrought in a nuclear war is not in and of itself, according to the warfighter, an adequate deterrent for their Communist counterparts.[64] Finite deterrence would then be a poor basis for strategy, because the Soviets do not accept its validity. It is an invalid deterrent posture, and because it cannot threaten the Soviets with a denial of victory, it is held to actually increase the risk of war.

The prospect of war is not all that frightened warfighters faced with a discrepancy between Soviet and American approaches to nuclear doctrine. The Soviet perspective offered its leadership increased political leverage. If a war can be fought and won, a particular outcome can potentially be predicted by both sides during a crisis. If that is the case, and the Soviets believed they had obtained sufficient military and strategic superiority to actually win a war, then such superiority could have been used to advantage without initiating hostilities. Thus, the acquisition of military superiority itself becomes a key Soviet goal.

Equality of forces, assumed by MAD authors to be the ultimate goal of Soviet arms programs, is not a desired endstate for the Soviets in the warfighter's interpretation. To them it is the hope of the Soviets that parity would "only define a transitory moment in time."[65] Superiority may be of use in a situation where war is inevitable. But it can also be used to turn nuclear asymmetries into "practical instruments of policy."[66] Caravelli indicates that this is accomplished in the following manner: "In peacetime, superiority can be used to deter a crisis. In other words, perceptions of strategic superiority and expectations by other nations of the confidence of the superior power in employing that advantage can translate into what Colin Gray has referred to as 'preemptive political accommodation.' "[67]

The goal of force development, deployment, and configuration was to reach a level of superiority where the United States could not threaten or make demands of the Soviet Union—in any region of interest. The fact of superiority functions "to seal off local conflicts from influence by U.S. strategic forces,"[68] ensuring "the neutralization of American strategic capabilities."[69] This "lies at the heart of the Soviet strategy to 'win without war.' "[70] The goal is to achieve a position where they would, by merely threatening a war that they could clearly win, force the United States to back down no matter the stakes. The Soviets seek in Luttwak's terms, "not a nuclear Pearl Harbor but rather the *political neutralization* of our strategic nuclear forces"[71] [my emphasis].

Such analysis relies on interpretations of Soviet force procurement and structure to establish proof for its validity. Doctrine and procurement both emanate from directives at the very highest level of government. Bureaucratic models of procurement are not held to be applicable to Soviet decisions. Rather, all decisions are depicted as conscious and centralized, reflecting the doctrinal decisions of the government.[72] Whereas MAD advocates distinguish between the roles of military and political officials, asserting that force structures may not reflect doctrine, warfighters contended that the civilian leadership had been so "militarized" that there was no discernible difference between the positions of the two groups.[73]

This perspective on Soviet military doctrine leads to a sustained critique of MAD as a guiding strategic theory for the U.S. force posture. Warfighters begin the development of an adequate deterrent posture with the categorization made explicit by Gray.

it is possible to identify three conceptually distinctive "core ideas" around which US nuclear weapons policy could rally: these are:

1. deterrence by anticipation of massive societal punishment;
2. deterrence by anticipation of being denied victory; and
3. deterrence by anticipation of US victory.[74]

Whether denial of victory would serve as an adequate deterrent posture is a source of some dispute among warfighters. But there is little question for any warfighter that "concepts of stable deterrence do not serve to rescue the ideal of threats of societal punishment from the waste dump of policy and intellectual history."[75] They understand that MAD authors are correct in arguing that deterrence requires credible threats against the values of the leadership (an appropriate message) in order to prevent nuclear war from ever taking place.

All deterrence theorists agree that a credible threat is needed to assure deterrence, but the schools diverge as to what it is that ought to be threatened. Warfighters argued that since the portrait of the Soviet leadership, its attitudes and values, provided by MAD was incorrect, the analysis of what should be threatened was inevitably incorrect. Warfighters held that threats of societal punishment were inappropriate and unpersuasive because nothing is threatened that the Soviets would not be willing to sacrifice under the right circumstances. A punishment approach is particularly inadequate because it fosters significant asymmetries in the power of deterrence on different actors. The United States has far more at stake in avoiding hostilities than does the Soviet Union, the warfighters claimed.

Initially it was argued that the Soviet leadership would accept staggering loss of life as an acceptable price to pay for victory. "The Soviets know that they can take high levels of human and industrial loss, and still emerge victorious."[76] This is presumably a lesson derived from the Soviet interpretation of history. Miller, for example, argued that the Soviet view of the past is clear, with unambiguous import for the present. "If the Soviet leaders have drawn one lesson from [their losses] it is that although such casualties must be avoided at all reasonable costs, should this prove impossible, the system is resilient enough to endure incredible levels of damage and survive."[77] This would be especially true "if Soviet arms could acquire Western Europe in a largely undamaged condition to serve as a recovery base."[78]

An American deterrent posture that threatened anything besides military and political targets was in fact useless because of tremendous "asymmetry in values between the Soviet and U.S. political system."[79] In fact, an effort to make plans consistent with any humanitarian values is useless for Gray, who takes the position that "[t]he great care shown by the U.S. JSTPS [Joint Strategic Targeting Policy Staff, the targeteers] to avoid unwanted collateral damage probably is effort wasted in the Soviet perspective."[80] If a war did break out, effects on the population would be of so little concern that it would not alter Soviet targeting strategy or its timing.[81]

What had to be threatened was the Soviets' ability to "win." That they were willing to accept horrendous casualties if the projected gains justified such losses was not to be taken as a sign of recklessness. The American deterrent posture needed to convince the Soviets that they could not win, because absent victory losses could not be adequately compensated. The debate among warfighters centers on what should be threatened to effectively persuade the Soviets that their war aims would be denied in actual combat operations.

Most warfighters have argued that the Soviets needed to be convinced only that a military victory would be denied them. This is best accomplished through Escalation Dominance. Where MAD authors called for a finite deterrence ordered around the concept of Crisis Stability, most warfighters believed that the Soviets had to be convinced that they would lose at any conceivable level of conflict. To the extent that the United States sustained effective options to counter any Soviet actions deterrence is "robust," for Soviet planners can look ahead to potential escalatory moves and understand that those will fail as badly as the initial moves.

A minority view among warfighters, primarily that of Keith Payne and Colin Gray, asserted that targeting of military capabilities was also insufficient to ensure a Soviet perception of American Escalation Dominance. If the only costs of conflict were general casualties and some increment of military power, the Soviet leadership would in this view risk war because it cares only about preserving the power structure. Effective targeting doctrine requires that the highest values of the state be threatened. And, these "principal assets are the political control structure of the highly centralized CPSU and government bureaucracy; the transmission belts of communication from the center to the regions; the instruments of central official coercion . . . ; and the reputation of the Soviet state in the eyes of its citizens."[82] The whole point of deterrence is to persuade the Soviets to not risk a war. But if the Soviets were guaranteed that after a war the state would remain intact even if specific war aims had been denied, the gamble might appear dangerously attractive.[83] If the state itself were threatened the Soviets would not be willing to take risks, even if the potential gains were enormous. Threats to the state are threats to those making the decision to go to war. Thus with "a clear political war aim—to encourage the dissolution of the Soviet state—much of the military war might not need to be fought at all."[84] The implication of this line of reasoning is that "[d]eterrent effort should be maximized if the advertised bottom line of U.S. strategic policy is . . . that the United States had the means and the strategy to effect the dissolution of the Soviet state."[85] Without the capacity to threaten the leadership's political control, deterrence cannot be assured. Indeed, loss of life is not a persuasive threat to an authoritarian regime. "The loss of 30 or 40 million people might well be compatible with a context defined by a Soviet leadership as victory: it would depend very much on who was among the 30 or 40 million."[86] Thus for Payne and Gray, key party officials and organs of control at the national, republic and local level must be targeted if U.S. nuclear policy is to send a persuasive message. Leadership relocation centers, both airborne command posts and hardened bunkers, and the several hundred thousand people expected to be in them, must be the object of a single "decapitation" strike.

This view is as much based on the need for persuasion as the victory/ denial position. That this is a rhetorical strategy is made clear in that, despite their forceful advocacy, Payne and Gray admit that such targeting strategy in an actual war would be not just unworkable but probably counterproductive. Operationally, such a strategy demands targeting major population centers. Even if more accurate and lower yield weapons were used, the Soviets would not have been able to distinguish a decapitation strike from a counterpopulation strategy.[87] Additionally, targeting what the Soviets most value at the outset of a war leaves no incentive for restraint. No deterrent remains because the United States would already have done its worst.[88]

All warfighters (whether looking to an American victory or Soviet defeat, or to the dissolution of the Soviet state) agreed that one element was absolutely key to preventing war: Damage Limitation. As with many concepts in warfighting, Damage Limitation is argued to have real operational benefits. Operational capacity then contributes to the effectiveness of deterrence, which then makes the operational benefits moot. The only way to deter nuclear war is to be able to fight one. Thus items of operational utility construct a persuasive, credible message so that there is no *need* to fight one. Preparation for war, then, is the only way to avoid war.

Damage Limitation is the ability to hold levels of damage in a strategic exchange to tolerable or acceptable levels. This is accomplished not so much through active defenses such as Ballistic Missile Defenses (primarily because they are currently unavailable) as through the capacity to inflict damage on an enemy's military capacity. No threat to use nuclear weapons is credible without Damage Limitation.

The "logic" of the paradigmatic persuasive situation in events leading to war works in the following manner. The asymmetry in Soviet and American values (the assumption that an American president would presumably care about American casualties) is known to the Soviets. Therefore "[a]s long as American society is essentially unprotected . . . the United States will have to lose any process of competitive escalation."[89] Threats by the United States to escalate would be unpersuasive to the Soviet leadership because they believe America will not act and risk its population. The threats of an American president would never be credible. "If escalation discipline is to be imposed upon the Soviet Union, even in the direst of situations, potential damage to North America has to be limited."[90]

Independent of assumptions about nuclear war, warfighters construct a view of the Soviet leadership that places primary emphasis on the *Soviets'* assumptions about nuclear war. Because they are believed to assume such a war can be fought and won, we must convey a similar attitude. Whether it is objectively correct or not (that is, whether it is physically possible to fight and "win" a nuclear war) is irrelevant. To avoid such a war we must persuade the Soviets that war would not be in their best interests. This demands that the United States adopt force structures that convey, at least in appearance, a warwaging, warwinning capability.

Assumptions about Nuclear War

While warfighting authors do not underestimate the physical destructiveness of a nuclear war, they reject the belief that such a war could have only one, necessarily apocalyptic, outcome. Actions can, and should, be taken that would limit damage to every sector of American society in the event of war. And again such actions are supported for both operational and rhetorical (deterrent) purposes.

So long as deterrence might fail, war must be anticipated. That the risk exists is clear for, as Colin Gray put it, "peace may be its profession [but] one day . . . SAC [Strategic Air Command] might discover that war is its business."[91] In other words, "so long as nuclear war is possible, it is prudent and responsible to seek to limit the degree of the catastrophe that would be unleashed."[92] While 20 million casualties would be a tragedy of unprecedented proportions, 60 million would be still worse. Thus the "defense" of population, industry, and agriculture serves a wartime function. (Authors who support the Strategic Defense Initiative tend to share the assumptions of warfighting. While warfighters explicitly addressing strategic theory tend to support SDI they did not emphasize it. Since defensive deployments are at best years off it was simply not believed to be relevant to discussion of what American force structures should be today or in the near future.[93])

Damage Limitation at the time was primarily comprised of defense through attack: destroying enemy forces before they could be used. The more Soviet missiles destroyed before launch, the fewer would remain to be exploded over American territory. It is this belief that nuclear war can have a range of outcomes that led warfighters to vigorously reject MAD. The refusal to contemplate alternative outcomes to nuclear war is seen as not just an ineffective deterrent, but as self-fulfilling prophecy. A nuclear force developed with the intent of avoiding options could lead the Soviets to believe that we would not be able to respond to an attack since our only available option would be to initiate an uncontrolled series of massive attacks. This posture is unpersuasive to the Soviets because if we did retaliate with a massive attack their only response would be to destroy our cities.[94]

As an alternative, weapons deployments signalling warfighting intent are powerful persuasive messages. The existence of options helps communicate not just the ability to conduct nuclear war but also the will. Warfighting deployments say that we intend to defend ourselves, and not to commit suicide, even if it is reciprocal. Damage Limitation confines war to military targets. In a counterforce exchange, a population is a target of last resort. As articulated by Gray, the maintenance of such an option is the only responsible policy.[95]

Central to a strategy that purports to minimize the effects of nuclear war is the ability to conduct operations in a controlled fashion. From a technical standpoint, it is held that command, control, and communications (C3) can be constructed to survive a nuclear strike and be usable in a prolonged war setting.[96] With secured command technology, nuclear exchanges can bring about war termination on favorable terms.

MAD authors postulated a force structure that functions as a communications medium, but when deterrence fails, the potential for persuasion would end. Warfighters agreed that force structures communicate but went farther. They thought that persuasive messages could be sent *during* a nuclear war. Even if the Soviets did not recognize the full range of intermediate escalation options,[97] it is likely that in a war they would quickly discover them.[98] American ability to control a war, then, must be communicated through the diversification of options. The capacity to choose a special response to Soviet provocation would assure the most appropriate message be sent. This is the only way to minimize the chances of war and its consequences.

FORCE STRUCTURE AS THEORY OF PERSUASION

Like MAD authors, warfighters put little faith in the use of Declaratory Policy as a means of communication. They did not believe that the Soviets looked seriously to American statements about nuclear war when the more solid and credible form of evidence—deployments—was available.[99] However, where MAD advocates said nuclear wars cannot be fought, and constructed a theory of persuasion based on those physical constraints, warfighters generally accepted the constraints—but argued that strategic doctrine must ignore them. Because the Soviet leadership prepares for nuclear warfighting only a force structure that can fight and win—empty though such a victory may be—will be persuasive. Force structures and characteristics of weapons systems are thus a medium of communication, as is the case with MAD. The doctrines differ as to determinations of what is persuasive, not on the importance of developing and sending the appropriate message, for after all "the primary target of our strategic forces is the mind of the enemy."[100] Whatever critique one may offer of the warfighters, it is not the case that they were eagerly searching for an opportunity to "push the button." They perceived themselves to be advocating a form of deterrence, and a prudent strategy. Indeed, some analysts found the very term "warfighting" misleading. Thus Gray stated that "[t]he American public is being informed today . . . that it has a choice between a policy of nuclear deterrence and a policy of nuclear defense or nuclear warfighting. This is a false opposition."[101] Such pleas for understanding must be evaluated against proposals for weapons systems.

Force Structure

Like MAD advocates, warfighters support the maintenance of the current triad structure. Not only does such a structure provide critical force redundance in the event of a deterrence failure, each leg has a different rhetorical and operational strength.[102] Though MAD advocates support a triad as security through redundancy, warfighters concentrate on the advantages and defects of any given leg in isolation from the others. Submarines are not only highly survivable, being difficult to track and able to stay on station for months, they can also operate close to the United States coast, receiving additional protection. Bomber-deployed weapons are useful because, being under human guidance until the last second, they can be aimed at targets left standing after a first exchange. ICBMs as well as submarines can be held "in reserve" for weeks or months in a prolonged war.

Despite agreement on the triad concept, differences emerge over ICBM survivability. For the MAD advocate there was little apparent motivation for the Soviets to take advantage of the vulnerability of the Minutemen and MX force, especially since an attack on American ICBMs would cause so many casualties countervalue retaliation would be inevitable. Warfighters completely disagree. That ICBMs are vulnerable is taken as a given.[103] While Soviet ICBMs may also be vulnerable, this was not seen as an equal trade-off deterring both sides. Since we were presumably not planning an attack, survivability was not considered a deterrence issue for the Soviets.[104]

The vulnerability of land based missiles, an entire leg of the triad, tempted a Soviet attack.[105] Without this particular leg being available, we would essentially be made unable to respond selectively after a Soviet first strike. Lacking weapons capable of destroying Soviet military forces, the United States would move to attack Soviet cities. "The best Soviet city in war is one which is alive: a live Soviet city is a hostage that saves an American city."[106] Without the capacity to take out threatening weapons offered by American ICBMs, the Soviets might assume they would be striking with impunity, for any American response would guarantee the devastation of American cities, and would therefore be "self-deterred."

As our ICBMs have grown more vulnerable, the land-based missiles' "disadvantages have grown in absolute and relative terms compared to the other two triad legs."[107] However, warfighters did not and do not suggest replacing the land-based leg because its advantages—accuracy, assured "penetration," promptness, control—are even at this time irreplaceable.[108] The fondness for the ICBM will be explored in the next section, but the vehemence with which the warfighters rejected the proposed "Midgetman," a small, mobile (survivable) replacement is telling. Typical is the position essayed by Stewart Blair: "Such a move [a small ICBM chosen over the MX] would merely confirm to the world that the United States is prepared to concede the arena of meaningful prompt counterforce capability to the Soviet Union and to continue what amounts to a 'sanctuary status' for Soviet ICBMs."[109] The triad must be preserved at all costs: if a leg is weak it should be modernized or "shored up," but it certainly should not be eliminated. The benefits of each leg are not redundant, they are interactive. Each is needed.

Force Characteristics: Options, Size, Accuracy, Survivability

As with MAD authors, warfighters believed that the three characteristics of a weapons system (size, accuracy, and survivability) and perhaps a fourth, speed, could be altered to influence Soviet perceptions. Both sets of warfighters agreed on types of characteristics that were desirable. While advocates of all types of weapons improvements, it was clear that the resulting multiplication of options undercut the communicative value of force acquisition and deployment. Intentions, except within an extremely narrow range, cannot be expressed. Only capabilities, and hence options, can be faithfully communicated. Where there are too many options, some differentiation of intent disappears.

This limitation makes the dispute over target sets, or at least Payne and Gray's part in that debate, purely academic. It is clear that the weapons characteristics one would select for counterpolitical targeting are identical to those chosen for countermilitary targeting. Since capabilities are the only medium of exchange that is trusted, there is no way for the Soviets to distinguish between the two approaches in order to determine which we would actually employ. This undermines the counterpolitical targeting position: by the author's admission it will not work operationally, and it cannot work persuasively.

At this level, then, the whole debate appears to collapse. The point of using deployments as a persuasive tool is that stated intentions are not reliable in an atmosphere of distrust. It is difficult then to support Payne and Gray's position on the weakness of countermilitary targeting (relative to counterpolitical). From their own assumptions about force structures and persuasion, and acceptance of constraints operating on counterpolitical targeting, the position appears indefensible. It not only does not work, it cannot even be communicated, hence made an effective threat within the physical constraints of the chosen communications medium. The reason Payne and Gray are *not* irrelevant is the emphasis placed on the ability to communicate options.

Four approaches to targeting are possible. Countersociety targeting (MAD) involves direct attacks on population centers, industrial and agricultural bases. Counterrecovery targeting is similar. The difference is that under this approach the United States would target, not currently valuable societal assets, but rather those that would become relevant in the post-attack environment. Counterforce or countermilitary strategy targets military capabilities in order to meet the dual goals of victory/denial and Damage Limitation. Counterpolitical targeting seeks to destroy organs of state control and those responsible for them.

The problem in communicating these distinctions is that force characteristics necessary for countersocietal and counterrecovery targeting are the same. One also acquires the same weapons systems for counterforce and for counterpolitical targeting. It is highly unlikely that the U.S. force structure could be refined sufficiently to communicate, with any level of precision, a single targeting set. No suggestions as to how this may be accomplished have been made in the literature. The choice to be made is between communication of the option of *either* countersocietal or counterrecovery targeting *or* countermilitary or counterpolitical targeting. The second set of options appeals to the warfighter. It is this choice that leads to a set of criteria for the development of American force structures at odds with the MAD advocate.

The dispute is clear, for example, in the debate about the ideal size of weapons. Where MAD authors express a clear preference for large weapons (and large weapons only), warfighters want every possible size nuclear weapon developed and deployed. Escalation Dominance assumes a series of steps up an "escalation ladder,"[110] making it necessary for the United States to have appropriate weapons for any level of conflict. If, for example, the Soviets had superiority at lower levels of escalation, where small weapons are necessary, they could be tempted to initiate hostilities not believing that the opponent would take the risk of escalating to higher levels of violence. Luttwak asserts that the desire to neutralize American strategic forces is part of a plan to confine conflict to levels at which the Soviets can win.

> The strategy that one may properly infer from the current pattern of Soviet force-building does not suggest an "all nuclear" war scheme but precisely the opposite: the increasingly powerful intercontinental nuclear weapons of the Soviet Union are meant primarily to inhibit any use of our own. Similarly the greatly enhanced theater and tactical nuclear weapons are intended to deny us any resort to those weapons.[111]

In such a world, the United States must appear able to conduct military operations at any conceivable level of escalation under any imaginable scenario. Every size of nuclear weapon is therefore justifiable in that it is always possible to construct a scenario for which it is necessary. The warfighter sees justification for small nuclear weapons.[112] Where MAD authors believe small weapons are "useable" and are therefore danger-ous, warfighters believe "thinkability" is essential for a credible threat-ening posture, which is in turn necessary at all levels of stability. To MAD authors this is "worst-case analysis." To the warfighter it is "pru-dence."

These differences again go back to differences in the portraits of the Soviet leadership. MAD authors hold that nuclear war would be so horrible that there is no plausible motive for initiating one. Motives that are plausible stem not from anyone's desire to gain in some way, but from the fear of loss engendered by the weapons themselves. Warfigh-ters see world domination as the motivation for war, and hold that this compulsion characterizes the Soviet Union. That desire for hegemony was there before nuclear weapons existed, and it will remain so long as there are independent power centers standing in the way of the Soviet goal. Not only does it exist, it is strong enough that only the clear expression of American will to create sufficient losses to offset Soviet gains deters it.

Thinkability is not an issue for warfighters, for they believe that to the Soviet audience war is already thinkable, consequences aside. All that is at issue is military capacity and the will to deny military and political goals. This requires the clear communication of the ability to wage war, and the willingness to do so, up to a desirable termination. Of course, to be effective, the communication system must be clear, reliable, and univocal prior to the outbreak of hostilities.

The next relevant characteristic is accuracy. Where MAD authors reject highly accurate weapons, warfighters believe accuracy is valuable. The more accurate the weapon the better. This is in large part the motivation underlying strategic force modernization. Currently a gap exists between the accuracy of ICBMs and SLBMs (Sea Launched Ballistic Missiles). Warfighters support any weapon system that can upgrade the accuracy of bomber-launched missiles and SLBMs such as the Trident D-5 SLBM.[113] While Circular Error Probable (CEP) is still the measure of accuracy, this is important only in so far as it supports a Hard Target Kill capability (HTK) and in particular prompt HTK.

HTK is the capacity of a nuclear weapon to land and explode so close to a target that even if it is hardened to withstand blast overpressures (such as a missile silo) the target will be destroyed. Since such targets are "time-urgent" (they must be destroyed before they can be launched), flight times become almost as important as accuracy alone. This is why even with almost equivalent accuracies, the other two legs of the triad still will not be considered acceptable replacements for ICBMs. For, as Gray makes clear,

Although it is true that the D-5 should have a nominal hard-target kill capability comparable to that of the MX (or SICBM), [Small ICBM, i.e. the Midgetman] it cannot be regarded as a candidate substitute for a modernized ICBM force. Military effectiveness (in this restricted context) is not solely a matter of the theoretical lethality of warheads against targets; it also includes consideration of the timeliness for assured transmission, receipt and execution of the actions that might be ordered.[114]

A high level of HTK capacity is important to assure Damage Limitation. Although the operational benefits of a Damage Limitation posture are not believed to be ultimately necessary (a persuasive deterrent means this capacity will never have to be put to the test) nevertheless, all other things being equal, the more accurate U.S. weapons, the more stable the deterrent. I have already discussed the argument that Damage Limitation is necessary to lend credibility to nuclear threats. It is also necessary to persuade the Soviets not to launch in a more direct way.

The Soviets were believed to judge the potential benefits of any hostile moves based on the correlation of forces equation. But if a nuclear strike is considered (as opposed to conventional moves carrying the risk of later nuclear escalation) the key equation becomes the *post-attack* correlation of forces, who, in other words, is ahead after the first exchange. In this scenario, the Soviets judge war to be likely or necessary and begin with a large, preemptive (preferably surprise) attack.[115] This is presumed to be a scenario motivated explicitly by Damage Limitation concerns on the Soviets' part. "[S]ince the survival of the homeland bears a direct relationship to reducing the weight of the enemy attack, whatever the proportion of the opposing force destroyed in the first strike contributes to that goal."[116] What would determine the Soviets' judgment as to whether such a move would be feasible was an assessment of the correlation of forces *after* a first strike.

Development of a persuasive American deterrent must keep in mind that the "side with the greater power before the exchange is an important factor, but it is not the determining factor. The determining factor is who ends up stronger after the exchange."[117] It would be extremely dangerous to lead the Soviets to believe they could emerge in the stronger position after an exchange, for the "idea is that the party with the most nuclear weapons after the exchange will dominate the world."[118]

The central goal of the American force structure, then, is to convincingly persuade the Soviets that after a surprise attack they could not be in a position so superior as to be able to end the war on their terms. At a minimum they must be convinced that the United States will retain enough forces to require a prolonged, costly war whose outcome would remain uncertain throughout. "This targeting philosophy substantially increases the chances that nuclear war may be avoided."[119]

HTK is central to the persuasive effort. The capability to strike opposing weapons makes it possible for a nation to engage in a prolonged war, while protecting military resources necessary for later salvos, and protects populations by keeping exchanges purely military. This scenario, of course, came from the perception that the Soviets would find our vulnerable ICBMs an irresistible target. Vulnerability creates the problem, HTK presumably solves it. Warfighters will not give up the ICBMs because they are necessary components to deterrence—but they seem to ignore the fact that they are also necessary for there to be a problem to solve.

Thus accuracy is strategically related to the final weapons characteristic, survivability. Although survivability is desirable to the warfighter, it is in no sense an ultimate criteria for procurement, as it is for the advocate of MAD. In the MAD view, if a weapon is not survivable its other benefits are moot. For the warfighter survivability is a luxury. An otherwise desirable weapon that is not survivable can perhaps eventually be made survivable in some way, like launch-on-assessment, a strategy requiring launch of American weapons upon determination of the size and type of an incoming attack; MAD proponents consider such a strategy dangerous and prefer the capability to "ride out" any attack before response.[120]

Despite the fact that vulnerable weapons are deployed, warfighters did attempt to discern methods for increasing survivability. If weapons became too vulnerable, or too large a percentage of them were too exposed, the Soviets may have evaluated their own potential for launching a Damage Limitation strike positively. In such a situation they could again calculate a benefit to themselves from merely threatening escalation. They could initiate hostilities at a lower level of violence, made confident by an ability to either "deter our deterrent" or to later moot it out if necessary.

A related rationale justifies the deployment of survivable weapons.

Survivable weapons communicate the ability to participate in prolonged salvos. Weapons that can be held in reserve without fear of loss make possible graduated series of exchanges over prolonged periods of time. Thus, according to Gray, the following elements are crucial to the development of a force posture adequate for convincing the Soviets that they could not win through a single, decisive blow: "The United States needs a hard-target counterforce capability that enjoys enduring survivability; a National Command Authority that is truly survivable . . . survivable and/or reconstitutable overhead surveillance and reconnaissance assets for target identification for controlled and discriminating attack purposes in the course of war."[121] It is not, therefore, the case that the warfighters ignore the benefits of survivability. Rather, they consider this characteristic as one of many to be evaluated in determining the benefits of a given weapons system.

Force Size

In evaluating the warfighter's position on force size it is important to remember that the warfighter did not believe it to be either desirable or necessary to divorce the strategic relationship from broader questions of American foreign policy. To the MAD advocate strategic theory is nothing more than a struggle to define strategic concerns in such a way as to remove them from any real bearing on political or military affairs. The warfighter, in sharp contrast, believes that nuclear weapons can, without being launched, exercise a profound influence on America's attempts (or inability) to achieve goals in international relations. The caveat is that political "usability" comes only with an indisputable superiority in every component of the strategic arsenal.

Parity, then, is inadequate as the basis for a deterrent posture. In fact, we should provide ourselves with options "the adversary either cannot or dare not match (or overmatch.)"[122] The central concept of MAD, that nuclear weapons forces should be structured in such a way that they have no use, is completely unacceptable. It is in fact "an idea it would be hard to improve upon were one seeking to minimize the relevance of (American) strategic weapons to world politics,"[123] which is, of course, the whole point of MAD. It is that goal which the warfighters reject. Parity is certainly better than inferiority, which would deny political leverage, but superiority is still better. Parity creates stalemate, hence diminishing leverage necessary to influence Soviet actions. The relationship between political utility of nuclear weapons and overall force superiority is linear.[124]

In contrast to the MAD position, strategic superiority is not seen as an inherently dangerous situation. The danger only comes when the wrong side is dominant. Gray argued that "[a] military imbalance is a source of danger to international peace and security only if the imbalance favors a state that is not committed to the upholding of the current structure of order."[125] Just so that there is no confusion over which side is which, he continues: "NATO-Europe . . . [and the] United States, can be trusted with whatever degree of military superiority it can secure and sustain—the Soviet empire cannot be so trusted."[126]

Superiority, furthermore, must be present at every level of every weapons category. Because of the importance MAD places on secure second strike capability, mutual levels of armament is judged sufficient if the relationship can be described in terms of "rough equivalence" or general parity. This concept is based on an understanding of the way each system (and launch platform) interrelates and trades off with every other weapons system. ICBM inferiority, for example, might be acceptable if it were coupled with superiority in SLBMs. Such a method of accounting for overall numerical balance is anathema to the warfighter. It is irrelevant that inferiority in intermediate range weapons might be balanced by superiority in submarines targeting the same points. Each category, as a separate and discrete element in the overall balance, must reflect American superiority. It is this difference in the approach to counting, more than a difference in counting methods, that led different theorists to provide opposite accounts of the same data. While MAD advocates differed as to whether the United States was ahead or equal during the 1980s, warfighters argued about whether the United States was already behind, and if so by how much. While most would not go as far as Douglass, who asserted that "we now stand totally defenseless,"[127] most would probably agree that "over the last two decades the Soviet Union has worked with extreme tenacity to remove one by one the western military counterweights to its strength."[128] Certainly these authors would agree that "it is no longer merely one or two categories of military power that we have to worry about, but rather the whole spectrum of capabilities with only a few exceptions."[129]

The count itself assumes additional importance in that it supersedes other methods of determining the strategic balance. Additional elements such as technological superiority, increased weapons reliability, and superior fueling methods are significantly undervalued. For the MAD advocate, the determination of strategic posture requires balancing a complex analysis and interrelating factors in an ultimately holistic determination of relative strength. For the warfighter these other factors are important and deserve attention. But they have little effect on the calculation of balance, which remains a straightforward mathematical relationship of more, less, or the same. The fact that a Soviet missile is less reliable, slower, or more difficult to launch than an American missile is not adequate compensation for smaller numbers.

MAD authors were willing to accept larger Soviet missiles, because they judge size to be compensation for lower accuracy and reliability. Warfighters saw the larger size as in and of itself a Soviet advantage and a threat to already vulnerable ICBMs.[130] MAD authors treated Soviet numerical superiority in certain weapons systems with complacency, since the United States was judged to be ahead in the quality of its weaponry. Warfighters saw any imbalance as potentially dangerous, because the Soviets would surely retain higher numbers, given a greater commitment to production, while continuing to search for technological breakthroughs.[131] Thus the debate over relative positions in the strategic balance was never resolved, for there was little real clash between the advocates. MAD authors based their position on an understanding that went beyond the numerical. Warfighters doggedly insisted that the numbers are all that count.

Command and Control

Command, control, and communications (C3) poses nowhere near the theoretical difficulty for warfighters that it does for MAD advocates. The requirements are simple. The C3 system must be able to function and survive through a post-attack environment and must be able to do so for a prolonged period of time. This was necessary in order to persuade the Soviets that the United States had the capability to wage war in a controlled fashion. Damage Limitation and victory/denial required on-going assessment of how successful each salvo was in a war, if only so that the authorities could determine which targets remained and which must be given priority.[132] This capability demands the continued ability not just to receive and interpret data but also to transmit orders to the field. If nuclear weapons are used, they will be interjected into a fluid military environment. In such a situation predetermined orders, target lists, and timetables are rarely adequate.

The need to convince the Soviets of a survivable C3 capacity was made more urgent by the fact that "while there is a Western propensity to think in terms of preserving the hostile government so that someone would be left to negotiate a war settlement or termination, that is not a Soviet concept."[133] If the C3 system was visibly vulnerable (or dependent upon only a few key "nodes"), the Soviets might have been tempted to initiate a strike. If the system was weak enough, the opportunity for a single decisive blow could have been perceived, based not on destroying military facilities but on rendering them effectively inoperable.

Intra-War Deterrence

For MAD authors, it is not just useless but actually counterproductive to discuss scenarios for the prosecution or termination of a nuclear war.

However, warfighters believe that actions taken during the course of a war can have, not only operational benefits, but rhetorical ones as well. If war efforts can be controlled then the possibility exists to use war efforts, particularly limited nuclear strikes, themselves as a way of communicating intent. Not striking Soviet cities in an initial attack is a direct way to communicate a desire to limit the war to a controlled, military effort. Similarly, if one believes the Soviets value their own political leadership above all else, then the organs of control should not be targeted in an initial exchange. This serves to communicate that the United States is attempting to avoid "doing its worst" and further, that it retains that capacity and the will to exercise it if pushed too far.

Aside from the operational questions concerning how communication can be received when warning and assessment facilities have been destroyed, this approach has other credibility problems. The Soviets were presumably preparing to win a nuclear war, preferably in a decisive way. How is the United States to ensure that, if subtle gradations can be discerned, such gradations will be interpreted as something other than weakness or mere tactical ineptitude? It is in part to address these concerns that warfighters who believe denial of Soviet war aims is inadequate postulated a theory of American victory.

These theorists argued that detailed war plans and targeting options and the concommitant hardware are of little benefit without an overall goal.[134] Contemporary strategic doctrine therefore was berated for a "visceral" unwillingness to consider ways the United States could prosecute a war to victory.[135]

A theory of victory enhances deterrence prior to a war. It is not that war aims could be effectively communicated per se. Rather, the argument is that plans guide the development of a more coherent (hence more easily communicable) deterrent posture. "A deterrent without a war plan cannot be credible, and a war without objectives cannot be meaningful."[136] The lack of a coherent war plan "feeds back into an impoverished deterrent posture and doctrine."[137] A coherent war plan is by definition one that makes possible a meaningful victory, and victory "means no more and certainly no less than that the United States achieve its political objectives."[138]

This raises an interesting question. Just what are the political objectives of the United States: To take any opportunity to "roll back" communist governments? To return to the status quo antebellum? These authors provide no answer. Political objectives are the objectives held by a nation in war. Would they differ from conflict to conflict? If so, how are objectives determined far enough in advance to impact on procurement decisions? Again the warfighter is silent. They do believe "weapon system procurement can make no sense except in terms of a guiding strategy, which itself is meaningless if isolated from the political purposes for which military power is purchased."[139] So the purpose of political objectives is quite clear. What is not clear is how, when, by whom, or, in what manner those objectives are to be determined. In fact even the nature of a victory is unclear. Gray states that while we should not begin a war in order to structure the world as we please, we may be faced with a choice between waging such a war and surrendering.[140] This appears to argue that although we (as the moral player) cannot initiate a war in order to eliminate Communism, we can take advantage of the opportunity when it is presented to us.

This may be unfair. Warfighters apparently believed that a theory of victory would enable the United States to prosecute a war in which escalation discipline could be imposed upon the Soviets, forcing them to sue for peace on terms favorable to the United States. In other words, a theory calling only for Soviet defeat could lead to acceptance of a stalemate such that, after a Soviet invasion of NATO, for example, Soviet troops would pull back to the German border. These authors would not support such an outcome. If not a return to the status quo with reparations, at minimum, then perhaps there might be an opportunity to reunite the Germanies under Western control.

Such scenarios will be covered in more detail in the next chapter. But a theory of victory calls for sufficient superiority to enforce escalation discipline on the Soviets and to be able to force them to back down, whatever the stakes. "Political objectives" remain undefined because they stem from the given conflict and cannot be predetermined. Ambiguity provides needed flexibility in the actual instance. A theory of victory calls for adequate thought and preparation to accompany the procurement of hardware. For example, Kennedy indicts the Maritime Strategy on this basis:

In the [Naval Secretary John] Lehman version of a maritime strategy the new and larger Navy is to carry the attack, in the event of war, directly to the shores of the Soviet Union . . . the principal deficiency of this strategy is that it doesn't say what is to happen if the naval attacks on the Soviet shoreline were to be successful. This lack of a "thought-through" element is characteristic.[141]

It is only the threat that the United States could exact significant losses on the Soviet leadership in such a situation that would persuade them to accept American peace terms.

Thus, warfighters were as concerned with the creation and maintenance of a persuasive message as were MAD authors. Because they begin with a radically different set of assumptions about nuclear war and about the Soviet Union, they postulate a radically different set of criteria for message construction. Yet the fundamental structure of the doctrine, and the need to manipulate American force structures in order to manipulate Soviet perceptions (and thus reactions) is the same. It is only the content of the desired messages that is altered.

CRITIQUE

As I indicated in the last chapter, numerous authors have indicted the warfighting position on the technical ground that it is impossible to conduct controlled, meaningful military operations in a nuclear environment. While probably true, such arguments in no way advanced the debate over strategic doctrine. They served merely to mire us down in such irresolvable technical questions as the level of EMP (Electromagnetic Pulse) command systems must be able to withstand. And, in fairness, such arguments additionally distort the warfighting position.

That warfighting is as much a theory of persuasion as MAD is clear. It is viable as an alternative to MAD only to the extent that its projection of audience response is superior. This becomes clear as soon as warfighters argue that the proof that the Soviet leadership does not care about its population is that collerateral damage from American attacks would not alter Soviet strategy or tactics during a war. For if that claim is true, then our possession of options that would leave civilians untargetted has no strategic operational benefit. Options are only relevant in so far as we can convince the Soviets that we have them. They are a persuasive tool, designed around a particular portrayal of a given audience. Employing them or not employing them in a war would not alter Soviet behavior.

In fact, although warfighters berated MAD advocates for ignoring the question of responsible behavior after deterrence had failed, they themselves demonstrated in a different way the identical problem: How do rational people prepare for an irrational event? MAD advocates attempted to make the question irrelevant. (It will not occur and if it does there is nothing we can do.) Warfighters ignored the physical constraints imposed by the weapons, arguing for distinctions that could not have been meaningfully communicated to the Soviet Union in the event, and thus arguing that rationality could be imposed. Both answers are unsatisfactory. The warfighters ignored the fact that their very attempt to deal with the constraints of war might have been making it dramatically more likely. Making purely physical constraints irrelevant (or rather, refusing to consider the constraints that do exist) to their conception of deterrence introduced purely technical dangers into the strategic relationship.[142]

The question of whose portrait of the Soviet Union was superior is difficult to resolve. The warfighters' portrayal is as circular as the MAD advocates'. Deployments provide conclusions, which are supported by documents that are selected as legitimate on the basis of their congruence with the conclusions already gleaned from physical evidence. The war-fighters reject the MAD proponents' attempts to discern motivations for deployments, but in so doing they assume the motivation, without examining or defending it. Thus "one must suppose, that this all but self-energizing mode of [Soviet] arms accumulation is a product of conscious leadership choice (or acquiescence) rather than merely the manifestation of a mindless military bureaucracy rolling about like a loose cannon without a rational purpose or political discipline."[143] The conception of Soviet forces as reflective of far-seeing intentional conceptions of strategy thus assumes primacy over all other potential explanations. Given the centrality of physical evidence to the warfighters, this assumption is absolutely critical, and yet it is never defended in any way as anything other than self-evident. If it were self-evident, however, there would hardly be strategic debate in the first place. Only a true believer could assert that "the Soviet system is almost pristine in its simplicity."[144]

As with the MAD position, warfighting is a theory of communication, but it is so mechanistic as to be deeply flawed. Our force structures are meant as communicative; those of the Soviets are meant to be used. One should not be misled by the idea that the Soviets are believed willing to use their forces politically to impose American acquiescence without the use of force. This in no way is meant to indicate Soviet manipulations of procurements and structures in order to send a nonverbal message. The Soviets see nuclear weapons as politically useful. Force levels are increased to support and enforce a single crude message demanding that the United States not become militarily involved in certain conflicts. The postulated Soviet strategy is "less concerned with manipulating the peacetime perceptions of potential adversaries"[145] (which is of course the whole point of ours), as with winning battles, preferably by being able to foreclose American participation in those battles.

It is additionally the case that as much weight was placed on the procurement process itself as on any other method of communicating with the Soviets. It is literally impossible to overprocure.[146] If a weapon can be developed to the prototype stage, it must be purchased. To not do so would be to raise questions about our "commitment" to a strong defense. Within the overall framework of warfighting, however, this approach makes strategy the slave of technology, for once purchased the weapons must be given some mission somewhere.[147] The classic example of this is the now-vulnerable ICBM. If its vulnerability is as destabilizing as warfighters suggested then it should be replaced. Yet it is retained because only a prompt HTK solves problems of vulnerability and no other leg of the triad can offer this solution. What is ignored is that no other leg of the triad has the problem either. But to unilaterally decommission the ICBMs, no matter the benefit, would have been to call our credibility into question.

This leads to consideration of the question of how refined policies and strategies can be communicated when everything, even if it is virtually useless, is purchased. It is clear that preparation must be made to fight every hypothetical scenario. If it can be thought of, it must be prepared for, to the point where warfighters such as Gray resent the demand that any given scenario should be defended at the level of plausibility.

Long-range planning is beset with, even embattled by, what may be called the plausibility problem. The immediate circumstances that trigger great events are rarely predictable and typically would be dismissed as irresponsibly fanciful had one dared to elicit them. Those who debate security issues in public are challenged constantly by the demand to "provide a plausible scenario." The actual events that trigger a war cannot be predicted. If a military planner keys the defense of a particular military program to a particular story of unfolding events, he is always liable to meet a fatal level of disbelief in the details that are provided.[148]

This argument neatly eliminates the need to so much as define priorities, since everything is a priority of equal urgency.

The limits of the communication medium are stretched, perhaps to the breaking point. This, I believe, is why the strategic balance for the warfighter must come down to a strictly numerical analysis. The medium chosen is clearly a rhetorical one. As such its power comes from the "resources of ambiguity."[149] The demand that all scenarios be seriously anticipated enhances this natural ambiguity. How can a specific communication be sent or received when the ultimate demand on the system is the communication of option and option requires choice?

The warfighters' perspective demands that all options be given the same respect within the system. Priorities cannot be chosen (hence cannot be communicated). Strictly numerical methods become essential. No matter the option the recipient of the message interprets into the message, superiority in numbers provides the flexibility (operationally) that a persuasive message demands. The MAD attempt to counterbalance inferiorities and superiorities is then unacceptable for it makes assumptions about which scenarios the Soviets had in mind when they interpreted our message. When any scenario has as much credibility and importance as any other, however, the assumption of selectivity upon which warfighting is based self-destructs.

CONCLUSION

In this chapter I sought to demonstrate that, like Mutual Assured Destruction, warfighting reveals itself to be a theory of state-to-state persuasion. Given the assured unreliability of discursive communication, the characteristics of American forces become a media through which a predetermined persuasive message can be sent. Both MAD and warfighting are theories constructed based on assumptions about the Soviet Union in order to regulate the U.S.-Soviet relationship. That relationship, however, is made additionally complex due to its global character and the fact that it is embedded within an alliance structure.

Assumptions made about the bilateral relationship may or may not apply in situations where allied states are involved and conflict is likely to begin at a conventional level. The attempt to apply these theories in such a setting, that is, in order to deal with the NATO-Warsaw Pact confrontation in Europe, can be expected to be less than perfect. Such a case, then, is likely to reveal tensions and strains in both theories. The characteristics of weapons have been considered to this point. The following chapter deals in greater detail with the range and location of weapons as these were seen as methods of communication on the Central Front.

NOTES

1. John Payne, "Threats and the Appeasement Theory of War," *The American Threat: National Security and Foreign Policy* (College Station, Tex.: Lytton Publishing Co., 1984), 4.

2. Payne, "Appeasement," 4.

3. Payne, "Appeasement," 4.

4. Colin Gray, "Planning for US Security Interests," *Proceedings: U.S. Naval Institute* 110, no. 12 (December 1984): 39. (Hereinafter cited as *Proceedings*.)

5. Edward Luttwak, *On the Meaning of Victory* (New York: Simon and Schuster, 1986), 173.

6. Richard Foster, "From Assured Destruction to Assured Survival," *Comparative Strategy* 2, no. 1 (1980): 67.

7. Luttwak, *Victory*, 34.

8. Luttwak, *Victory*, 260.

9. Mark Miller, "Soviet Strategic Thought: The End of an Era?" *International Security Review* 5, no. 4 (Winter 1980): 488.

10. Gray, "Planning," 42.

11. Luttwak, *Victory*, 86. This is portrayed as an infinite and circular process. Gray, "Planning," 42. "But the stability of Soviet control of Eastern Europe is threatened by the attractive power of Western Europe, and the political independence of Western European politics is underwritten by the U.S. security guarantee."

12. Dimitri Simes, "Gorbachev: A New Foreign Policy?" *Foreign Affairs* 65, no. 3 (1987): 485.

13. Colin Gray, "Maritime Strategy," *Proceedings* 112, no. 2 (February 1986): 36.

14. Simes, "Gorbachev," 491.

15. Gray, "Maritime Strategy," 36.

16. Gray, "Planning," 42.

17. Colin Gray, "War Fighting for Deterrence," *Journal of Strategic Studies* 7, no. 1 (March 1984): 7.

18. Simes, "Gorbachev," 479.

19. Luttwak, *Victory*, 31.

20. Richard Foster, "On Prolonged Nuclear War," *International Security Review* 6, no. 4 (Winter 1981–1982): 503.

21. Luttwak, *Victory*, 271.

22. The doctrinal concept of an inevitable all out nuclear war has been abandoned. See Charles Gati, "The Stalinist Legacy in Soviet Foreign Policy," in Robbin Laird and Erik Hoffman, eds., *Soviet Foreign Policy in a Changing World* (New York: Aldine, 1986), 16–28.

23. Foster, "Assured Survival," 62.

24. Thus, for example, Foster says ("Assured Survival," 60): "The Soviet strategic concept and objectives are the dialectical opposites of the US concept and aims. The Soviet objective is global victory both in a state of peaceful coexistence and, if deterrence fails, in a general nuclear war fought for global objectives." Soviet documents are almost treated as if they were composed of a "code" that warfighters believe they have properly interpreted. MAD authors are then indicted for having read the documents at face value. For an analysis of this mode of interpretation see Edward Zuckerman, *The Day After World War III* (New York: Avon Books, April 1987), 245. For examples see J. A. Vermaat and Hans Bax, "The Soviet Concept of Peace," *Strategic Review* 11, no. 4 (Fall 1983), and Keith Payne, *Nuclear Deterrence in U.S.–Soviet Relations* (Boulder: Westview Press, 1982), 79–122.

25. Robert Levgold, "The Nature of Soviet Power," in Laird and Hoffman, eds., *Soviet Foreign Policy*, 38; Joseph Douglass, "U.S. Strategy for General Nuclear War," *International Security Review* 5, no. 3 (Fall 1980): 291; John Caravelli, "The Role of Surprise and Preemption in Soviet Military Strategy," *International Security Review* 6, no. 2 (Summer 1981): 230; Karen Dawisha, "Soviet Ideology and Western Europe," in Edwina Moreton and Gerald Segal, eds., *Soviet Strategy Toward Western Europe* (Boston: George Allan and Unwin, 1984); 26–35; Colin Gray, *Nuclear Strategy and National Style* (Lanham, Md.: Hamilton Press, 1986), 16.

26. It is important to remember that this is not solely a hardware comparison: Multiple factors would have to be considered.

27. Colin Gray, "Letter to the Editor," *Comparative Strategy* 2, no. 4 (1980): 367.

28. Foster, "Assured Survival," 62.

29. Luttwak, *Victory*, 39.

30. Miller, "Soviet Thought," 484.

31. Miller, "Soviet Thought," 484.

32. Colin Gray, "Strategic Forces and SALT: A Question of Strategy," *Comparative Strategy* 2, no. 2 (1980): 116.

33. Although in some instance they are not working from their own translations this is true for all the cited authors.

34. Foster, "Prolonged War," 510; Benjamen Lambeth, "What Deters? An Assessment of the Soviet View," in John Reichart and Steven Sturm, *American*

Defense Policy, 5th ed. (Baltimore: Johns Hopkins University Press, 1982), 196; Caravelli, "Surprise and Preemption," 228.

35. For example, Miller, "Soviet Thought," merely states (483) that: "[*Military Strategy*] has remained consistent in all three editions," which is certainly not the claim of the MAD authors who have examined the book.

36. Gray, "Planning," 38.

37. Caravelli, "Preemption," 231.

38. Miller, "Soviet Thought," 477.

39. Miller, "Soviet Thought," 478.

40. Miller, "Soviet Thought," 478.

41. Gray, "Strategic Forces and SALT," 115–116.

42. Lambeth, "Assessment," 192.

43. Douglass, "General War," 308.

44. Miller, "Soviet Thought," 478.

45. Lambeth, "Assessments," 189.

46. Gray, "Strategic Forces and SALT," 118. See also, Luttwak, *Victory,* 185.

47. Gray, "Strategic Forces and SALT," 119.

48. Miller, "Soviet Thought," 487. See also Colin Gray, "What Deters? The Ability to Wage Nuclear War." in Reichart and Sturm, *Defense Policy,* 179; Lambeth, "Assessment," 190. See also 191.

49. Luttwak, *Victory,* 42. See also Gray, "Strategic Forces and SALT," 119–120.

50. Lambeth, "Assessment," 188.

51. Lambeth, "Assessment," 195.

52. See Lawrence Freedman, *The Evolution of Nuclear Strategy* (New York: St. Martin's Press, 1983), especially 225–272, for a relevant history.

53. Miller, "Soviet Thought," 479.

54. Miller, "Soviet Thought," 478.

55. Miller, "Soviet Thought," 478.

56. See Miller, "Soviet Thought," 479, and Lambeth, "Assessment."

57. Miller, "Soviet Thought," 501.

58. See Foster, "Assured Survival," 56; and Lambeth, "Assessment," 189.

59. Miller, "Soviet Thought," 479.

60. Douglass, "Strategy," 291.

61. Miller, "Soviet Thought," 485.

62. See Caravelli, "Surprise," 230; and Lambeth, "Assessment," 190.

63. Caravelli, "Surprise," 230.

64. Caravelli, "Surprise," 229, and Lambeth, "Assessment," 189.

65. Luttwak, *Victory,* 42.

66. Foster, "Prolonged War," 501.

67. Caravelli, "Surprise," 228.

68. Gray, "What Deters," 178. See also Lambeth, "Assessment," 191, and Foster, "Assured Survival," 60.

69. Luttwak, *Victory,* 41. (Emphasis in original.)

70. Foster, "Assured Survival," 60.

71. Luttwak, *Victory,* 41.

72. See Miller, "Soviet Thought," 503, and Simes, "Gorbachev," 479–480.

73. "Contemporary U.S. defense policy is less characteristically American

than merely civilian. Soviet strategic views for their part, are less uniquely Soviet than simply military. The differences between the two stem principally from assymetries in the composition of the strategic elites of the two countries." Benjamen Lambeth, "Contemporary Soviet Military Policy" in Roman Kolkowicz and Ellen Propper Mickiewicz, eds., *The Soviet Calculus of Nuclear War* (Lexington: Books, 1986), 35.

74. Gray, "Warfighting," 5.
75. Gray, "Warfighting," 23.
76. Gray, "Strategic Forces and SALT," 124.
77. Miller, "Strategic Thought," 480. See also Gray, "What Deters," 179.
78. Gray, "What Deters," 175. See also Foster, "Prolonged War," 508.
79. Gray, "Warfighting," 16.
80. Gray, "What Deters," 175.
81. Gray, "Warfighting," 16.
82. Gray, "What Deters," 175.
83. Gray, "What Deters," 175.
84. Gray, "What Deters," 180.
85. Gray, "Strategic Forces and SALT," 124.
86. Gray, "What Deters," 179.
87. Gray, "Warfighting," 6.
88. Keith Payne, in interview with author, October 31, 1986, Fairfax, Va.
89. Gray, "What Deters," 182.
90. Gray, "What Deters," 182.
91. Gray, "What Deters," 174.
92. Gray, "Strategic Forces and SALT," 125.
93. For a balanced treatment of the strategic debate over SDI see "Weapons in Space: Vol. II: Implications for Security," *Daedalus* 114, no. 3 (Summer 1985): entire issue.
94. Douglas, "General War," 292. Luttwak explains (*Victory,* 236):

Far from seeking more destructive power against the peoples of the Soviet Union, the aim rather has been to uncover ways and means of making retaliatory threats more selective, more flexible, and much less destructive—threats which could in turn plausibly deter Soviet threats themselves less catastrophic than the all-out nuclear attack upon America which is most easily dissuaded by a very small nuclear force.

95. Gray, "Warfighting," 9.
96. For a detailed analysis of current weaknesses in U.S. C3 and what can be done to strengthen the system see Ashton Carter, John Steinbrunner, and Charles Zraket, eds., *Managing Nuclear Operations* (Washington, D.C.: The Brookings Institution, 1987).
97. Miller, "Soviet Thought," 496.
98. Gray, "Warfighting," 21.
99. See for example, Gray, *National Style,* 16–20. Also Keith Payne in interview with author, October 31, 1986.
100. Miller, "Soviet Thought," 505.
101. Gray, "Warfighting," 5.
102. Douglas Dagleish and Larry Schweikart, "Trident and the Triad," *Proceedings* 112, no. 6 (June 1986): 74.

103. See Dagleish and Schweikart, "Triad," 79; Luttwak, *Victory*, 37 and Lambeth, "Assessment," 194.

104. Stewart Blair, "Question for U.S. Strategic Modernization: Why 'Ride Out' A Soviet Attack?" *Strategic Review* (Spring 1982): 47.

105. Blair, "Ride Out," 47.

106. Foster, "Assured Survival," 70. See also Blair, "Ride Out," 47.

107. Dagleish and Schweikart, "Triad," 79.

108. Luttwak, *Victory*, 109. Thus, for example, he similarly implores us (*Victory*, 45) to reject a submarine-only option, since doing so allows the Soviets to focus all their attention on anti-submarine warfare, so that even though submarines are invulnerable *today*, they could be vulnerable *tomorrow*, and therefore must be treated as vulnerable.

109. Blair, "Ride Out," 49. It is also argued that mobility would be no aid to survivability because Midgetman bases could simply be "barrage attacked." See Colin Gray, "Strategic Forces," in Joseph Kruzel, ed., *American Defense Annual 1987–88* (Lexington: Lexington Books, 1986), 76.

110. The "escalation ladder" is described in detail by Herman Kahn who serves the warfighters as the initial author to conceptualize their position, much as Bernard Brodie serves the MAD authors. For a detailed list of escalatory "rungs" see Herman Kahn, *Thinking About the Unthinkable in the 1980s* (New York: Simon and Schuster, 1984), 123–151.

111. Luttwak, *Victory*, 105–106.

112. This is why, for example, they may oppose the development of the single warhead "Midgetman" because it is presented as trading off with the MX for budgetary reasons, but would support it if the development of both programs simultaneously was possible.

113. Gray, "Strategic Forces," notes (78): "In principal, at least, a twenty boat Trident force by 1999 could carry 3,840 warheads, each in the half-megaton range. With an accuracy capability in the same class as the MX, there can be no doubt that the D-5 [warhead] will pose a truly formidable threat to most of the hardened targets in the Soviet Union that are of particular interest to US defense planners."

114. Gray, "Strategic Forces," 78. Dagleish and Schweikart confirm that ("Triad," 76): "technology currently employed in Trident missiles or imminently available will make the SLBM equivalent or superior to the ICBM in every category except communications reliability."

115. See Caravelli, "Surprise," 226; Foster, "Assured Survival," 62, and Douglass, "General War," 291. In fact Caravelli takes pains to point out (232): "the consistency of the Soviet views on key elements of doctrine such as surprise and preemption has been remarkable in that it has not undergone significant change, in spite of what appears to be a more restrained approach to these topics since the early 1970s."

116. Miller, "Soviet Thought," 495. See also Caravelli, "Surprise," 231; Douglass, "General War," 291; and Foster, "Prolonged War," 506.

117. Douglass, "General War," 291. See also Caravelli, "Surprise," 233, and Foster, "Prolonged War," 506.

118. Douglass, "General War," 291.

119. Foster, "Prolonged War," 514. See also 497; Gray, "What Deters," 172, and Luttwak, *Victory*, 236.

120. This is the argument made in Blair, "Ride Out." Similarly Douglass argues ("General War," 301) that: "A launch-under-attack option appears almost essential. The United States cannot wait until the full force of the Soviet attack has been delivered and then expect to launch a counterstrike." Blair takes the position that, if announced, this would enhance deterrence (48).

121. Gray, "Warfighting," 24.

122. Gray, "What Deters," 177.

123. Gray, "What Deters," 177.

124. Foster, "Assured Survival," 67. "As we gradually weaken our strategic forces, we increase the strategic utility of the superior Soviet conventional and nuclear forces."

125. Gray, "Warfighting," 7.

126. Gray, "Warfighting," 7.

127. Douglass, "General War," 309. Luttwak has argued (*Victory*, 46) that "Now, by contrast it is only the grossly ill-informed, the self-deceived and the willfully deceiving who will still argue the point."

128. Luttwak, *Victory*, 35.

129. Luttwak, *Victory*, 47.

130. See Luttwak, *Victory*, 186 and 211.

131. See Luttwak, *Victory*, 200. And indeed Foster ("Assured Survival," 54) has argued that "The technological lead we once enjoyed is shrinking, and new generations of Soviet weapons are in many cases superior in quality to corresponding weapons in the United States."

132. See Blair, "Ride Out," 50, and Luttwak, *Victory*, 188.

133. Douglass, "General War," 295. See also 294.

134. Gray, "What Deters," 174.

135. See Gray, "Warfighting," especially 9.

136. Foster, "Assured Survival," 63.

137. Gray, "What Deters," 174. See also Foster, "Assured Survival," 54, and Gray, "Warfighting," 6.

138. Gray, "Warfighting," 6.

139. Gray, "Strategic Forces," 68.

140. Gray, "Warfighting," 12.

141. William Kennedy, "The U.S. Defense Organization," in Ray Bond, ed., *Modern U.S. War Machine* (New York: Crown Publishers, 1987): 38.

142. They deserve the criticism when they advocate giving launch authority to field commanders at the onset of any international crisis (Douglass, "General War," 302) or bemoan nonproliferation policies since more nuclear armed countries meant less territory the Soviets could take easily in a war (209).

143. Lambeth, "Assessment," 192.

144. Lambeth, "Assessment," 191.

145. Lambeth, "Assessment" 189.

146. Thus Gray argues ("Strategic Forces and SALT," 115):

Deterrence and war are at least a two-person business, and it is the duty of Western defense professionals to make it as difficult as possible for a group of Soviet staff officers to design not-implausible blueprints for victory. On this reasoning, the West may end up over deterring and worrying about vulnerabilities that have no military and political meaning—but that is an acceptable price to pay.

147. Some have argued that technology "drives" strategy, in the sense that what is possible technologically determines the strategic choices argued for. That is not my position. Rather, I am arguing that overarching strategic assumptions demand that what is possible technologically be produced. Given that strategy of procurement, weapons are purchased which may or may not fit gracefully into pre-existing force structures, missions and planning.

148. Gray, "Planning," 39. See also Douglass, "General War," especially 311.

149. Kenneth Burke, "What Are the Signs of What," *Language as Symbolic Action* (Berkeley: University of California Press, 1966), 359.

Chapter Four

Strategic Doctrine and the Defense of NATO

MAD and warfighting are similar in that each doctrine was designed to provide a conceptual basis for the bilateral nuclear relationship between the United States and the Soviet Union. The internal logics of the strategic theories best met the problem for which they were designed: to deter nuclear attacks on the territory of one nuclear superpower by the other. Given the overriding importance of deterrence this bilateral orientation is understandable. However, precisely because the United States and the Soviet Union were superpowers, their interests were global. Conflicts between the superpowers occurred at diverse geographic areas and affected the superpower relationship as a whole. These conflicts had to be resolved with the understanding that the potential for escalation existed whenever and wherever the desires and interests of the superpowers were in collision. Theorists seeking to minimize the risks of nuclear confrontation had to simultaneously find the means to extend or protect national self interests while avoiding a direct clash between superpowers leading to a nuclear war.

From the American perspective, a strategic posture was needed that discouraged the Soviets from actively challenging United States and allied interests. Threats and acts of violence below the level of strategic war had to be deterred as effectively as homeland attacks. Though the tactical needs of deterrence differed in each specific confrontation, the perspectives on policy were derived from the major strategic doctrines: MAD and warfighting.

MAD and warfighting were devised to deal with an extremely limited range of circumstances. Yet these theories have been applied to less intense forms of conflict, potentially involving Third World countries and alliances.[1] When theories are stretched in this way, tensions and inconsistencies in their application emerge. This chapter explores the contradictions and paradoxes that appear when strategic doctrines are expanded to encompass tactical and theater roles. Specifically, it will discuss one of the most important areas where the United States sought to constrain the actions of the Soviets: Western Europe.

The shared assumptions of MAD and warfighting as they applied to the defense of Europe must be examined in order to provide a complete critique. No doctrine exists in a vacuum; the constraints imposed by the goals which actors seek to accomplish must be preserved within existing situations. Those constraints are not constant, but are shaped by the scenarios devised to describe the potential for a land battle in Europe and choices which were emerging in the mid- to late 1980s for dealing with the situation. Furthermore, discussing the potential for a land battle is not contained by issues relating to territory only, but inevitably raises questions of broader uses of force at sea: the maritime strategy. This analysis will move from defining areas of commonly perceived constraints to an examination of how solutions differed between advocates of warfighting and MAD, given the presuppositions of doctrine, and finally the way extensions of the doctrines generated contradictions with the strategic levels of analysis.

Two elements of the United States' attempt to deter Soviet encroachment into Western Europe will therefore be examined: the proposed use of so-called "Emerging Technology" weapons on the Central Front (generally defined as the inter-German border and the border between Germany and Czechoslovakia), and the attempts to articulate a coherent strategy for naval action in the event of a land war in Europe. The attempt of both MAD and warfighting advocates to adapt their theories to these scenarios will be analyzed in order to further illuminate the functions and limits of strategic doctrine.

SHARED DOCTRINAL ASSUMPTIONS
CONCERNING NATO

By the mid–1980s there was growing ambivalence on the part of both MAD and warfighting authors about the force planning dictates of their doctrines for Western Europe. Stabilizing the balance of nuclear power at the strategic level, party had posed near unresolvable dilemmas for the application of strategic doctrine to the need to deter lower levels of violence in Europe. Consider first the position of the MAD authors. The very basis of the MAD position is that no policy gain can justify the horror of nuclear war. At a normative level, nuclear weapons are useful and should be used, only to deter Soviet nuclear strikes on American territory.[2] Nuclear weapons should be worthless as instruments of foreign policy. Yet these authors are forced to compromise their ideal position, for if this assumption is taken as a given, how can the United States enforce its policies is areas vital to its interests?[3]

No one concerned with the development of strategic doctrine advocated a unilateralist position that permitted American indifference to a Soviet takeover of Western Europe. NATO Europe had to be defended by the United States for moral and cultural reasons. It was (and still is) also believed to be a region vital to American national security. Yet it was clear that neither the United States nor the West European governments were willing or able to provide sufficient levels of manpower or material to deter a conventional attack on Western Europe using conventional weapons. MAD authors were therefore forced to defend an exception to their preferred rule that nuclear weapons not be used in support of particular policies. There was apparently one event short of a strategic nuclear attack on the United States that might justify the use of nuclear weapons: a Soviet invasion of Western Europe using conventional weapons. That exception somehow had to be defended within the overall framework of the MAD position. And it had to be defined as a singular exception if the position was to retain its integrity.

While far more willing to tolerate risks of escalation, warfighters also had problems in integrating the defense of Europe into their position. Escalation Control requires Escalation Dominance. At every point across the spectrum of violence, allied forces must be prepared to counter and win against aggression. By maximizing the chances of success at each level of violence, the burden of escalation was ideally to be placed on the Soviet Union. Consequently, the chances of successful deterrence were increased. But the inadequacy of NATO's conventional defense led warfighters to call for immediate escalation to the nuclear level in case of a European war. This strategy cedes both Escalation Control and Escalation Dominance at the lower levels of conflict to the enemy. Like MAD theorists, warfighters were forced by the constraints they found operating on the Central Front (especially on the West German border) to manipulate doctrine in important ways.

Discussions of strategic forces from MAD and warfighting perspectives rarely take economic or political constraints into account. In discussing the American side of a bilateral system, U.S. theorists are free to advocate force structures in a normative manner. When analyzing approaches to the defense of Western Europe, however, proposed actions had also to be considered in light of an alliance structure. Even actions taken unilaterally by the United States directly affected the entire alliance and would have substantial political consequences. The assumption was, and in fact still is, that, as a practical reality, proposed force structures must be acceptable to the European allies. This places an additional burden on force deployments and announced strategy.

Doctrine must take into account political constraints upon allied actions. Both MAD and warfighting advocates share similar views about which political factors were operative. These factors served as constraining assumptions held jointly by both sets of authors during the 1980s.

1. *Western Europe must be defended.* All discussions presuppose that NATO-Europe faces a significant military threat from the Soviet Union, and that it is not capable of defending itself. The question of Soviet motives is assumed rather than argued. MAD and warfighting advocates therefore reject proposals for a "fortress America" posture that would result in European neutralism. They find many reasons to extend military support. Aside from cultural ties, the nations of Western Europe are held to be vital to American security. From a military perspective, a friendly Western Europe is a geopolitical necessity for the United States. As a maritime power, the United States must prevent any hostile nation from gaining hegemony over the "world island" of Eurasia because a conquering state could use the resources of these continents to lay siege to North America.[4]

2. *An imbalance of conventional forces existed between NATO and the Warsaw Pact which favored the Pact.* The weakness of allied conventional forces in comparison to Soviet troops has been of concern since the demobilization after World War II. This situation was still of concern to strategic theorists as late as 1988, even though MAD authors believe that that imbalance had been greatly exaggerated for years.[5] Jonathan Dean, for example, argued that when qualitative factors were taken into consideration the disparity between conventional forces was far less than generally assumed.[6] No one doubted the Pact's military superiority, but the level of threat imposed by such imbalance was never clear. Nevertheless, recent studies "argue for less pessimism about Western conventional capabilities than is prevalent, but they do not argue for optimism sufficient for conventional [only] deterrence."[7] For it is also clear, given demographics,[8] and increasing fiscal constraints,[9] that a general commitment on the part of NATO to redress the imbalance was always unlikely.

3. *The Soviet attainment of nuclear parity badly undermined the deterrent power of NATO.* During the era of clear American nuclear superiority, NATO's conventional forces were intended essentially as a "tripwire," a line which, if broken, would alert NATO to a massive Soviet attack. In the event of such an attack, nuclear forces in Western Europe and the United States would be launched. This strategy had gradually been modified, but the risk of nuclear escalation remained an important element of NATO policy.[10] In particular, American strategic forces had been "coupled" to the defense of NATO Europe. In order to convince the Soviet Union that the United States would be willing to escalate to strategic nuclear war in Europe's defense, the United States took the

position that for military purposes the territory of the European allies is the equivalent of American territory. Once the Soviets acquired an assured second-strike capacity, this version of coupling became less credible. To this day the question of whether the United States would have risked nuclear retaliation on American cities in defense of allies remains open.

Some began to fear that America's strategic deterrent had been "decoupled" from the defense of NATO-Europe. For them, the essential question became: Can anything be done to "recouple" and, if so, is there anything to be gained in the attempt? There are obvious thresholds that can be crossed in the scope and intensity of violence. The distinctions between peace and war, small and large conventional war, conventional and nuclear war, and limited and all-out nuclear war are clear. The "lines" between one level of violence and another are referred to as firebreaks. Because the strength of the firebreaks (that is, whether or not a particular firebreak is perceived as easy to cross) is believed to be manipulable, a large part of the dispute over deterrence on the Central Front concerned which firebreaks ought to be made strong and which weak. Those seeking strong firebreaks between wars limited to the European theater and intercontinental nuclear war faced the problem of "selling" a policy that ran counter to the expectations of some European allies. A strong firebreak raised the specter of a nuclear war fought between the United States and the Soviet Union, but contained to European soil. Coupling serves to create shared risks as well as to increase the perceived cost of Soviet adventurism. Coupling is meant to ensure that a decision by NATO to use nuclear weapons would involve all the allies equally, because it conceptually ties the use of nuclear weapons in Europe to a strategic exchange between superpowers. Thus the devastation of Western Europe could not be accomplished without incurring the destruction of the United States and Soviet homelands as well. As Hirschfield summarizes: "Basically coupling means continued visible assurance that the United States would risk Chicago to save Frankfurt."[11]

4. *A nuclear defense should be neither too automatic nor too cumbersome.* There is an inherent tension between attempts to reduce risks of escalation in Europe for the sake of crisis management and attempts to increase assurances that nuclear weapons will be used when necessary. The NATO allies did not want a defense that was too dependent upon resort to nuclear options, yet neither did they want too little reliance on nuclear weapons, for that appeared to reduce the risks for the Soviets should they desire to go to war. The European need to seek a middle ground became an additional persuasive constraint for American authors discussing European security.

Despite sharing similar views on constraints, MAD and warfighting authors argued for much different policies. Differences are generated by the need to adapt their theories in a manner consistent with their respective strategic doctrines. Yet, as examples will show, these adaptations extend the contradictions within the doctrines rather than resolving them. Consider the first example, war on the Central Front.

THE LAND BATTLE IN EUROPE

The stated purpose of the NATO alliance is the defense of its members.[12] The goal of the alliance (as distinct from the goals of individual member states) excludes offensive actions, as well as power projection in regions beyond Europe. Forces were structured and deployed in order to deter a Soviet attack on Western Europe and to defend Western Europe should deterrence fail. These requirements placed MAD advocates in a difficult position when trying to reconcile alliance requirements with the suppositions of strategic doctrine. At the strategic level, the goal of MAD is to make nuclear weapons militarily unusable, to create a situation where no possible policy objective can be served by their use in war. At the theater level, the goal is to tie the use of nuclear weapons to the deterrence of purely conventional attacks.

Finding an appropriate role for nuclear weapons at the theater level is not an easy task. The debate has been long, complex, and politically volatile. This section pursues the argument by analyzing NATO doctrine and by reviewing the MAD critique. From there, my discussion moves to consider problems with some major alternatives that were under consideration for shoring up NATO weaknesses. Finally, I will review what may become a significant change in the overall strategy of the United States: Emerging Technologies. The section will close with a discussion of the warfighter's response to the MAD position.

NATO Defense Doctrine

The compromise between the desire to avoid nuclear warfare if at all possible and the perceived need to use nuclear weapons to deter conventional attacks was at the root of NATO's defense strategy through the 1980s, called "Flexible Response." Intentionally ambiguous, this doctrine called for a Soviet attack to be met initially with equivalent force, reserving the right for NATO to initiate the use of nuclear weapons to retrieve victory in extreme situations. Freedman, for example, argues that Flexible Response is not even a strategy in the traditional sense of that word.[13]

There may be no clearer example of Burke's concept of the resources of symbolic ambiguity than that offered by this doctrine.[14] The refusal to specify the criteria for determining threshold points for the use of nuclear weapons and the strategy of escalation is intentional. If the

Soviets cannot predict what actions will result in NATO escalation, they cannot manipulate NATO doctrine by, for example, engaging in offensive operations designed to halt just short of predetermined thresholds.[15] As Freedman argues: "The somewhat vague and indefinite quality that would render it virtually useless at a time of serious confrontation does have value in peacetime, reminding a would-be aggressor that there can be no certainties as to how apparently rational governments would act when they found themselves in an utterly irrational situation."[16] Thus ambiguity increases uncertainty and, presumably, deterrence. Ambiguity can be useful in other ways. A vague doctrine can be used to "paper over" differences between alliance members. Each defense ministry can plausibly argue that its opinions have been adopted by the alliance as a whole.[17]

MAD's Critique of NATO Strategy

Flexible Response posits a force structure where, in the event of war in Europe, nuclear weapons would be weapons of last resort. For this strategy to be viable NATO must be able to wage conventional war for a reasonable period of time, Although Flexible Response had been NATO doctrine since the early 1960s, and although this element of the strategy has been clear since its adoption, NATO has never had sufficient conventional forces to match the Warsaw Pact.[18] There are ways to compensate for quantitative inferiority in conventional weapons, but the techniques involved were politically unacceptable to the West German government.[19] The only alternative judged to provide NATO with a sufficiently "robust" deterrent was the deployment of nuclear weapons virtually on the border between the Germanies. This force structure hardly made for "flexibility." Without adequate conventional forces, NATO might be forced to use nuclear weapons (as a last resort) very quickly.[20] Indeed, since nuclear weapons close to the border were vulnerable to conventional attack, the political leadership faced the risk of a "use them or lose them" situation regardless of the way the conventional battle may have progressed.

MAD authors were deeply troubled by Flexible Response. For while they supported it in theory, they did not believe NATO force structures to be truly flexible. The forward positioning of nuclear weapons was at odds with the doctrine of Flexible Response. The proponents of forward deployment justified the policy on the grounds that it created a high risk of the immediate use of nuclear weapons and so increased deterrence. But such a rationale vitiated the virtues of Flexible Response. Hines, Peterson, and Trulock noted:

Ironically, some in the West would hope to avert war by further narrowing the range of NATO choices during a crisis, which they believe would reinforce the credibility of NATO's first-use threat. This view demands continued reliance for security on the frightening specter of global nuclear war, a specter that now serves to undermine rather than to enhance the Western defense consensus and opens the door to Soviet warfare.[21]

But this is not the only problem caused by forward positioning of nuclear weapons. The construction of an "automatic" nuclear threshold was regularly used as a justification to avoid deploying the conventional forces necessary to sustain Flexible Response.[22] Perversely, forward deployment also increased the incentives to initiate an attack. If the Soviets believed they could destroy allied nuclear nuclear weapons quickly with conventional forces, they might then consider a blitzkrieg strategy to capture weapons before a decision on their use could be reached. They would then face only the weak deployed conventional forces and the risk that the United States would retaliate with strategic forces. A credible deterrent, MAD authors held, should include a conventional force that can pose a plausible defense for a reasonable amount of time. For example, Posen wrote:

If the Soviets believed that they can achieve victory with conventional forces alone, then overall deterrence of Soviet aggression is surely undermined. As John Mearsheimer has pointed out, in the world of conventional deterrence, it is confidence in quick, cheap victory that causes the aggressor to attack. In NATO's case, Soviet confidence in a speedy conventional victory may also undermine the deterrent effect of the Alliance's nuclear weapons, providing hope to the Pact that NATO could be overrun before a decision to use nuclear weapons were taken.[23]

It was, therefore, the rapid "blitzkrieg" style invasion of Western Europe that the MAD authors fear, and it is the chance of such invasion that their doctrine had to anticipate and reduce.[24]

If forward basing creates a dangerous situation by its overemphasis on nuclear weapons, as opposed to conventional ones, it also calls into question the overall strategic posture of the United States. In a situation where Europe is lost to a Soviet conventional attack, any threat of escalation becomes incredible. A strategic exchange would lead to mutual annihilation and would not win back European territory. Thus forward basing risks de facto decoupling in the event of a theater war. To remedy this problem, MAD authors argued that NATO must increase the nuclear threshold by increasing conventional forces so that nuclear weapons would not have to be used in defense of Europe.

MAD authors supported Flexible Response because they wanted to see capabilities developed that would have assured a nonautomatic recourse to nuclear use and escalation in time of war. Then nuclear escalation could remain a strategy of last resort to be employed only when a conventional defense was about to collapse.[25]

The need for a stronger conventional force can be seen in detail when the MAD literature addresses the question of deploying the cruise and Pershing II missiles. From the moment the decision to place these missiles in Europe was made, MAD authors argued against the location of these weapons on the inter-German border.[26] Such positioning, they held at the time, greatly increased the likelihood that nuclear weapons would be used in a crisis. Their proximity to the border, where Pact forces would attempt to break NATO lines, would make them vulnerable.[27] MAD authors isolated a number of policy options available to the alliance designed to reduce the vulnerability of nuclear weapons. In each instance MAD theorists rejected the option on the grounds that it was destabilizing or ineffective.[28] They thus rejected the chosen basing mode as ultimately counterproductive. MAD authors sought a force structure that would have enhanced stability without sacrificing deterrence; that would satisfactorily communicate the risks of nuclear escalation without overrelying on them.

No First Use and No Early First Use

Almost all MAD indictments of NATO nuclear policy pertained to the forward basing of nuclear weapons. MAD theorists did not seek to redress problems by eliminating NATO's nuclear options altogether, but they did advocate a policy of "transarmament," requiring a restructuring of NATO's forces. "Transarmament" evolved only after some experimentation with doctrinal options.

In 1982, MacNamara and several other eminent MAD theorists called for a NATO declaration of "No First Use" (NFU) of nuclear weapons.[29] Prompted by the contradictions in forward deployment policy, the pledge to forego nuclear escalation was advanced as a way to force greater reliance on conventional defense.[30] The authors included a critical hedge: they were not, they said, so much advocating NFU as seeking to promote discussion of it.[31] The resulting discussion made it clear that nuclear weapons had to remain an inherent part of NATO strategy. In fact, by 1986 the original group of authors had joined with several others to call for "No Early First Use" (NEFU) of nuclear weapons.[32] This position holds that NATO ought to reserve the right to use nuclear weapons first, but that it should remove the incentives to use them by eliminating front line deployments. NEFU emphasizes conventional defense and improved chances for deterrence and Crisis Stability.

The rationale for No Early First Use was widely, if uncomfortably, accepted by MAD authors. It was believed that NATO could not deter Soviet attack without resorting to the threat of nuclear war. "Without the realistic threat to use nuclear weapons, NATO can never achieve a confident defense within its limited personnel and economic resources," Cotter said.[33]

Military theorists believe that because of advantages intrinsic to defense, an attacker requires a 3 to 1 numerical superiority to mount a successful invasion.[34] Because the Pact was forced to echelon its troops behind the FEBA (Forward Edge of the Battle Area, or front line) to decrease their vulnerability to a nuclear attack, Warsaw Pact forces could not be massed to achieve the necessary ratio of offense to defense. Thus, NATO's inferior conventional forces provided an adequate deterrent— so long as the Soviets had to take into consideration the possibility of nuclear use when deploying their conventional forces.[35] In fact, since the late 1940s Soviet troop density had declined from 500 per square kilometer to 20.[36] Thus the nuclear threat was seen as neutralizing, to a large extent, the Pact's conventional superiority.

Maintaining a nuclear option was also important to the NATO alliance because of political constraints on warfighting strategies. Traditionally, military theorists have called for the defense to "trade space for time" in any conventional war. This tactic requires fighting a running battle of maneuver against blitzkrieg tactics and counterattacking when sufficient forces can be brought to bear. On the Central Front, such tactics would have required initially ceding up to one third of the Federal Republic. The Germans would not accept any such strategy.

Responding to this political limitation, the allies adopted a conventional doctrine that required "forward defense," where forward meant as far forward as possible.[37] Forward defense is less flexible than the traditional defense in depth, since it is less responsive to enemy activity. It will work only if the number of Pact forces at the FEBA is kept to a minimum. Renunciation of nuclear options would, therefore, badly undermine NATO's ability to sustain a viable forward conventional defense.

If the consequences of NFU upon conventional deterrence were not bad enough, many MAD authors argued that NFU would increase the chances of nuclear war. Because the Soviet Union according to the MAD authors did not believe nuclear war could be limited, deterrence could be achieved by maintaining even low probability of the use of nuclear weapons as a possible response to nuclear war—but the threat has to be maintained. This requires that the threat, and the concomitant risk of nuclear war, be structured into force configurations. This intentional creation and maintenance of risk is really what coupled NATO to the American strategic deterrent. As Mearsheimer argued: "Given the consequences of using these horrible weapons, it is not necessary for the likelihood of use to be very high."[38] He explained that it is "the fear of these consequences, of course, that motivates the NFU movement; it is, however, the utter horror we associate with these weapons that makes them so dissuasive."[39] Even a small probability of the use of nuclear weapons, according to this argument, creates a robust deterrent. Renunciation of the use of nuclear weapons, or at least the first use of such weapons, would require that NATO's conventional forces be sufficient to repel an attack.[40] A defense relying solely on conventional weapons, by reducing the costs of failure for the Soviets dramatically, encourages them to invade, particularly in a crisis.[41] If they fail, they have gained nothing but they have not suffered devastating losses either. Simply put, they would have very little to lose. This was particularly frightening since a growing consensus held that the Soviets would prefer to fight a conventional war if they had to fight in Europe.[42]

While the potential consequences of another conventional war in Europe are horrifying enough, any engagement involving American and Soviet troops also risked nuclear war. It was therefore quite dangerous to create a situation that could embolden the Soviets. This analysis led Mearsheimer to conclude that,

[i]f there is a great risk of nuclear escalation in any European conventional war, it is best to make this explicit in NATO's declaratory policy. Otherwise NATO's leaders risk deluding the Soviets into underestimating the risks of aggression, while moreover denying themselves the deterrent effect that comes from recognizing the risk of escalation.[43]

Betts also makes the link between conventional deterrence and nuclear risks explicit:

Pure conventional deterrence raises the danger of nuclear war by making the potential consequences of resort to conventional war less unthinkable for the attacker. As long as nuclear weapons exist, so does the danger that any war between the superpowers could escalate despite declared doctrines or actual intentions. Short of abandoning deterrence altogether, the best way to minimize the danger of nuclear war is to minimize the chance of conventional war.[44]

The internal tension in the MAD position is pronounced. On the one hand, doctrine makes it clear that under no circumstances should nuclear weapons be used to advance particular policies. On the other hand, a vital policy objective—the defense of Europe—could not be accomplished without credibly threatening the first use of nuclear weapons. Even as MAD authors embrace the deterrent power of the threat, they shy from its consequences. The risk should be high enough to frighten the Soviets, but not so high as to frighten them to the point of provoking them. "Pure" Crisis Stability must be abandoned, since it trades off with deterrence. But just as Crisis Stability cannot be overemphasized at the expense of deterrence, deterrence cannot be taken to such extremes that it jeopardizes Crisis Stability. MAD authors are not unaware of these tensions. As Sigal writes:

Although it is possible to reconcile apparent contradictions between deterrence and stability, internal contradictions in the logic of deterrence remain. That logic rests on a central paradox: how can NATO deter the Warsaw Pact by nuclear threats that it manifestly has little or no incentive to carry out? This paradox generates policy dilemmas that put the credibility of NATO's doctrine in doubt.[45]

The question that plagues MAD authors and NATO strategists continued to be: Can the tensions that inhere in doctrine be reduced if not eliminated?

The MAD Dilemma and Emerging Technologies

MAD advocates wanted to retain enough nuclear weapons (and sufficient ambiguity about their use) to make a conventional defense of Europe viable. Nuclear risks are therefore seen as necessary from this perspective, but they must be managed prudently. The threshold at which NATO must use its nuclear arsenal is to be kept high. Linking the defense of Europe to nuclear forces generally and to the American strategic deterrent specifically couples European defense to the risk of all-out-nuclear war and therefore creates an apocalyptic price for the failure of deterrence. Because the No First Use proposal placed the nuclear threshold too high it was rejected. Then existing force postures were indicted by MAD critics because they placed the threshold too low. No Early First Use was said to strike a sound balance, if sufficient conventional forces could be created and nuclear weapons deployed correctly. Yet strategists faced political limitations on the resources available for conventional forces, and pressure against the use of nuclear weapons to make up the difference.

Emerging Technology weapons (ETs) appear, at first glance, to resolve this dilemma, but close inspection reveals that they simply posed the same problems in different form. Still in the early stages of development, ETs may eventually permit conventional weapons to play such a powerful role on the battlefield as to eliminate the need for nuclear weapons.[46] Technological developments promise increasing accuracy for conventional weapons, a factor more important than pure destructive power (or yield).[47] Weapons with sophisticated guidance systems could be directed to hardened targets (or troop concentrations) and achieve their missions with a high success rate. Such weapons could conceivably have forced the Pact to continue echeloning their divisions, thereby reducing NATO's dependence on nuclear weapons, had they been fully deployed prior to the Pact's dissolution. At a minimum, high accuracy weapons offered the hope that sufficient conventional power could be created to permit NATO to pull its nuclear weapons far behind the FEBA so that they would no longer be vulnerable to attack.[48]

The resulting situation would arguably have produced a reduction in the pressure on NATO to escalate a conventional war quickly to the nuclear level. A purely conventional defense could be mounted without giving up the deterrent potential from the (presumably now secure) nuclear forces. An end to the far forward deployment of nuclear weapons would constrain Soviet planning, and reduce their incentive to initiate conventional war in a crisis, by removing the possibility of a war begun with the elimination of NATO's nuclear forces with conventional weapons. Imposing such a constraint on the Soviets would strengthen NATO's deterrent without violating the political conditions imposed by its domestic audience. Slocombe says:

Raising the nuclear threshold requires greater NATO conventional capability. There are two ways to attain that capability; a large increase in the number of conventional units defending the Central Front or a significant enhancement of the technological superiority of NATO's conventional forces. The required increase in conventional units appears to be unaffordable, but fortunately trends in battlefield systems do hold out the possibility of a technology solution, provided NATO is willing to accept it.[49]

Examination of the strategy, however, reveals that it is not without problems.

The primary purpose in developing ETs was the interdiction of Pact second and third echelons. ETs are argued to enjoy the same force multiplier effect as nuclear weapons (which would have precluded the Pact from massing forces) but without the same escalatory potential attached to their use. The tactical doctrines that would govern the use of ETs are referred to collectively as "Deep Strike." The most relevant example of this doctrine is "Follow on Forces Attack" (FOFA), which is sometimes referred to as the Rogers plan.[50] FOFA was designed specifically to destroy echelons behind the front lines, limiting troop concentration, reinforcement, and resupply. Destruction of the echelons behind the FEBA not only promised to make NATO's conventional forces viable, but also to make forward defense a more realistic option. The possibility of maneuver is created without requiring NATO to yield territory because ETs permit the extension of the battlefield into enemy territory. "The Soviet Union would then face the choice of escalating the conflict by using nuclear weapons or withdrawing, "following a successful ET strike.[51] Thus, "Deep Strike" tactics seem to create a better fit between plausible military action and political constraints. Even if a "conflict erupts, the new generation of conventional arms should buy some time—six to eight weeks i[s] frequently mentioned—for a negotiated solution before the protagonists are backed into a nuclear conflict, with all its inherent uncertainties."[52] Other purely defensive approaches to deterrence appeared to MAD authors as either ineffective or unable to gain sufficient support among alliance members.[53] Yet when the implications of Deep Strike doctrines are considered, tensions begin to appear.

The basic paradox emerges from the doctrinal requirements to strike a balance between safely managing risks and communicating them. Deterrence requires creating a credible risk for the enemy by creating a plausible threat. The greater the threat the greater the deterrent effect. But since the risks of nuclear escalation are shared risks, there is a need to keep the threat under tight control, despite the fact that the "threat that leaves something to chance"—the threat that is structured to go out of control—may be the strongest deterrent. The two goals of credibility and manageability thus work at crosspurposes in the context of the nuclear force structure, and must be balanced against one another. The doctrines that would govern the use of ETs attempt to skirt the dilemma by creating a threat based on a risk great enough to deter the Soviets, but unshared. If possible this would satisfy both the perceived need to communicate great risk and the unwillingness to tolerate it. ETs were thought to be a possible solution to NATO's dilemma because they seem to offer a conventional alternative available within the financial, demographic and political constraints experienced by the allies. But the tensions that arise prevented MAD advocates from embracing ETs and the Deep Strike doctrines they make possible. As Sigal concludes:

[T]he very logic of nuclear deterrence is internally paradoxical, and the paradoxes create dilemmas in practice: inconsistencies in declaratory policy and strategic doctrine, trade-offs among weapons and force postures, predicaments for leaders in crisis and wartime. Most attempts to escape the paradoxes of deterrence merely pose them in new form.[54]

Because the Deep Strike doctrines extend the battlefield deep behind the FEBA, the strategy communicates an aggressive stance by NATO. Yet, according to MAD authors the ideal message would be nonoffensive, purely retaliatory and hence stabilizing. Only the threat of retaliation should be maintained. Obviously, this is not the message of Deep Strike. Thus, MAD authors are attracted to the strategy because it reduces dependence on early use of nuclear weapons, but repelled by it because it communicates intentions opposite from the MAD ideal.

Deep Strike in any of its specific forms is, in essence, an extremely aggressive posture for a defensive alliance to adopt. It is structured around one basic weapons characteristic: the ability to strike deep into enemy territory from positions at (or even behind) the FEBA.[55] It looks, as a result, exactly like a posture designed for offensive attacks on the Warsaw Pact. Because capabilities rather than words constrain interpretations of messages, NATO's declaration of defensive intentions would not have counteracted appearances. As Mearsheimer argues:

Even if NATO resists that pressure [for a preemptive attack] and maintains its commitment to a defensive strategy, those force improvements may well seem offensive in nature to the Soviets. What is offensive and what is defensive are all in the eye of the beholder. Consider, for example, what might happen if NATO increased the size and quality of its forces but still retained its strategy of forward defense. That strategy, although a defensive one, requires NATO to move the majority of its forces right up to the intra-German border. NATO might claim that executing this strategy in a crisis is a defensive move. The Soviets, however, are likely to see the movement of those strengthened NATO forces to the intra-German border as the final preparatory step for launching an offensive into East Germany. Given Soviet thinking on the advantages of striking first in a war, there would undoubtedly be much pressure on the Soviets to launch a preemptive strike. Of course, there is good reason to expect that NATO leaders would be subjected to similar pressure.[56]

Deep Strike is as potentially destabilizing as any other approach that has the potential to lead the Soviets to conclude that there is an advantage to striking first in a crisis. Because the context would appear to be denuclearized, the advantage might appear to be magnified. Yet any war, fought with any weapons, that involves the superpowers, automatically carries a risk of escalation to the nuclear level.

ET technology inherently carries the risk of an undesired escalation to nuclear war, therefore. It is additionally expected that ETs will rely heavily on the same ballistic missile technology as many nuclear weapons, such as the Pershing II.[57] To the Soviets, Deep Strike would not just have looked like an offensive strategy, but an offensive strategy relying on nuclear weapons. Radar cannot distinguish between missiles carrying conventional and nuclear warheads.[58] The use of ET weapons would hence be, to the Soviets, indistinguishable from a preemptive nuclear attack. This would hardly be conducive to restraining escalation once a war had begun. Nor does Deep Strike add to Crisis Stability. Battlefield nuclear weapons created risks, but they did not have the range to threaten Pact territory. Forward-deployed ETs share the problems of the Pershing II. They are accurate enough to threaten hardened targets, but it is that capacity that MAD authors claim to be destabilizing.[59]

If the Soviets responded by acquiring equivalent ET capabilities, the situation becomes even more dangerous.[60] Computer systems make higher levels of accuracy possible by integrating tracking, acquisition, and terminal guidance. Should ET become commonplace, all conventional forces would be structured around—and dependent upon—a small number of computerized command centers (called nodes). The nodes are exactly the type of targets ETs can destroy easily. Preemptive pressure in a crisis could, with Deep Strike, be even greater because of the susceptibility of the command and control nodes to destruction by ETs.[61]

Assessment of the MAD Position

So far, I have examined tensions recognized by MAD authors who extended their doctrine from strategic exchanges to the Central Front. At this point, I will sum up the contradictions that inhere because of a conflict between doctrinal assumptions and communicative needs.

MAD authors represented Soviet motives differently depending upon whether they were discussing a strategic exchange or a war in Western Europe. In the former case, it was generally claimed that the Soviets are not especially aggressive: they have no desires to attack the United States or to expand their territory. The Soviets are portrayed as a status quo power. In the latter case, MAD authors assumed the Soviet Union to be both aggressive and expansionistic. The capability to respond militarily had to be continually and effectively communicated to thwart Soviet plans for invasion. This implicit constraint is assumed to be a necessity for NATO defense policy.[62] As a consequence of these beliefs, MAD authors redirect the objectives of nuclear policy from deterrence by threat of punishment and toward deterrence by communicating threats to deny its opponent victory. At the strategic level it is argued that the threat of punishment is sufficient to deter the Soviets. To some extent, it was still true of the Central Front strategy as advocated through the 1980s. For example, MAD authors indict conventional only deterrence because it does not demonstrate clearly enough a threat to do more than frustrate Soviet ambitions. But denial begins to receive an emphasis not apparent at the strategic level.

The goal of strengthening the conventional leg of NATO's triad is to make deterrence more robust.[63] ETs ostensibly make a NATO defeat less likely. Should deterrence fail, victory could be achieved without recourse to nuclear weapons. Like effectively deployed nuclear weapons, ETs can enhance deterrence. After all, the threat of nuclear escalation is, in large part, sought for its beneficial effect on the conventional balance. Yet, the question of how NATO policy is linked to higher levels of nuclear escalation is still unresolved.

The Soviet acquisition of a secure second strike capability convinced MAD authors of the need for a potent NATO conventional defense. A nuclear attack by NATO that destroyed Soviet cities to punish the U.S.S.R. would surely have resulted in a retaliatory attack on American soil. A strategy based on the threat of massive societal destruction was no longer considered persuasive by the 1980s given the Soviet acquisition of secure second strike the previous decade; the defense of Europe may be a vital interest but it is not one of immediate national survival to the United States, and a deterrent posture that lacked credibility risked putting the United States in the position of having its bluff called. Although MAD doctrine worked to adjust NATO policy accordingly, it had yet to find a unified, consistent policy at the time of the Pact's dissolution.

The Warfighting View of the Central Front

Contradictions also arise in the warfighters' attempt to reconcile strategic theory and the need for deterrence on the Central Front. The goal of the warfighters was to make prospects for a nuclear response to a conventional invasion of Europe obvious and certain. The ambiguity of the Flexible Response doctrine, which MAD authors sought to restore by adjusting force posture, was rejected by the warfighters.[64] Forward deployment of vulnerable nuclear stockpiles, creating a "use them or lose them" mentality was, to warfighters, a positive aspect of NATO's force structure. It allowed NATO to clearly communicate to the Soviets that any war on the Central Front would necessarily become a nuclear war. The more automatic (and controlled) the escalatory process, the stronger the deterrent was judged to be.[65]

As a result, the warfighters' position on NATO is not fully consistent with their position on strategic policy. Obviously, the assumption of Soviet aggression underlies all policy considerations, but the message that is to be created to maximize chances of deterrence are different at the theater and strategic levels. Two important shifts are noticeable.

First, the very foundation of the warfighting position at the strategic levels demands the conscious attempt to proliferate options. Ambiguity becomes the very centerpiece of strategy, so that every time a potential enemy conceives of a strategy he finds something in the force structure that might be used to counter that particular strategy. For the Central Front, though, the warfighter wished to eliminate ambiguity.[66] By advocating the automatic use of nuclear weapons, the warfighters proposed that options be narrowed and flexibility structured out of NATO's defense posture. Second, advocacy of automatic escalation to nuclear weapons use required the warfighter to violate a basic tenet of strategy, Escalation Dominance. At the strategic level, the warfighter wished to see force structures that would permit the United States to clearly communicate its ability to control hostilities at any point a across the spectrum of violence. Yet when discussing NATO, the warfighter ceded control at the conventional level to the Soviets. Rather than building more conventional weapons to increase NATO's power to deter invasion, warfighters sought reliance on NATO's ability to threaten the Soviet Union with nuclear weapons. It was held that this "automatic" threat would be effective.

These arguments parallel the position taken by MAD advocates on the issue of ICBM vulnerability. They argued that the United States need not worry about preemptive attack on its land-based missiles because the fear of automatic escalation to general nuclear war was sufficient to deter the Soviets. To this argument, warfighters responded that if forces are not equivalent, Soviet incentives to execute a war winning strategy would increase. Yet, when considering the issue of conventional equivalence on the Central Front, warfighters eschewed this line of reasoning. Instead, they argued for immediate escalation to higher levels of violence. Slocombe captures the parallels between the scenarios:

The problem of extended deterrence is simply the international and political problem of the credibility of retaliation with potentially suicidal consequences against serious, but not inevitably fatal, threats. From this perspective, the debate over the extensions of U.S. nuclear deterrence to Europe finds its counterpart in the debate over U.S. capacity to deter less than all-out attacks on the United States itself. The whole debate about the window of vulnerability and the significance of the vulnerability of U.S. intercontinental ballistic missile (ICBM) silos simply recasts the question of extended deterrence in a nongeographic, nonnational context. Just as threats of mutual obliteration may be thought less than adequately credible to deter attacks on U.S. allies in Europe and elsewhere, so such threats may be thought less than adequate to deter limited attacks on military forces in the United States itself.[67]

At the strategic level, there should never be a need for all out war, according to the warfighters. Escalation Dominance is sufficient to deter and, presumably, to force termination of hostilities should deterrence fail. Escalation Dominance leaves enemies no motive to escalate, for it should be obvious to them that they would lose at any higher level of violence. The burden of risk is thus placed upon the enemy. It is they who must make any decision to escalate. The United States would retain the capacity to successfully respond. But on the Central Front, the force postures advocated by warfighters required the alliance to assume the burden of escalation. Escalation becomes an immediate necessity given the paucity of conventional forces. This leaves warfighters in the odd position of resting deterrence on the threat to "punish" the Soviets in case of a nonhomeland war.[68]

At the strategic level, the preference for denial of victory over punishment is absolute for the warfighter. Punishment alone is thought to have little or no deterrent (persuasive) effect relative to denial. The shift in emphasis at the theater level is patent. Nuclear weapons are indeed intended to deny the Pact its military goals in a Western European war.

Yet the levels of violence and the distance from the FEBA at which violence would take place are far greater than *just* a denial of victory requires. Nuclear operations would not be limited to the battle area in these scenarios if the warfighters had had their way. The war, at least in its nuclear aspect, would have been brought to the territories of the Pact. While this undoubtedly would affect Soviet ability to command and resupply troops at or near the FEBA, it is an extreme response to a limited mission. This policy is quite distinct from the judicious use of counterforce typically advocated by warfighters.

For both the MAD and warfighting doctrines, theoretical tensions become apparent as soon as they are applied to conflicts below the strategic level. Another element of the force structure intended to deter an attack on NATO is nuclear and conventional naval power. The discussion of the Maritime Strategy for a war on the Central Front also reveals the tensions in the two perspectives. An examination of the ways strategic theorists have sought to structure and deploy naval forces for deterrence reveals these theoretical tensions.

THE MARITIME STRATEGY

The Navy's 1980s strategy for supporting the alliance during a land battle in Europe was gradually articulated beginning in 1982. Depending upon one's view of the strategy, the emergent quality of the doctrine can be seen either as a sign of a slow process of building consensus among professional naval officers,[69] or as a calculated attempt to deflect criticism by creating a "moving target."[70] It is clear, nevertheless, that several issues arose as key elements of contention between strategists supporting and opposing the Navy's position, referred to as "the Maritime Strategy."

Although the Maritime Strategy discusses the role of the Navy in a variety of contingencies, the discussion of the strategy focused on the articulation of naval operations during war in Europe.[71] The focus of this discussion, in turn, was on the best way to deal with the Soviet northern fleet, based on the Kola Peninsula bordering on Norway. The Soviet fleet had capabilities permitting it to engage in conventional naval battles directly relevant to a land war in Europe, as well as strategic nuclear war. Two specific issues were discussed as a result.

The first issue raised by the Maritime Strategy was: In what way should the Navy protect the Atlantic sea lines of communication, or SLOCs? The SLOCs are the routes used by ships moving across the Atlantic from the United States to Europe. If NATO was to prevail in a conventional war in Europe, it was critical that the SLOCs remain open. For if NATO was to have any chance of prosecuting conventional war in Europe without recourse to nuclear weapons, reinforcement and resupply from the United States would be necessary. An airlift, by itself, is inadequate in such a situation, as was clearly demonstrated during the Gulf conflict. If sufficient material was to reach NATO forces, it would have to come by ship, and thus the Atlantic SLOCs would have to be defended against Soviet naval forces. The question was how best to accomplish this task. The Maritime Strategy, supported by warfighters, proposed "offensive" sea control. The argument was that aggressive attacks on Soviet naval forces in Soviet homewaters and on the Kola Peninsula, north of the Atlantic, would put the Soviet Navy on the defensive. If they are on the defensive, supposedly they would not be able to leave their homewaters to enter the Atlantic and attack Allied shipping.[72] MAD critics rejected this strategy, and instead defended "defensive" sea control as an appropriate alternative. This involves defending convoys as they cross the Atlantic and monitoring natural geographic chokepoints so as to destroy Soviet naval forces as they attempt to enter the Atlantic.[73]

The second issue raised by the Maritime Strategy is: Should the Navy have actively attacked Soviet ballistic missile submarines (SSBNs) in the event of conventional war? Although the SSBNs were part of the Soviet's strategic nuclear arsenal (indeed, they were the Soviets' most survivable and hence arguably most valuable strategic forces), the attack was in large part defended by warfighters on the grounds that such a strategy would contribute to sea control, and thus indirectly to the land battle. The warfighters point out that the Soviet weapons best able to threaten the SLOCs are the same weapons best able to protect threatened SSBNs: the attack submarines, or SSNs. Thus attacks on the SSBNs, whether they are successful or not, would serve an important purpose. Such attacks would force the Soviets to use their SSNs to protect their secure second-strike deterrent. If used in that way, the attack submarines would not be available for attacks on allied shipping in the SLOCs.[74] MAD authors responded that such attacks are unnecessary to further defense of the SLOCs. The SSBNs were so valuable to the Soviets, they argued, that Soviet homewaters would, in the event of war in Europe, be turned into protective "bastions" for them no matter what the U.S. Navy did.[75]

Of course, since the SSBNs are strategic nuclear weapon platforms, a strategy calling for attacks on them had implications beyond conventional war. And, in fact, advocates of the Maritime Strategy argued that if the Navy were to be successful in its attacks on Soviet SSBNs, the destruction of the second-strike deterrent would have important benefits. As long as the SSBNs survived, the Soviet leadership might feel confidence in their ability to deter American escalation to nuclear attacks on the Soviet homeland. The loss of the SSBNs could convince the Soviets not to escalate to nuclear use, particularly against the American homeland, since they would no longer be able to do so with impunity. The result would be significant "war termination leverage" for the

United States and its allies.[76] Critics of the Maritime Strategy argued that, precisely because the SSBNs are so valuable to the Soviets, it would be extremely dangerous and provocative to attack them in the context of a conventional war in Europe.[77]

Yet, despite the implications of the Maritime Strategy for nuclear strategy, both sides agreed on the criterion by which the strategy should be judged: Would the adoption by the United States of the force structures and deployments dictated by the Maritime Strategy aid in deterring the Soviets from initiating a land battle on the Central Front? Supporters and critics deal with this overarching question via analysis of a key issue—the desirability of threatening escalation of naval warfare. It is the position taken on that question that determined an analyst's position on the Maritime Strategy.

The Navy's Role in Escalation: The Warfighters' Position and the MAD Critique.

At the outbreak of a European war, strategic planners envisioned a choice for the use of naval forces: to go on the offense and destroy Soviet SSBNs and their protecting SSNs while in their homewaters, or to intercept Soviet SSNs as they sortied into the North Atlantic in order to attack allied shipping. The former was advocated by warfighters who supported the Maritime Strategy and who saw merit in escalation. The latter was advocated by MAD critics who wished to see the level and intensity of violence contained. The following analysis shows how each school tried to reconcile its advice with its strategic doctrine.

In considering the situation in the mid–1980s, analysis begins with an examination of divergent views on the time it would take to win a land battle on the Central Front. Many components of the Maritime Strategy are designed around the "time urgent" requirements of the land battle. To have their desired effect, naval forces must engage the enemy (and in some instances complete their missions) before NATO has lost the land battle in Europe. Since naval forces are intended to contribute to the outcome of this battle, they are of no use once the land battle is over. Brooks admits that the Maritime Strategy assumes that:

There will be no immediate collapse in Central Europe. Maritime power inherently requires time to take effect. If land and air forces in Germany are overrun in days, neither the Maritime Strategy nor any alternative use of seapower is likely to be able to prevent that event (although . . . there is an implicit assumption that loss of Central Europe is the loss of a campaign, not a war).[78]

If the conventional phase of a war on the Central Front were very short, there would be little reason to defend the SLOCs. If the war has no prospect of remaining conventional, but is likely to escalate rapidly, conventional material can make little or no difference to the outcome. Protecting convoys, is, therefore, of little importance in such a situation.[79] If on the other hand, the war has a prolonged conventional phase, or stays conventional, then effective defense of the SLOCs becomes critical. But the Maritime Strategy went far beyond a defense of shipping.

Resources that could be deployed to protect conveys could be used to attack Soviet submarines, a key component of the enemy's retaliatory capacity. Although such an attack would destroy Soviet nuclear weapons, it would not itself use nuclear weapons, and therefore could, presumably, be considered a nonnuclear escalation of violence. Is such an attack advisable? An answer to this question depends upon projected Soviet actions in a European war.

An expert consensus was developing that in a war, the Soviet SSBNs would not move through the Atlantic into the open ocean. Rather, the SSBNs and however many SSNs were assigned to protect them, would return to home ports, creating "bastions" or sanctuaries in order to safeguard the SSBNs.[80] At the time it was felt that there might be some additional submarine traffic in the North Atlantic, as a portion of the SSBN fleet (again with protecting escorts) left the bastions, but these forces were expected to go north away from the SLOCs, in order to hide under the polar ice caps.[81] The question is whether Soviet retention of a secure second-strike capacity provides useful stability during a conflict that risks nuclear escalation.

It is in such a situation that "the Soviets would almost certainly make worst case assumptions about American intentions—if U.S. attack submarines began to position themselves to destroy the Soviet SSBN force. This would probably intensify rather than defuse a crisis."[82]

Because the SSBN issue involves strategic forces, both MAD theorists and warfighters are able to develop positions consistent with their respective strategic theories. The MAD position is premised on the need for both sides to maintain secure second-strike forces. To threaten an opponent's second-strike capability is destabilizing, MAD proponents hold. This is especially true when a conventional conflict has broken out. It is when a conflict may still be contained at the conventional level that actions that threaten or appear to threaten the Soviet submarine force should most particularly be avoided. In fact MAD authors argue that if the warfighters are correct, and the Soviets do place a significant weight on the nuclear balance (or "correlation of forces") it is even more certain that threats to the Soviet SSBNs ought to be avoided. Rather than accept the destruction of their SSBNs and return to the status quo antebellum, the Soviets are likely to respond to any attack by attempting to assure a favorable strategic balance, say, by attacking the U.S. ICBM force.[83] And even if the anti-SSBN mission could be accomplished, it would not lead the Soviets to abandon efforts on the Central Front, since "the historical record suggests that navies should not be expected to play an important role in deterring major conventional wars."[84]

Warfighters, in contrast, see the anti-SSBN mission as critical to Escalation Dominance, increasing stability and avoiding higher levels of violence. To deter Soviet escalation requires guaranteed superiority at higher levels of violence so that the motive to escalate is eliminated. Gray makes the point:

One cannot evade the dilemma that the better NATO's nonnuclear forces fare on land and sea, the stronger the incentive will be for the Soviets to engage in nuclear escalation. The real action in a future war may involve maneuver battalions, tactical air wings, and carrier battle groups (CVBGs), but success for their endeavors will be possible only if escalation discipline can be imposed on the enemy.[85]

Destruction of the SSBN fleet is a method of assuring a balance which least risks escalation to nuclear war. Such an operation would be conducted at sea with conventional weapons, create no "collateral" damage, and not threaten Soviet capacity to wage nuclear war without leading to escalation.[86]

Defense of the SLOCs, however, is directly relevant to the land battle, and here the tensions in the warfighting position emerge. If forces are structured to ensure that a war in Europe goes nuclear almost immediately, defense of the SLOCs does not require offensive attacks on the Kola Peninsula, where the Soviet northern fleet was based. Even if the war is prolonged, it would ostensibly be fought with nuclear weapons predeployed in Europe. Additional weapons, if needed, would not be inserted into the theater via the SLOCs, but would instead come from American SSBNs, some of which were specifically assigned to the defense of NATO.[87]

Warfighters admitted that the Soviets wanted to bastion their strategic naval forces. But to assure that in the event of hostilities the Soviets used their SSNs, the attack submarines, to protect the bastions so that they would not be free to enter the Atlantic and threaten allied shipping, was assumed to require offensive American activity in the form of attacks on the bastioned homewaters and potentially the Kola base itself.[88]

Apart from an attack on the bastion, warfighters also advocated other measures that would have made the United States assume the burden of escalation. Warfighters hold that in time of crisis, some Soviet SSBNs are likely to be deployed under the polar ice caps for safety. Despite far superior American anti-submarine warfare (ASW) capabilities, it is almost impossible to locate a submarine hiding under ice. To guarantee the destruction of these forces (and their escorts, the SLOC-threatening

SSNs) American forces must destroy them before they reach their hiding places. This would require racing Soviet forces north at the onset of a crisis, much less a war, in order to prevent their access to the ice cap. If American forces could beat Soviet submarines to the ice cap, but were unable to create an impenetrable barrier there, or if Soviet submarines were caught actively trying to cross such a barrier, American forces could be compelled to initiate the war at sea. This could occur before hostilities even broke out on land; it certainly could happen before the outcome of a conventional war in Europe was clear. The strategy at sea, like the strategy on land, required American forces to assume the burden of escalation.[89]

The Maritime Strategy and the MAD Response

The MAD position on SLOCs and risk assumption is far more consistent with its strategic theory. The ultimate role for naval forces is the defense of SLOCs in time of war. "[D]eterring the Soviet threat to NATO, especially the Soviet conventional threat, is therefore the baseline case against which the Maritime Strategy should be measured."[90] This led critics to argue that the Maritime Strategy can play only a supportive or ancillary role.[91] The Navy's primary role must be designed to contribute to deterrence by making prospects of a successful Soviet war less likely.[92]

If deterrence fails, the goal of naval forces is to help a war in Europe remain conventional by making it possible to win without recourse to nuclear escalation. Defense of the SLOCs is necessary to guarantee adequate reinforcement and resupply to sustain a conventional war. Thus, the ability of the Navy to defend the SLOCs contributes to deterrence, since it conveys the message that the Soviets could not win in a protracted conventional war of attrition. NATO ground forces carry the burden of this message, but naval support is essential.[93]

For MAD advocates, protection of the SLOCs is best accomplished by passive sea control. Since the Soviets will bastion the bulk of their forces, the remaining attack submarines can be removed as a threat by a combination of barrier-defense and protective convoy escort.[94] This approach serves the needs of stability because it does not require an attack on second-strike forces. Protection of the SLOCs reduces Soviet incentives to disperse its fleet, since the SSBNs are not threatened.

A defensive Naval posture serves the communicative ends of MAD doctrine. Recall that for MAD theorists all strategy must signal shared risks. Because defensive or passive sea control demands that the U.S. Navy exclusively focuses on Soviet naval forces directly threatening to NATO conventional operations, it enhances prospects of conventional NATO success without threatening to escalate the war by attacking "bastioned" SSBNs and therefore making Soviet second-strike capabilities less secure.

CRITIQUE

Both MAD and warfighting are theories of persuasion designed to deter the outbreak of an intercontinental nuclear war. When extended to encompass different circumstances and scenarios, accommodations in basic positions must be made. Management of the bilateral relationship must be adjusted to take into consideration possibilities of multilateral conflict. Theorists could not ignore scenarios other than all-out nuclear war; for so long as the superpowers were involved in conflict, all-out war always remained an unfulfilled, but recognizable, potential. The problem MAD and warfighting authors faced in applying doctrines did not remove their obligation to generate and refine theories of persuasion. Such problems do, in fact, serve to illuminate the ways strategic theory is obliged to function in fashioning persuasive strategies.

Many of the problems in maintaining a consistent persuasive position stem from the fact that when considering the Central Front, strategic theorists must broaden their analysis to encompass additional audiences. In advocating an alliance force structure, it is no longer sufficient to determine a message's persuasiveness on the basis of a portrait of the Soviet Union and its motives. The analyst must also decide how the message will affect European attitudes and perceptions. The strategist must shape theory in accord with the answers to prior questions. What forces will NATO governments be willing to procure? What doctrines will they accept? And what will they feel they are able to do given the rhetorical constraints imposed by their respective domestic audiences? For example, there is no evidence that either school would reject a purely conventional defense strategy—indeed both would probably prefer it—if they believed adequate forces were feasible. Yet all American strategists believed—and many still do—that sufficient forces will not be made available to adopt such a posture. Consequently, their doctrines attempt to fashion a persuasive deterrent in light of this constraint. Even the capabilities of nuclear force deployments, in terms of range and survivability at least, are sometimes shaped with an eye to what European governments and their domestic audiences will accept.[95]

The need to deal persuasively with these additional audiences becomes manifest in the theorists' perceptions of the alliance itself. Both schools agreed that one important element of deterrence was the political unity of NATO.[96] The Soviet Union might not be deterred if it thought the alliance would fragment in a crisis. A key measure of NATO's strength, in other words, is how strong it thinks it is. It is not the number of tanks owned by alliance members that matters most, but the perception that the alliance is a unified political entity. The strategic need for political unity parallels the appeasement theory of war. Arms represent capability, but unity represents credibility and will. And just as a "victim nation" must find a way to communicate its will, NATO must find a way to communicate its unity. It is therefore essential that the member states—and the analysts attempting to device policy for them—avoid advocating doctrines or procurement policies that foment (or reveal) disunity.

Several examples demonstrate the significance of these rhetorical constraints in the work of deterrence theorists. Coupling is defined in the literature as assurance that the United States "would risk Chicago to save Frankfurt." Historically, this conception of "coupling" emerged from a time when the allies were unable to deploy conventional forces and the United States had a virtual monopoly on atomic weapons. But this is really a *form* of coupling; there are other policies that could demonstrate American commitment to Europe. What was needed was a visible assurance that American military power would be dedicated to the defense of Europe when needed. The allies have recovered from World War II, and the United States has had the manpower and material to provide a far greater conventional force in Europe. A policy that coupled European and American responses at a conventional level alone, however, was not acceptable so long as there was a perceived Soviet threat, because the Europeans also perceived the need for a specifically nuclear guarantee. To suggest alternatives was to raise fears of "decoupling."

Coupling is itself a rhetorical construct. Nuclear coupling requires American strategic retaliation in the event of war. Were the United States to deploy nuclear weapons only on its own territory and declare that it would use them in NATO's defense, coupling would not be assured. Only capabilities can be trusted. In this situation it is necessary to structure capabilities that intrinsically risk escalation. The deployment of American nuclear forces in Europe was seen as the only way to guarantee this structure because American weapons would be used against Soviet soil, therefore inviting Soviet retaliation on the American homeland. But what if limited wars can be fought? Then, strategic weapons are not really coupled.

Related to the issue of coupling is that of establishing automatic threshold points at which escalation becomes automatic. "Firebreaks" are pauses or thresholds built into a force structure. They are meant to make some decisions obviously more momentous than the ones preceding them and to provide enough time for combatants to be able to consider alternatives. Two firebreaks have been particularly relevant: that dividing conventional from nuclear war, and that dividing theater nuclear war from general nuclear war. Strategic theorists and their European audiences were undecided about the wisdom of making firebreaks clear or ambiguous.

The difficulty was as follows: If the firebreak between conventional and nuclear war is too weak, the risk of escalation is too great and a nuclear war could be unleashed in the densely populated countries of Europe. If it is too strong, the chances of conventional war may rise as the risks attached to attack decrease. No matter which alternative is pursued, one risk or the other is emphasized. American theorists tended to prefer a strong firebreak between theater and strategic nuclear war. Warfighters openly supported theater limits so that wars could be terminated successfully at the lowest levels of escalation. MAD advocates, by considering the use of nuclear weapons in Europe at all, were forced to search for opportunities to limit nuclear war, at least geographically, lest inadvertent escalation lead to total apocalypse once the nuclear threshold had been crossed. Yet this kind of control is exactly what Europeans did not want. Such a firebreak is automatically viewed as decoupling, for it eliminates shared risks and presumably raises the specter of a superpower war fought at the expense of the nations of Europe.[97]

I began the chapter by observing that any theory of deterrence in a nuclear age must construct doctrine so as to anticipate and resolve problems of strategy and tactics in complex situations where conflict emerges from interests and events not directly concerning the defense of national territory. By definition, events that spring from overlapping interests pose the question of whether violence can be resolved at levels short of nuclear war. The need to control the bilateral relationship between the nuclear superpowers generated deterrence theory, and so its extension to subnuclear situations is less than perfect. But lower levels of violence must be taken into consideration since it is these which offer opportunities for escalation into all out conflict. It is the risk of escalation that deterrence theories are designed to communicate.

What makes deterrence theory ultimately paradoxical is that the risk is shared; the message is addressed to oneself as much as to one's opponent. The attempt to turn the risk of holocaust into a manipulable message inevitably involves questions of control. The greater the level of control over events, the less the deterrent, but the less the level of control, the greater the level of threat communicated, not only to the enemy but also to oneself. It is not just a question of what a nation can do (capability) or plans to do (will) but what a nation appears willing to do. When it is incredible that a government would take a certain risk, the problem can be solved by structuring forces such that the relevant actions are inevitable under certain conditions. In nuclear chicken, too, the best way to play is to close your eyes and take your hands off the steering wheel. The "risk that leaves something to chance," that is based on the intentional relinquishing of control, may be the strongest deter-rent.[98] It is also the most dangerous, particularly if the other side employs the same strategy. There is not even a chance to back down when a bluff is called.

Different theorists advocate different levels of control. But the question of balancing the persuasive elements of deterrence looms over every move, particularly at lower levels of violence where mutual restraint is most likely to give way. MAD authors seek to reduce risks by imple-menting tight controls. But the result of failure can hardly be contem-plated. Warfighters tolerate looser controls, intentionally increasing risk but hoping to provide greater control over the consequences. Yet if the worst were to occur, the lack of control could backfire, yielding the same consequences as a failure of MAD.

The question of the consequences of war reveals still more about the theories. What exactly is a "lower order" consequence? Is a European war less desirable than a strategic exchange? By structuring a hierarchy of consequences some nuclear wars are implicitly sanctioned as "better" than others. For American theorists, any nuclear war involving attacks on the United States is worse than one which does not. In fairness, this partially reflects judgements of magnitude based on the number and size of weapons exploded. But the fact that nuclear wars are placed in a hierarchy, rather than considered generally unacceptable, reveals the ethnocentrism that underlies strategic theory as an endeavor. Again it should be pointed out that MAD theorists are not immune to this cri-tique. They would prefer to avoid nuclear war. Once they accepted the need for a nuclear risk to be used in Europe's defense, however, they forced themselves to contemplate and account for a nonstrategic use of nuclear weapons. And their desire to stop the use of nuclear weapons as quickly as possible reflects the assumption that geographically limited nuclear wars are "better" than intercontinental ones.

At the strategic level, MAD advocates have been outpaced techno-logically. That the United States has acquired a counterforce capability is beyond dispute. MAD advocates' response to that situation and to European defense is to continue to apply the original MAD framework. This inability to see beyond their own tragic frame demonstrates another key aspect of deterrence theory.[99] I have already argued that both schools are self-sealing in that they are nonfalsifiable. Self-sealing systems in a historical context, however, are self-perpetuating. Neither system ac-commodates the search for alternative communicative processes. Each has an internal logic that dictates that the strategies it advocates will be perpetuated and accelerated.

Because the logics of the two theories are different, assumptions are perpetuated in different ways. For warfighting, it occurs as an outgrowth of the need to demonstrate will and commitment. Without conflict national will becomes difficult to communicate because the forces in being, once deployed, show only capability. It is only *before* they are deployed, while in the procurement pipeline, that weapons signal national will. The logic of the theory therefore calls for constant additions to the force structure whether needed or not. This is the genesis of the "decade of neglect" argument.[100] MAD authors who argue that we "stopped racing" in the 1970s because we had "already won" miss the point.[101] To stop adding to the force structure at any point risks communicating a failure in American will, since it is the *act* of procurement that is important.

The Maritime Strategy demonstrates this point. Authors discussing the strategy, particularly after 1984, are obviously sincere in their attempt to develop appropriate naval tactics for a variety of contingencies. But this debate occurred after the Navy and its supporters demanded a "600 ship Navy." Strategy should determine force size, and indeed it did here: The strategy called for a buildup of naval forces, not to meet any particular need, but because it was judged important to communicate a willingness to procure naval forces. It was only after that point that the question of what message the forces should be used to send to the Soviets became an appropriate topic for debate.

MAD's preference for "finite deterrence" is also self-perpetuating. MAD authors display a decided preference for arms control when compared with their warfighting colleagues.[102] Arms control, however, is a vehicle for maintaining Crisis Stability, not for developing alternative modes of communication. Crisis Stability is meant as a way of perpetuating peace in a nuclear world for eternity. The doomsday balance is literally judged to be a perpetual and unchanging phenomenon.

The mechanistic forms of communication selected by the authors trap them. No change is possible because there is no opportunity considered that would break the system, its assumptions, or its structures. This is even more apparent when considering European defense. There is no debate over Soviet motivations, nor is there really any debate about Soviet tactics for a war in Europe. There is general discussion about how the Soviets would prosecute the land and maritime battles. What is never considered is why they ever would have prosecuted such a war. Even if the Soviets were as aggressive as warfighters believed, there were any number of reasons why the Soviets might have chosen to attack somewhere other than the point where they faced the largest military force ever assembled.

What is in contention is how the balance between risk and control can be safely achieved. What passed for debate over Soviet motivation was in reality a discussion of Soviet tactical doctrine. But the United States had tactical doctrines for war in Europe also. The existence of these doctrines without consideration of motivations tells us nothing— but was and is assumed to tell us every thing we need to know.

NOTES

1. I do not mean to suggest that either country would intentionally have risked the danger of escalation simply because a third nation's interests were threatened. A superpower would presumably believe its own vital interests to be threatened in some way.

2. For one of the clearest expressions of the discomfort MAD authors had concerning NATO policy and its reliance on nuclear weapons see Robert McNamara, *Blundering Into Disaster: Surviving the First Century of the Nuclear Age* (New York: Pantheon Books, 1986), especially 74–75.

3. Colin Gray, for example, has noted the ambivalence with which MAD advocates view technological developments which have out paced their theory. See Colin Gray, "What Deters? The Ability to Wage Nuclear War," in John Reichard and Steven Sturm, eds., *American Defense Policy*, 5th ed. (Baltimore: Johns Hopkins University Press, 1982), 177.

4. Thus Gray says ("Maritime Strategy," *Proceedings: U.S. Naval Institute* 112, no. 2 [1986] [hereinafter cited as Proceedings]: 38): "Just as Great Britain had excellent cause to be anxious lest an Imperial Germany dominant in continental Europe should build its High Seas Fleet to an unassailable strength, so the United States has good reason to anticipate that a Soviet Union dominant in Eurasia would be bound to begin what would amount to a siege of the United States." His analysis is based on an interpretation and application of MacKinder's work. See Colin Gray, *Maritime Strategy, Geopolitics, and the Defense of the West* (New York: Ramapo Press for the National Strategy Information Center, Inc., 1986). Not all authors support the defense of Europe for purely geopolitical reasons (as Gray uses that term). See, for example, Walter Slocombe, "The Future of Extended Nuclear Deterrence, in Richard Lugar and Robert Hunter, eds., *Adapting NATO's Deterrence Posture*, Significant Issue Series no. 7 (Washington, D.C.: Center for Strategic and International Studies, 1985), 26.

5. See, for example, Joshua Epstein, Kim Holmes, John Mearsheimer, and Barry Posen, "Policy Focus: The European Conventional Balance," *International Security* 12, no. 4 (Spring 1988): 152–202.

6. Jonathan Dean, *Watershed in Europe* (Lexington, Mass.: Lexington Books for the Union of Concerned Scientists, 1987), 38–43. Dean's argument is that purely quantitative comparisons are distortive since they do not account for factors such as training, preparedness, morale, and initiative, all of which were said to favor NATO.

7. Richard Betts, "Conventional Deterrence: Predictive Uncertainty and Policy Confidence," *World Politics* 37, no. 2 (1985): 159. For varying discussions of the balance which argue that the figures favoring the Pact are exaggerated see also, Anthony Cordesman, "Europe's Armies and Forward Deterrence: When Is Enough Enough?" in Lugar and Hunter, eds., *Adapting*, 27–59; John Mearsheimer, "Nuclear Weapons and Deterrence in Europe," *International Security* 9, no. 3 (Winter 1984–1985): 19–46, and Barry Posen, "Measuring the European Conventional Balance," *International Security* 9, no. 3 (Winter 1984–1985): 51.

8. Cordesman, "Europe's Armies," 27–59.

9. See, for example, Thomas Hirschfeld, "Tactical Nuclear Weapons in Europe," *The Washington Quarterly* 10, no. 1 (1987): 104–109.

10. For discussions of the historical development of alliance strategy see Lawrence Freedman, *The Evolution of Nuclear Strategy* (New York: St. Martin's Press, 1983), and David Schwartz, "A Historical Perspective," in John Steinbruner and Leon Sigal, eds., *Alliance Security: NATO and the No-First-Use Question* (Washington, D.C.: The Brookings Institution, 1983), 5–21.

11. Hirschfield, "Tactical Nuclear Weapons," 102.

12. See Betts, "Conventional Deterrence," 172.

13. Lawrence Freedman, "Flexible Response and the Concept of Escalation," in The Royal United Service Institute for Defence Studies, ed., *RUSI and Brassey's Defence Yearbook* (Washington, D.C.: Brassey's Defence Publishers, 1986), 89. As Sigal notes (Leon Sigal, *Nuclear Forces in Europe* [Washington, D.C.: The Brookings Institution, 1984], 15):

Were Warsaw Pact forces on the verge of breaking through NATO defenses, NATO doctrine calls for selective nuclear strikes to deter advances on the ground without provoking further escalation. These could take one of three forms: an attack by LRTNF [Long Range Theater Nuclear Forces] against military installations in the USSR, an attack by medium-range missiles or aircraft against Warsaw Pact Force concentrations behind the lines in Eastern Europe, or the use of short-range artillery shells or nuclear bombs against enemy forces on the battlefield.

14. Kenneth Burke, *A Grammar of Motives*, 2nd ed. (Berkeley: University of California Press, 1969), xix.

15. These are the so-called "salami tactics." See Donald Colen, *The ABCs of Armaggedon: The Language of the Nuclear Age* (New York: Pharos Books, 1988), 129.

16. Freedman, "Flexible Response," 113. Freedman bases his analysis on Schelling's theory of manipulating risks. Thus (94):

There was an avoidable risk of things moving beyond responsible control in the move from limited to general war. Drawing attention to this possibility could reinforce deterrence; if necessary allowing the situation to begin to slip away, would force the adversary to confront the possibility of matters getting completely out of hand. This might make him more accommodating. . . . Schelling calls this *The Threat that Leaves Something to Chance*. "The key to these threats," he explained, "is that, though one may or may not carry out, *the final decision is not altogether under the threatener's control.*

17. See Sigal, *Nuclear Forces*, 14.

18. Freedman, *Evolution*, 283–302.

19. The defensive measures available were rejected by the Federal Republic on the grounds that they would contribute to the appearance of a permanent division between the Germanies.

20. McGeorge Bundy, et al., "Back From the Brink," *The Atlantic Monthly* August 1986: 37. "Despite the current doctrine of flexible response in Europe, NATO military planners have warned that in reality the response during a crisis would hardly be flexible. The deployment of battlefield nuclear weapons in forward areas could, in fact, negate the doctrine, because it could require that a decision to 'use or lose' nuclear weapons be made very early—even before a purely conventional defense had been attempted."

21. John Hines, Phillip Peterson, and Notra Trulock III, "Soviet Military Theory from 1945 to 2000: Implications for NATO," *The Washington Quarterly* 9,

no. 4 (1986): 134. This strategy reverses the understanding of risk implied in Flexible Response. Freedman, "Flexible Response," 100–101.

At issue has been whether these thresholds represent natural *firebreaks*. That is, would the opposing forces be driven over them by the dynamics of warfare—*involuntary escalation*—or would the passage require, or at least allow for deliberate political decision—*voluntary escalation*. Particular weapons are often discussed in terms of whether they would support or undermine the setting up of firebreaks. For example, enhanced radiation weapons ("neutron bomb") were criticised and promoted as blurring the line between conventional and nuclear weapons.

22. Fred Haynes, "Emerging Technologies and Deep Attack Concepts," in Lugar and Hunter, *Adapting*, 60.

23. Posen, "Measuring," 48. Bundy has argued ("Brink," 38) "To discourage limited Soviet military actions NATO can continue to rely on a nuclear deterrence of low credibility or it can emphasize a conventional response of high credibility. The second alternative provides a more reliable deterrent and promises a lower risk of nuclear war."

24. Sigal, *Nuclear Forces*, 13. This is in part based on the assessment that the Soviets would not initiate war in Europe unless they calculated a rapid and decisive victory was a likely outcome. See Hines, et al., "Soviet Military Theory," 123–124; John Mearsheimer, "A Strategic Misstep: The Maritime Strategy and Deterrence in Europe," *International Security* 11, no. 2 (1986): 6, and Mary Fitzgerald, "Marshal Ogarkov on the Modern Theater Operation," *Naval War College Review* 34, no. 4 (1986): 6–25.

25. See Fitzgerald, "Ogarkov," 22; Hines, et al., "Soviet Military Theory," 125–133; Hirshfield, "Tactical Nuclear Weapons," 108–109; Sigal, *Nuclear Forces*, 2–4; and Slocombe, "Extended Deterrence," 13.

26. The deployments of the so-called Euro-missiles stemmed from the 1979 "dual track" decision. Intermediate range weapons would be deployed, while arms control agreements with the Soviets were pursued to ban the missiles at the same time. See John Cartwright and Julian Critchley, *Cruise, Pershing, and SS-20: The Search for Consensus: Nuclear Weapons in Europe* (New York: Brassey's Defence Publishers, 1985) for a political history of the decision that includes an appendix of NATO Assembly resolutions. It is fairly clear that, as a political decision, dual track satisfied none of the parties involved. See Sigal, *Nuclear Forces*, 1.

27. The stockpiles are clearly identifiable as nuclear storage facilities.

28. Some of these options were under consideration by NATO; others were never really likely to be employed. The first is the predelegation of launch authority: releasing launch codes to commanders in a crisis and permitting them to use nuclear weapons as they saw fit. The fear was that given the vulnerability of NATO command and control structures NATO governments would have felt pressured to take this step, permitting the use of nuclear weapons based solely on a localized tactical situation. This would involve the renunciation of all responsibility and control over escalation of the war by National Command Authorities. The prospect of hundreds of second lieutenants launching uncoordinated nuclear strikes at will may or may not have frightened the Soviets, but it horrified MAD authors. For a complete description of release and dele-

gation procedures during the 1980s, see Bruce Blair, "Alerting in Crisis and Conventional War," in Ashton Carter, John Steinbruner, and Charles Zracket, eds., *Managing Nuclear Operations* (Washington, D.C.: The Brookings Institution, 1987): 75–120; Bundy, "Brink," 36, and Daniel Charles, *Nuclear Planning in NATO: Pitfalls of First Use* (Cambridge: Ballinger Publishing Co., 1987), 156. The second option, which was employed, is the use of "dual capable launch platforms," weapons capable of firing either nuclear or conventional warheads. MAD authors argue that, for a number of reasons, such weapons degrade NATO's ability to fight a conventional war. See Bundy, "Brink," 36–37; Hirshfield, "Tactical Weapons," 110, and Slocombe, "Extended Deterrence," 25. The third option is dispersing nuclear weapons into the countryside in the event of a crisis. Should hostilities appear likely, NATO faced an extremely difficult choice. It could have delayed mobilizing its nuclear weapons, leaving warheads at vulnerable sites, or it could have dispersed the weapons, thus reducing vulnerability. The former choice could have increased Soviet confidence in their ability to keep a war conventional, thus weakening deterrence when it was needed most. The latter option risked convincing the Soviets that NATO was preparing a preemptive attack undermining Crisis Stability and eliminating any incentive to attempt to resolve the crisis. See Charles, *Planning*, 49, and Bundy, "Brink," 37. The fourth option was to better harden and defend nuclear weapons storage facilities. MAD authors believed such efforts would ultimately be ineffective and might have been counterproductive since they had the potential to exacerbate NATO's reliance on forward defense. See Sigal, *Nuclear Forces*, 19–20. The final option is preemptive nuclear attack. Whether or not NATO was planning such an attack, some of the weapons that were forward deployed could have been used in such an attack. The Pershing II and Ground Launched Cruise Missile are both accurate enough that they could have been used against Soviet command and control structures. When forward deployed, their range is such that they could hit targets outside of Moscow. MAD authors therefore saw these weapons as destabilizing in a crisis, since they gave the Soviets an incentive to launch first in a crisis. The argument is that the Soviets would have believed that if they did not launch first they would not have had an opportunity to launch at all. See Charles, *Planning*, 124–125; Sigal, *Nuclear Forces*, 65; and Hines, et al., "Soviet Military Theory," 128.

29. McGeorge Bundy, George Kennan, Robert McNamara and Gerard Smith, "Nuclear Weapons and the Atlantic Alliance," in William Bundy, ed., *The Nuclear Controversy: A Foreign Affairs Reader* (New York: New American Library, 1985), 23–38. Originally published in 1982, the article was republished in book form along with several others.

30. "The deeper purpose of the No-First-Use idea is to induce internal structural changes in NATO's defense preparations." John Steinbruner, "Introduction," in Steinbruner and Leon Sigal, ed., *Alliance Security*, 2–3.

31. Bundy, et al., "Atlantic Alliance," 37–38.

32. This is the article "Back From the Brink" previously cited. The full list of authors is McGeorge Bundy, Morton Halperin, William Kauffman, George Kennan, Robert McNamara, Madeline O'Donnell, Leon Sigal, Gerard Smith, and Paul Warnke.

33. Donald Cotter, "Peacetime Operations: Safety and Security," Carter et al., etc., *Nuclear Operations*, 39.

34. Joshua Epstein, *The 1988 Defense Budget* (Washington, D.C.: The Brookings Institution, 1987), 41.

35. Thus Slocombe notes ("Extended Deterrence," in Lugar and Hunter, *Adapting*, 23): "Militarily, the possibility that the allies will use nuclear weapons against mass Soviet conventional forces must influence Soviet judgements as to the prudence of massing armor sufficiently for the conventional breakthrough their doctrine requires. In time, perhaps, those tank concentrations will be as vulnerable to conventional assault as to nuclear, but there is little reason to believe that that time has come." See also, Fen Osler Hampson, "NATO's Conventional Doctrine: The Limits of Technological Improvement," *International Journal* 41 (Winter 1985–1986): 178–179.

36. Hirschfield, "Tactical Nuclear Weapons," 103.

The need for dispersal also raises questions about the significance of the mentioned Soviet tank superiority along the expected axes of approach to the allied forward area. As Donald Cotter pointed out, planned troop density for Soviet forces in the attack has declined from some 500 per square kilometer in the immediate postwar period to around 20 by the mid–1970s; Cotter speculated that with further modernization of tactical nuclear forces the density can be cut to 8 per square kilometer, not a trivial benefit if true. Thus, tactical nuclear weapons still have value, although less than previously; using them has become less credible, but not incredible.

37. See Betts, "Conventional Deterrence," 163–164; Hirschfield, "Tactical Nuclear Weapons," 103; Mearsheimer, "Nuclear Weapons," 30; and Posen, "Measuring," 51.

38. Mearsheimer, "Nuclear Weapons," 22.

39. Mearsheimer, "Nuclear Weapons," 21. See also Betts, "Conventional Deterrence," 154, 177–178; Freedman, "Flexible Response," 114; Hampson, "Conventional Doctrine," 168–169 and 179; Sigal, *Nuclear Forces*, 3 and 8.

40. Mearsheimer, "Nuclear Weapons," 20 and 26–27.

41. See Betts, "Conventional Deterrence," 154–157, 171, 173, 175–177; Bundy et al., "Brink," 39; Mearsheimer, "Nuclear Weapons," 20 and 25; and Sigal, *Nuclear Forces*, 15.

42. Hines, et al., "Soviet Theory," 122, 125, and 135. See also Mary Fitzgerald, "Marshal Ogarkov and the New Revolution in Soviet Military Affairs," *Defense Analysis* 3, no. 1 (1987): 3–19.

43. Mearsheimer, "Nuclear Weapons," 43.

44. Betts, "Conventional Deterrence," 154–155.

45. Sigal, *Nuclear Forces*, 14.

46. Yves Boyer, "Strategic Implications of the New Technologies for Conventional Weapons and the European Battlefield," in Catherine Kelleher and Gale Mattox, eds., *Evolving European Defense Policies* (Lexington: Lexington Books, 1987), 102." Consensus seems to be developing on areas in which the emerging technologies could be of most benefit: the exercise of command, surveillance, attack against enemy first echelon forces and deep attack against fixed targets."

47. Boyer, "Strategic Implications," 104. Gervasi argues that the relative

importance of accuracy to yield is eight to one. Tom Gervasi, *The Myth of Soviet Military Supremacy* (New York: Harper and Row Publishers, 1986), 81.

48. Freedman explains ("Flexible Response," 95):

The basic dilemma that continues to vex NATO planners stems from the belief that a Soviet conventional attack on Western Europe cannot be thwarted without resort to nuclear threats that themselves lack credibility because of the extent of the Soviet counter-threat. One approach to the dilemma has been to challenge the defeatism of the conventional situation. If the conventional option could be shown to be more promising than generally accepted then it might be possible to reduce the dependence of NATO on the threat to use nuclear weapons first.

See also Boyer, "Strategic Implications," 103; Haynes, "Deep Attack," 64.

49. Slocombe, "Extended Deterrence," 60, see also 19 and 25; Hines et al., "Soviet Theory," 134–135; and Hirschfield, "Tactical Nuclear Weapons," 105 and 110.

50. After General Bernard Rogers, Supreme Allied Commander Europe (SACEUR) at the time the plan was devised. FOFA is often grouped with the Army doctrine of AirLand Battle (ALB). This must be done cautiously. FOFA was intended to reduce the dependence of NATO on nuclear first use and to raise the nuclear threshold. ALB is similar in that it calls for attacks on follow on echelons, but different in that it calls for an "integrated battlefield": that is, the initial deployment of forces will combine conventional, nuclear and chemical weapons. See Hampson, "Conventional Doctrine," 166–167. Hampson also points out that the two propose different depths of operation. ALB would go 100 to 150 km. deep. FOFA would go 200 km. and beyond.

51. Hampson, "Conventional Doctrine," 165–166.

52. Boyer, "Strategic Implications," 116.

53. Examples of defensive alternatives that have not proven persuasive include defensive barriers along the border such as prepared mines and obstacles for tanks (Dean, *Watershed*, 73–74; Hampson, "Conventional Doctrine," 180–181), small "stay behind" units of mobile antitank weapons (Mearsheimer, "Nuclear Weapons, 28), and preplaced explosives that create ditches (Epstein, *Budget*, 39). It is also clear that West German acquisition of nuclear weapons along the lines of the French *Force d'Frappe* would have been unacceptable to the rest of the alliance. Sigal, *Nuclear Forces*, 11.

54. Sigal, *Nuclear Forces*, 7–8.

55. See Boyer, "Strategic Implications," especially 113.

56. Mearsheimer, "Nuclear Weapons," 42. See also Betts, "Conventional Deterrence," 174–175; Fitzgerald, "Theater Operations," 14. Dean explains (Watershed, 66):

Although they may be conceived by their supporters as a purely defensive response to possible Warsaw Pact attack, if deployed in large numbers these weapons can be used for attacks. Already the Soviet force posture, with heavy armored forces concentrated in a forward position in Central Europe, creates great ambiguity as to Soviet intentions. Although this deployment pattern reflects announced Soviet strategy for defense against Western forces in the event of war in Europe—a massive armored counterattack on the aggressor force—it could also be used to launch an aggressive attack on Western Europe. It should be the object of Western policy through arms control and political negotiations to bring the Soviet Union gradually to change this deployment pattern. Yet the tank-heavy equipment of NATO forces concentrated in forward positions currently forms a mirror image of Warsaw Pact forces, creating a strong inducement to competition in force improvements on each side. With both NATO and Pact forces structured and equipped to carry them out, the adopting of deep penetration strategies on both sides would increase the possibility that tensions in Europe, or a conflict outside Europe, would lead to a panicky Pact decision to launch a preemptive attack against the West.

57. In the Gulf War, for example, in which United States forces relied heavily on many of the technologies and strategies discussed here, many of the weapons employed against Baghdad, such as the now famous Tomahawk, do in fact have nuclear variants.

58. See Hampson, "Conventional Doctrine," 176–177.

59. Potential target sets are listed in Hampson, "Conventional Doctrine," 163–164. See also Haynes, "Emerging Technologies," 64.

60. Nor are they particularly likely to create less damage (except radioactivity, admittedly a large exception) than nuclear weapons. They are intended for attacks on hardened targets, thus they are necessarily powerful. Indeed, one author projected yields of 2.5 kilotons. (Many currently deployed nuclear weapons have lower yields.) See Mary Kaldor, "Beyond the Blocs: Defending Europe the Political Way," *World Policy Journal* 1, no. 1 (Fall 1983): 8. And, in fact, Boyer argues ("Strategic Implications," 117):

The reduction of collateral damage is presented as one of the most positive aspects of high-tech weapons. It is a very dubious argument. To suppress antitank defenses, for example, the enemy might decide to use massive artillery bombardments and infantry. The first would eliminate defensive positions, the second would seize the territory. Given the degree of urbanization in Western Europe, there is no chance of sparing the civilian population caught in an uninterrupted crossfire. Not only will the battle be carried on in depth, but one of the objectives will be the compartmentalization of the theater by cutting major transportation axes. The population would then be trapped, unable to flee. Civilian casualties would probably equal those caused by nuclear strikes.

This projection, however, is based on employing extremely optimistic assumptions about the ability to control and limit use of nuclear weapons.

61. Frans-Bauke van der Meer, "Impact of Emerging Technologies and Military Doctrines on Crisis Stability, Arms Control and Disarmament, and Detente," in Frank Barnaby and Marlies Ter Borg, eds., *Emerging Technologies and Military Doctrine: A Political Assessment* (New York: St. Martin's Press, 1986), 254.

62. Jonathan Dean is an exception. The whole point of his argument in *Watershed*, a book that today reads as fairly prophetic, is that political conflict in Europe is over and that the challenge now is to construct a way to dismantle the military structures of both sides in such a manner as to avoid provoking conflict through military destabilization.

63. Whereas the U.S. triad is defined by launch mode (air, land, and sea launched weapons) the NATO triad is conceptualized by level and intensity of violence. Thus it is composed of conventional forces, theater nuclear weapons, and the American strategic deterrent. This is obviously biased to the extent that superpower war is viewed as a higher (worse) level of escalation than is nuclear war confined to Europe.

64. As Sigal articulated the distinction (*Nuclear Forces*, 11):

Extending nuclear deterrence to Europe means, by longstanding NATO policy, contemplating first use of nuclear weapons. At issue is how to do so credibly under conditions of nuclear interdependence. Some strategists feel that first use need only remain a possibility. As long as that possibility exists, they argue, it introduces enough risk into Soviet military calculations to deter them from a deliberate attack on Europe. Other strategists insist that first use must be a near certainty, not just a possibility. Only by making nuclear war seem inevitable, they feel, can NATO be sure of deterring the Soviet Union.

65. Thus, for example, the problem Luttwak saw with the system at the time was not theoretical, but rather the fact that the Soviets had obtained strategic parity. Thus the answer is not a change in NATO force posture but an American strategic buildup in order to regain superiority. Edward Luttwak, *On the Meaning of Victory: Essays on Strategy* (New York: Simon and Schuster, 1986): 170–173.

66. Soviet parity made "massive retaliation," as that was understood in the 1950s, incredible as an intentional strategy. An automatic nuclear response continued to rely on conventional forces as a "tripwire." Yet the relevant nuclear weapons were ostensibly small enough to be thinkable—yet large enough to establish Escalation Dominance at the theater nuclear level. It should be emphasized that this automaticity of response is viewed as an alternative to an adequate conventional defense in part because such a defense is not believed feasible.

67. Slocombe, "Extended Deterrence," 13.

68. If there was not an element of punishment involved, there would be no need for weapons with the range to strike deep into Soviet territory.

69. Linton Brooks, "Naval Power and National Security: The Case for the Maritime Stategy," *International Security* 11, no.2 (1986): 60.

70. In contrast to Brooks, Mearsheimer writes ("Strategic Misstep," 17–18):

It is important to emphasize, however, that it is not easy to describe this strategy since the Navy has often been vague in describing it. . . . As a result, the public debate on this subject is often carried on without any reference to the specifics of the strategy. Moreover, the core aim of the strategy appears to have changed over time. . . . This fact, coupled with the often vague descriptions of the strategy offered by the Navy, lends the Maritime Strategy an ambiguous or elastic quality.

He specifically refers to it as a "moving target" (18).

71. The fullest articulation of the strategy in the open literature was published as a supplement to the Naval Institute *Proceedings*. The Naval Institute itself is a private organization unaffiliated officially with the Department of the Navy, but which automatically makes the Chief of Naval Operations its president and which is housed in a building on the Annapolis campus. See *The Maritime Strategy*, January 1986 supplement to the *Proceedings*. Brooks identifies four elements in the strategy (although I deal here with only two), "Naval Power," 66–67. He quotes the piece in the supplement by Admiral Watkins, then Chief of Naval Operations (*Maritime Strategy*, 14). And Mearsheimer admits that although the Navy has occasionally shifted its rhetorical emphasis from one to another of these four postures, all four have remained elements of the Maritime Strategy since it was formulated in 1981 ("Strategic Misstep," 25).

72. See, for example, E. F. Gueritz, "NATO Strategy and Extended Deterrence: The Changing Role of Sea-Based Forces," in Institute for Foreign Policy

Analysis, ed., *NATO's Maritime Strategy: Issues and Developments, Special Report 1987: The Atlantic Alliance and Western Security: The Maritime Dimensions, Vol. II* (Washington, D.C.: Pergamon Brassey's International Defense Publishers, 1987), 1–22.

73. Mearsheimer, "Strategic Misstep," 42. He also points out (44–45) that part of the problem may stem from the uses of the labels "offensive" and "defensive," since there is probably a stigma associated with "defensive" activities from the standpoint of the professional military.

74. See Colin Gray, "The Maritime Strategy 1988: Bad Strategy? or Global Deterrent?" *Proceedings* 114, no. 2 (February 1988): 54–59.

75. Soviet SSBNs are too noisy (hence detectable) to patrol the open ocean the way American SSBNs routinely do.,

76. Linton Brooks, "Conflict Termination Through Maritime Leverage," in Stephen Cimbala and Keith Dunn, eds., *Conflict Termination and Military Strategy: Coercion, Persuasion, and War* (Boulder: Westview Press, 1987), 168.

77. See William Lind, "The Maritime Strategy 1988: Bad Strategy? or Global Deterrent?" *Proceedings* 114, no. 2 (February 1988): 57–58.

78. Brooks, "Naval Power," 67 (emphasis in original); Robert Weinland, "The Soviet Naval Buildup in the High North: A Reassessment," in Sverre Jarnell and Kare Nyblom, eds., *The Military Buildup in the High North* (Boston: University Press of America, 1986), 21–44.

79. Thus Gray admits "If World War III is a brief and bloody passage of arms in Central Europe, followed inexorably by explosive nuclear escalation, then maritime strategy in any shape, manner, or form is, by definition, an irrelevance." Colin Gray, "The Maritime Strategy in U.S.-Soviet Strategic Relations," *Naval War College Review* 42 no. 1 (Winter 1989): 9. See also Harry Train II, "Seapower and Projection Forces," in Joseph Kruzel, ed., *1986–1987 American Defense Annual* (Lexington, Mass.: Lexington Books, 1986), 124–125.

80. The most sophisticated work to date on Soviet naval policy supports this thesis. See Michael MccGwire, *Military Objectives in Soviet Foreign Policy* (Washington, D.C.: The Brookings Institution, 1987). Of particular interest are the appendixes, 406–476. See also J. Breemer, "U.S. Maritime Strategy: A Re-Appraisal," *Naval Forces: International Forum for Maritime Power* [hereinafter cited as *Naval Forces*] 8, no. 2 (1987): 64–76. This consensus cuts across disagreement on the Maritime Strategy itself. See Mearsheimer, "Strategic Misstep," 42–43, and Train, "Seapower," 128. Even Brooks, who believes offensive or active sea control is absolutely necessary agrees ("Naval Power," 63) that "The most important Soviet navy roles in global war would be protecting . . . Soviet ballistic missile submarines (SSBNs) and protecting the approaches to the Soviet homeland." He also agrees (63): "This essentially defensive initial role for the Soviet navy is confirmed by the overwhelming majority of Soviet naval exercises." See also Robert Wood and John Hanley, Jr., "The Maritime Role in the North Atlantic," in James George, ed., *The U.S. Navy: View From The Mid–1980s* (Boulder: Westview Press in Cooperation with the Center for Naval Analysis, 1985), 335.

81. Mearsheimer, "Strategic Misstep," 16

82. Mearsheimer, "Strategic Misstep," 46–47. He points out:

The United States will soon have, with Trident D–5, MX, Minuteman III A, nuclear-armed Tomahawk cruise missiles, and the Pershing IIs, a substantial counterforce capability against Soviet land-based ICBMs. This development, coupled with the fact that the Soviets have a small, antiquated, and vulnerable bomber force, means that the two land-based legs of their triad would be in good part vulnerable to an America strike. The survivability of their SSBN force would therefore loom as a much more important matter.

83. Mearsheimer, "Strategic Misstep," 51. He does admit that this option is unlikely. Epstein suggests (*Budget*, 52) that a more likely response would be nuclear strikes against American carriers.

84. Mearsheimer, "Strategic Misstep," 8.

85. Gray, "Maritime Strategy," 39. Brooks, "Naval Power" (80–81) agrees, although he explicitly disagrees with Gray's position on the need to threaten the Soviet political apparatus (68).

86. Brooks, "Naval Power," 81. See also James Tritten, *Soviet Naval Forces and Nuclear Warfare: Weapons Employment and Policy* (Boulder: Westview Press, 1986), 230.

87. William Kaufmann, *A Thoroughly Efficient Navy* (Washington, DC: The Brookings Institution, 1987), 50.

88. See Brooks, "Naval Power," 92. One author argued that although attacks on the Kola base make the carriers targets, being a target is a legitimate role for American carriers. In effect, the carriers become decoys, drawing attack submarines away from the convoys. See F. Drury, "Naval Strike Warfare and the Outer Air Battle," *Naval Forces* 7, no. 4 (1986): 47.

89. Horizontal escalation, one of the four elements comprising the Maritime Strategy, is also in tension with strategic doctrine. Horizontal escalation calls for the Navy to initiate battle in theaters important to the Soviets but not part of the original conflict in order to draw Soviet forces off the Central Front. The strategic theory calls for direct responses to hostilities at an equivalent level of violence. Obviously a strategic war would have no geographic or spatial limits. An intercontinental nuclear war, if it is to be restricted, can be limited only by the nature of the targets. Nevertheless, the idea of meeting violence with equal violence calls for some clear link between the targets after a strike on American silos, bases, or ports. By contrast, horizontal escalation calls for retaliatory strikes on targets having no apparent link to those initially attacked.

90. Mearsheimer, "Strategic Misstep," 4. Actually advocates of the Maritime Strategy agree. See Brooks, "Naval Power," 71 and 76. This is because after the first month 90 to 99% of NATO supplies will have to come by sea. Ronald O'Rourke, "U.S. Strategic Sealift: Sustaining the Land Battle," *Naval Forces* 7, no. 3 (1986): 30–39.

91. Mearsheimer, "Strategic Misstep," 30. See also Cordesman, "Forward Deterrence," 29, where he argues that only ground forces are relevant, failing to even mention the naval balance. Again, advocates of the strategy agree. See Brooks, "Naval Power," 74. Train repeats an oft-used phrase when he comments ("Seapower," 124): "Navies do not win wars, but they can cause them to be lost."

92. Mearsheimer, "Strategic Misstep," 35, argues that there must be a strong enough naval force to prevent the Soviets from concluding that they could sever the SLOCs completely, therefore guaranteeing the success of a blitzkreig strategy on the ground.

93. See Boyer, "Strategic Implications," 105.

94. Epstein, *Budget*, 53. See also Barry Posen, "The U.S. Military Response to Soviet Naval Developments in the High North," in Jarvell and Nyblom, eds., *Buildup*, 45–58.

95. This was clear in the original decision on the deployment of intermediate range nuclear weapons in Europe. Deployment on submarines would have been a militarily superior option, but a politically unacceptable one since the weapons would not be visible enough to provide a clear statement of commitment to Europe. See Strobe Talbott, *Deadly Gambits* (New York: Vintage Books, September 1985), 33.

96. See, for example, Slocombe, "Extended Deterrence," 13; Benjamin Lambeth, "Theater Forces," 90.

97. Strong firebreaks are decoupling because they suggest an attempt on the part of the United States to structure conflict to avoid meeting its commitment to escalate to a strategic exchange. It therefore also suggests the possibility of a war fought by the superpowers without damage to the superpowers. This abrogates the shared risk of the alliance members.

98. This does seem somewhat in tension with the warfighters' position on C3. On the one hand, they want command and control improved so that control can be maintained during weeks or months of nuclear exchange. On the other hand they rely in part on the Soviet's knowledge of the weakness of C3 and the inability to control exchanges to deter war in Europe. I believe this again reflects the fact that warfighting is a theory of persuasion. Protracted warfighting under controlled circumstances may not be possible, but we must act as if it is in order to deter. At the same time, we can benefit from Soviet doubts as to whether or not it is possible to maintain deterrence whatever the Soviets believe.

99. Kenneth Burke, *Attitudes Towards History*, 3rd ed. (Berkeley: University of California Press, 1984), 92–105.

100. For an example of the "decade of neglect" argument see Colin Gray and Jeffrey Barlow, "Inexcusable Restraint: The Decline of American Military Power in the 1970s," *International Security* 10, no. 2 (1982): 27–69.

101. Gervasi, *Myth*, 85.

102. This is the outgrowth of the different perspectives on the Soviet Union. If they are pragmatic it is reasonable to assume they would look for areas of interest where negotiation was possible. If they are ideological and aggressive, it is reasonable to assume that they see negotiations as an opportunity to manipulate and institutionalize Western weaknesses.

Chapter Five

Conclusions

This study has demonstrated that strategic doctrine emerges from a series of competing theories of persuasion. Authors advocating MAD and warfighting in their pure forms, and as they were applied to the case of extended deterrence, construct persuasive messages based on their analyses of the audience, which, through the 1980s, was considered to be the Soviet Union. In this chapter I will summarize the conclusions that can be drawn regarding strategic doctrine as communication by considering standards for argument and evidentiary validity, the self-sustaining nature of deterrence theory, and the mechanistic model of communication employed. Because these conclusions apply to both MAD and warfighting, it is possible to draw conclusions about the role communication plays in strategic doctrine.

Several assumptions underlie the structures of deterrence theory and strategic doctrine as persuasion. I will specifically consider the importance of communicating risk and the need to avoid "mirror imaging" in the development of effective messages. Finally, I will describe additional research projects that are suggested by this study.

SUMMARY OF FINDINGS

This study establishes the claim that, although presented as essentially different, the two strategic doctrines developed out of deterrence theory are predicated on identical models of communication. They are, in other words, structurally identical in that they share common assumptions about the role of communication. Both are circular. The doctrines are tautological because they lack standards for textual analysis, for argument, and for evidentiary validity. Arguments about strategic issues have not moved to a level where *how* what one knows is *known* or even arguable. As a result, standards are not developed for testing claims.

Hence, debate does not move beyond the extension and application of unexamined assumptions. Both doctrines, therefore, generate arguments in defense of interpretations rather than advancing proof claims that can be tested. This lent a self-perpetuating quality to discussions of U.S. military posture in a nuclear age, evidenced in part by the near complete lack of calls for disarmament despite the dissolution of the primary target audience. Finally, although the doctrines are about communication, the model of communication employed in both instances is naive.

Standards of Validity

Because they are theories of persuasion, both strategic doctrines must begin with audience analysis. Since Aristotle, rhetorical theorists have recognized that since it is audiences who ultimately interpret messages, message construction should be predicated on an understanding of the audience at which the message will be aimed. If that audience analysis is in any way incorrect, then the message construction process will necessarily be flawed, and the message itself unpersuasive. The Soviet government was essentially closed to the United States. Certainty in evaluations of the Soviet leadership as an audience for strategic messages was impossible. The accuracy of any given conclusion about the Soviets was inevitably arguable. Conclusions about the nature of the appeals likely to persuade Soviet leaders were speculative, and the grounds upon which the speculation was based were themselves subject to argument. Because the Soviets did not tell theorists what would deter them, evidence had to be identified and interpreted. Yet, neither school developed standards that could be used either to determine what counted as legitimate evidence of Soviet intentions or to test competing interpretations of what has been categorized as evidence. Soviet doctrinal texts, statements of military and political leaders, force structures, and historical actions all have been used in support of claims about Soviet values, beliefs, and doctrines. It is a paradox of the nuclear age that for deterrence to work, communication must be effective—yet because of the adversarial relationship between the United States and the U.S.S.R., the processes of reciprocity, trust, and cumulative understanding that ordinarily underlie communication could not be assumed. Thus, what would usually be taken for granted becomes the ground for extended interpretation and perpetual argument in defense of competing interpretations.

Deterrence theories made categorizing judgements about the authenticity of Soviet messages. Hence, the question was always raised: Which text, weapons deployment, or action, accurately represents Soviet motivations? Based on critical practice, this question needed to be answered *prior* to any attempt at interpretation. But, as there were no agreed upon standards for determining the quality of evidence, the legitimacy of interpretive questions was always at issue. Indeed, such questions were raised as part of the attempt to properly categorize evidence. Thus, what should have been the first stage in the exegetical process was not only enacted *after* what should have been a later stage of analysis, it was also made to be dependent on analysis that should have been dependent on *it*. For both schools, the claims that could be drawn from the evidence affected the ways in which it was interpreted, at least in part due to the order in which the analysis of evidence was conducted.

As each side in the debate developed classification procedures and evidence standards compatible with its view and discounted alternatives, proof claims became unfalsifiable. Evidence was decontextualized in this way, since no particular category of evidence was ever used to crosscheck any other category of evidence.[1] Evidence stood alone, without regard for the way any given item or category modified subsequent judgments. Resolution appeared impossible, since although many of the disputes between theorists centered on competing interpretations of texts,[2] no explicit methodology existed to guide interpretation. Several evidentiary questions should be critical to the development or defense of any strategic doctrine. In this context, the questions should have been: What counts as evidence of Soviet intentions? How can legitimate and illegitimate interpretations of Soviet intentions be differentiated? And, finally, what methodologies are able to answer questions about Soviet intentions?

Although there are many discussions of critical methodology in rhetorical studies, strategic theorists appear to be innocent of them all. There was no reciprocal theory of communication guiding interpretation of the Soviets. In fact, it is no exaggeration to say that they did not in any way perceive what they were doing as textual criticism. Strategic theorists did not believe they were engaged in interpretive analysis: therefore, they saw no need to develop interpretative schemes. Theorists "just" read texts, examined force structures, and explained historical events. These forms of evidence were thought to be objective and self-evident, not requiring methodologically guided application.[3] Theorists assumed that the evidence they used was univocal and unambiguous, that it spoke in the same voice and conveyed the same meaning to all who encountered it. If there was a dispute over meaning, it was attributed to inaccuracies in translation, carelessness, or ideological bias on the part of the opposing author.[4] The debate between the schools was therefore stagnant, a matter of exchanging unexamined preconceptions. There is no opportunity to distinguish between high and low probability claims. Evidence was not used inductively to buttress positions and cement proof claims on the way to conclusions about Soviet intentions. Rather, a priori judgments about Soviet intentions were used deductively to generate arguments explaining evidence as evidence of Soviet motives. If one does not agree with the assumptions generating the defense of evidence, one will not agree with the interpretation of the evidence. The debate over Soviet motivations proceeded without resolution. It would no doubt have continued, barring nuclear holocaust, because the disputants provided no mechanism for resolving it. It will continue, even now, via disputes over what ultimately caused the dissolution of the Union. The strategic debate is self-perpetuating. It is not a matter of pronouncing one side right and one wrong. Even within schools of deterrence theories evidentiary standards break down, as I have tried to show in discussing the NATO question.

Self-Perpetuation of Doctrine

MAD and warfighting as argument structures posit complex systems for the prevention of nuclear war. Each is entrenched by its own logic. Both provide guides for the proper construction and manipulation of messages of threat and risk. Threatening nuclear war becomes a way to harness the risk of war. Such threats are embraced and sustained as the only way to avoid actualizing that risk. But the communication of the risk via threats can only be achieved within exceedingly narrow boundaries, offering no way to escape the self-sustaining dictates of doctrine.

MAD begins with the assumption that the ideal state of affairs would be a balance between communicating states. Crisis Stability requires a definable, precise, and reciprocal relationship between the states threatening one another. The United States and the U.S.S.R. must act within the constraints of a shared abhorrence of mutual destruction. This can only be assured if each side acquires and maintains secure second-strike capability. If either side has more weapons than are needed for a secure second strike (or higher accuracy weapons than are required), the system is destabilized by the resulting vulnerability of the opponent. MAD has been associated with arms control and the attempt to negotiate reductions in nuclear arsenals, but only because of the perception that arose that both the United States and the Soviet Union possessed more weapons than required for a second strike. Once the proper balance was achieved, further efforts at arms reduction would grind to a halt, for Crisis Stability would be destroyed if either (or both) sides had less than a secure second-strike force. MAD, therefore, posits the need for a static system, but safety only results if the system is static in perpetuity. In a MAD world, cooperative U.S.-Soviet relations would be possible only as long as each side's population remained hostage to the other's. There can be no escape from the Doomsday System and the shared risk of annihilation it offers—and depends upon. Again, this is demonstrated by the cautious support for various arms control proposals on the table with the Commonwealth of Independent States: the concern now is not that the arms race might spiral out of control, but rather that in our mutual relief at the end of the Cold War, we might be foolishly tempted to cut too much.

Warfighting begins with an acceptance of the appeasement theory of war. This doctrine too offers a structure from which there can be no escape. Because the theory distinguishes between capability and will, each side must take actions that communicate its will directly. The obvious method for communicating will is to engage in armed conflict, but that is too costly to be acceptable. Indeed, that is the outcome the entire system is designed to avoid.

Weapons procurement is thus structured to communicate in addition to the simple possession of weapons. *Having* weapons communicates a level of capability. Procuring additional weapons, especially if doing so involves sacrifice, conveys will. The need to demonstrate will remains regardless of one's capabilities or the capabilities of an opponent. Because will is an intangible, it can only be demonstrated through *action*. The only action available as an alternative to on-going acquisition of additional weapons is war—as unacceptable an outcome to warfighters as to advocates of MAD. Warfighting creates a structure that is stable only when it constantly demonstrates both capabilities and its intentions. As in a cell, an end to growth signals stagnation and impending death. Stability comes from change. Any attempt to end the process communicates a dangerously destabilizing failure of will. Thus today, in an era of dramatically reduced defense budgets, there is still a willingness to sacrifice manpower and weapons stocks in order to protect projects currently in the development pipeline.

Even while models of communication are based on the threat of death, or annihilation of the United States or perhaps of humanity, deterrence theorists recognize that the systems they advocate to hold the threat in check perpetuate and entrench the threat. Yet that is tolerated, for to speculate on the existence of alternatives is a destabilizing act of heresy within the logics of both schools. Both models create structures to stop a threat to humanity of human origin. But doing so in a manner that leaves humanity subject to the perpetual threat of nuclear annihilation for all time is the only way of achieving human freedom from threat.

Mechanistic Communication

Deterrence theorists sought effective ways for the government of the United States to communicate with the government of the Soviet Union.

Propaganda does not concern these theorists, nor does public or private summitry. The sole purpose of strategic doctrine, even now when other channels of communication are opening up between the United States and the various Republic governments, is to communicate threats so that there is no doubt, no ambiguity, in the superpower relationship. Unfortunately, in the desire to communicate a perfect message, the necessary imperfection of all human communication is ignored and finally forgotten. It is, therefore, an assumption of the systems that communication is mechanistic, for the costs of even a single communication breakdown may be infinite. Thinking thus hardens into doctrine, and the result for both systems is a limited model of communication.

What was ignored in the process is the most fundamental element of communication: That it is reciprocal, a means for sharing between parties. In both the MAD and warfighting systems, the Soviets were denied an authentic "voice." When it was believed that an artifact was produced because of a Soviet intent to communicate, that artifact was immediately discounted as inauthentic and disingenuous. The United States is portrayed as "textualizing" its armed forces; using them as symbolic structures for communicative purposes. Weapons are built and deployed in order to convey a message. Operational characteristics are considered, from both systems, from one overriding point of view: What will a weapon with certain capabilities convey to the Soviets?

By contrast, Soviet deployments and activities were considered to be data for interpretation. What was procured and deployed in relation to other priorities and what was said between Soviets might have offered insights into their real intentions to the astute critic, but were never considered to be part of an intentionally constructed message-system. The United States builds weapons based on criteria formulated out of the demands of its communicative needs. The Soviet Union built based on what would be needed to actually fight a war. Theorists reserve to themselves the ability to construct precise and accurate messages, but they did not consider that the Soviets might have been doing the same. The Soviets were presumed to have the ability to understand our messages: Ostensibly they could decode our symbolic language of CEP and megatonnage. But although they could receive and understand our messages, the United States alone actually engaged in communication. The United States sent and the Soviets received. In both MAD and warfighting this assumption is implicit and unquestioned.

The model of communication used is one that was rejected by communication analysts thirty years ago. The Sender-Message-Receiver (SMR) model posits a linear system, where an individual constructs and conveys a message to a receiver, who interprets it clearly (assuming no background static). It was rejected as being so simplistic as to be misleading. Most obviously no room exists in the model for feedback; responses to the message from the receiver that the sender responds to. While the model accommodates interference, it treats it as a mechanical breakdown that can eventually be corrected. The model does not acknowledge the inability of human beings to communicate perfectly, without interpretation. For, while we must interpret Soviet behavior (since it is not *meant* as a message) our behavior is intended to be communicative. It ought, therefore, be quite clear.[5] There is no room in the model for misinterpretation. Actions on the part of the receiver will be intentional (although they may feign misunderstanding in order to further their own ends).

COMMUNICATION ANALYSIS

In the previous section, I have examined the ways that a naive understanding of communication led strategic theorists to the development of doctrines which are mechanistic and self-perpetuating. Having demonstrated the way this model of communication underlies strategic theory, I will now critique the two theories *as* models of communication. Such a critique permits a deeper understanding of the functions, flaws, and paradoxes of contemporary deterrence theory.

Both MAD and warfighting seek to develop communicative systems in order to regulate a relationship whose rupture means catastrophe, but which is assumed incapable of sustaining meaningful discursive communication. The enterprise led both sets of theorists to defend and sustain a "perspective by incongruity."[6] Instruments of death, nuclear weapons, are symbolically transformed into instruments of life, because they create the risk that stays the hands of those with the ability to use them.

Each theory is self-sustaining. The dialectic between the two continues without hope of resolution. In order to provide a communication-centered critique of the doctrines I will first examine two issues central to the deterrence enterprise—the communication of risk, and the need to avoid "mirror imaging." I will then explore the manner in which these two issues transform deterrence into an on-going dialectic, inescapable so long as traditional assumptions remain in place and unquestioned.

Communication of Risk

One of the basic assumptions shared by MAD and warfighting authors is that relations with the Soviet Union cannot be trusted to reasoned discourse alone. Whether communication is verbal or not, reasoned attempts at persuasion were an insufficient basis for affecting Soviet behavior. To merely request of the Soviets that they refrain from a particular activity—say, invading Western Europe—and then trust to their good will was hopeless. The Soviets had to be in some way threatened if their behavior was to conform to American desires. However, for threats to be effective, they must be communicated in a convincing manner. The recipient must recognize and understand the threat and must believe that it will be carried out as promised. The point of making a threat is, after all, not to carry it out, but to obtain the desired change in behavior.[7] Deterrence theorists assumed that only threats would persuade the Soviets to act in ways consistent with American interests.

Deterrence theory, in both its variants, assumes that the United States can clearly communicate an appropriate threat, have its force postures and doctrinal statements recognized as a threat, and have that threat believed. These requirements are the root cause of a paradox so deeply embedded in deterrence theory as to be a truism: For a threat to be persuasive, it must be real. In a nuclear age such threats, however, generate a risk of destruction that is shared. Deterrence then, depends on credibly threatening exactly the action all parties—especially the one making the threat—wish to avoid. This is the "rationality" paradox. Rational people wish to avoid nuclear war, but rationality dictates that the best way to avoid a war is by credibly threatening to start one. And the most credible threats of all come from those who behave irrationally. After all, threats of a potentially self-destructive nature are easiest to believe when they come from someone with bloodshot eyes.[8] Thus a balance must be struck. Risks must be high enough to communicate a legitimate threat yet low enough to be both manageable and tolerable.

The Soviet Union had to be able to confidently interpret changes in force deployments, or structures, as intentional. If the Soviets could not invest actions with meaning, the entire system would have collapsed. Unintended risks are counterproductive: They interfere with the fidelity of the message. For this reason, elaborate guidelines and complex structures were created to ensure political control at the highest level over deployed weapons.[9] This ensured that changes and manipulations could be assumed to reflect the desires of the National Command Authority. The messages must be interpreted in a probabilistic manner—but it is at least fairly certain that it is a message of some sort.

The mechanisms used to guarantee political control can be manipulated in any given situation in order to increase the apparent risk. Such flexibility permits risk to be kept manageable in ordinary circumstances and then dramatically increased when the need for a stronger message is perceived. The need to manipulate levels of risk stems from Schelling's "threats that leaves something to change."[10] The classic metaphor used to describe the situation is "nuclear chicken."[11]

Nuclear chicken is important, not only for what it reveals about deterrence theory, but because it demonstrates the influence of game theory on deterrence. Chicken is a game where two drivers direct their automobiles at one another at full speed. The first driver to swerve demonstrates less will, and loses. The best way to play chicken, it has been said, is to throw the brake and steering wheel out the window, for then there is no question of swerving. What is particularly interesting about the adoption of chicken as a model for deterrence, is that winning gains the winner no substantive benefit. The only goal for the players is to avoid losing.

Before examining the assumptions of this model and the way they became embedded in deterrence theory, a consideration of the reasons theorists have found this game so compelling will be useful. Chicken has proven a popular and long-lived metaphor for deterrence because of the symbolic resources with which it is invested.

Games as a model for international relations were popular almost from the beginning of the application of deterrence theory to the nuclear age. Although this approach has been qualified and indicted,[12] its influence, particularly on views of communication, remains. As Lawrence Freedman explains:

A game of strategy was one in which the best course for each player depended on what the other players did, and could be distinguished from games of skill or chance. This emphasis on the interdependence of the adversaries' decisions provided the essence of the theory. The second important assumption was that of rational behavior, based on calculations aimed at maximizing values. No particular set of values was associated with "rational" behavior in this sense. All that was required was that whatever the values, they were held in an explicit, transitive and internally consistent manner.[13]

This approach, and its problems as a communication model, becomes clear when nuclear chicken is subjected to critical analysis.

Using chicken as a metaphor for international relations in the nuclear age allows the problems of deterrence to be discussed in a benign way. Several authors have argued that the power of nuclear weapons "jargon" lies in its ability to symbolically recontextualize the hundreds of millions of deaths that could result from a nuclear war.[14] The chicken metaphor places the risk of nuclear holocaust into a familiar and reassuring "boys will be boys" context. Chicken is, after all, merely a manifestation of adolescence, although admittedly a potentially dangerous one. The metaphor implies that the risk is under conscious control, manipulated by and responsive to a single rational actor at all times. The actor in the scenario makes the decision to *reject* control: It is not that the brakes simply fail at an inopportune moment. The metaphor portrays both opponents as identical. Both actors are under complete control and operate under the same assumptions of rational cost-benefit analysis.

Each actor is rational enough to understand that at a certain point—

when the brakes are discarded—there is no longer any reason to continue the game since loss is certain. One final element in the metaphor's rhetorical power can be seen in an application of Wander's work on the Third Persona.[15] Wander argues that in any text there will be an ignored, excluded audience. The portrayal of the nuclear superpowers as unitary actors excludes the audience that matters most: the hundreds of millions of people who have no say, but an ultimate stake in the outcome. Despite its rhetorical power, the metaphor makes assumptions about communication that are unrealistically optimistic.

The metaphor assumes that the irrevocable signals can be sent clearly, and received without distortion. The actions that renounce control—discarding the steering wheel and brake—must be perceived, understood and acted upon for the metaphor to be correct. It will be difficult enough to recognize that a signal has intentionally been sent. On a dark night with headlights blazing it may be impossible to see the action take place. In terms of nuclear deterrence, the opponent's intelligence apparatus may be malfunctioning; or it may not be sufficiently streamlined for the individuals interpreting the raw intelligence data to report appropriately to the relevant decisionmakers.

Even if the action is seen, understanding does not necessarily follow. In terms of the metaphor, it one opponent drives a car with a handbrake then the brake thrown out the window by the other opponent may not be properly identified. Discarding it then becomes a meaningless gesture. In terms of deterrence, opponents may exercise political control over weapons in completely different ways. Yet the metaphor assumes that meaning will be reciprocally understood, and that interpretation will be rapidly followed by the appropriate counteraction.

If the action is understood, the metaphor further assumes that the significance of the act will be assessed in equivalent terms. Almost any game move may be perceived as a trick, suggesting the need for a devious counterstrategy—or a more resolute one: in the metaphor's terms, driving even faster. Opponents may perceive a loosening of control procedures for nuclear weapons as an attempt to streamline command procedures in order to prepare for a preemptive strike. This may signal that war is inevitable, and convince the opponent to make every effort to launch first.

No consideration is given to what happens when each side duplicates the other's actions in an attempt to "win." What happens when both drivers simultaneously renounce control? Or when both superpowers initiate a self-reinforcing cycle of alerts, stripping away political control over their weapons? The metaphor posits discrete sequences of action. It is unable to generate means for sorting out simultaneous or near simultaneous events, particularly when they interact to reinforce one another.

Finally, it is assumed that each side values the outcome equally and in comparable terms. Jettisoning control is a rational way of feigning irrationality in order to achieve rational ends. If one's opponent is truly irrational, or suicidal, an intentionally irrational action will hardly generate the desired response. If one of the superpowers believes initiating a nuclear war is the only way to salvage anything of its society, then deterrence is highly unlikely.

Deterrence is necessary all the time, not just when occasional crises raise tensions. Or perhaps it is more accurate to say that the world exists in a permanent state of crisis. The deterrence system both tolerates a high level of risk on a day to day basis and accepts the need to selectively heighten risks in certain circumstances.

There is a self-limiting quality to the discourse generated that stems from its origins in game theory. Deterrence theories as theories of persuasion stem from a worldview that holds communication to be a mathematical phenomenon that can be understood, calculated, and predicted, with precision. Thus deterrence theorists of both schools believe that force structures can be devised that can restrain apocalypse through the use of rationality. This is the original source of the rationality paradox. The paradox is so deeply embedded in discussion of strategic doctrine that it manifests itself in virtually every discussion of policy. Consider one important example, war termination.

For many years, little was said about how a nuclear war might be ended. Strategic theorists focused on ways to avoid starting nuclear wars because their scenarios all expressed ways in which opponents would think about nuclear war prior to such a war beginning. Hypothetical scenarios of potentially real events did not mesh with the internal logics of either MAD or warfighting. Consideration of termination strategies from within those perspectives is either useless or counterproductive. From a MAD standpoint war, if it comes, will be total. Even to propose termination strategies is to foster the dangerous illusion that wars can be fought in a nuclear age. For the warfighter, termination would simply be the natural outgrowth of Escalation Dominance. To consider other scenarios for termination smacks of a defeatist neutrality that could be interpreted as lack of will. Nevertheless, some authors were beginning to examine options for terminating nuclear conflict within the context of force structures as they existed in the late 1980s.

In the literature on War Termination, communication is portrayed as completely mechanistic. Even the diagrams used are exact parallels of the Sender-Message-Receiver (SMR) model of communication.[16] The decision to use force is made by the sender, who translates it into a strategy, which then constitutes the message. The actions taken in response, by the receiver, determine the decision to terminate the conflict. But it is clear from the text accompanying the diagram that the decision to resolve the conflict is made exclusively by the sender. In other words, the feedback in the system comes from the sender: It is a completely closed system.

The mechanism implied by such a perspective is apparent in the different assumptions about the ways a war would begin and end. It is assumed, for example, that a war in Europe would terminate when the Soviets recognized that a rapid, conventional approach would not work, either because NATO's conventional forces were stronger than they had appeared or because NATO's use of nuclear weapons were too great a threat. As Treverton writes:

Yet, if they [the Soviets] were capable of making those kinds of cost-benefit calculations during the war, they ought to be before it. Hence they would never start the war in the first place. Limited war is not compatible with unlimited objectives. That point, apparently trivial, has been true since the beginning of the nuclear era. Yet our customary notions of how a war in Europe might begin seem to presume unlimited Soviet intentions, and thus to belie the limited objectives which form the basis for our imaginings of how such a war might end.[17]

What Treverton points to, although he does not see it in these terms, is that the communication system is believed sound. It may suffer breakdowns in which case rational analysis would cease and war would begin, but would quickly reestablish itself, and the war would end with the return of reason. The assumption of rationality ignores the fact that people begin wars in panic and desperation and fight them in confusion. An objective assessment of cost benefits would be extremely difficult in such situations. As Freedman notes, "[i]t was as if police offers were being taught the art of homicide detection in terms of opportunity and murder weapon, but never motive."[18] As in the game of nuclear chicken, the theory ignores all the aspects of communication likely to produce misinterpretations when clear communication was needed most.

It is difficult to conceive of the risk as tolerable or the system as rational except within its own logic. That logic is in part perverted because it is based on a need to communicate about risks that arise from a flawed view of persuasion and communication.[19] The logic of calculated irrationality derives from the need to construct a system of communication within a context that misunderstands communication.

Despite the substantive differences between the doctrines, the concern with communicating risk is central to both of them. Thus the doctrines also share the paradoxes and problems that emerge from this particular vision of communication. Because the doctrines are theories of communication, and hence of persuasion, they also share in the problems inherent to a system based on analysis of motivations. I will now consider the way such problems are dealt with by the two sets of theorists, and what those problems reveal about the deterrence enterprise.

Mirror Imaging

Flawed assumptions about communication form the basis of MAD and warfighting. This distortion is embedded at the most fundamental level, where deterrence theorists argue about audience analyses of the Soviet Union. The respective portraits of Soviet leadership are a natural point of stasis because for both doctrines the audience analysis was the starting point for their entire conceptual framework. Should the assumptions held about the Soviets have been disproven, either doctrine would have collapsed. It is not surprising, then, that some of the most vociferous disputes between MAD and warfighting authors centered on discussions of Soviet motivations generally, and on the accusation of "mirror imaging" specifically.

An accusation of mirror imaging charges an author with imputing his or her orientation and motivations to the Soviets. Soviet reasoning is assumed to "mirror" the values and assumptions of the theorist. The argument, therefore, is that the accused author *assumes* that his or her motivations would provide a satisfactory explanation for Soviet actions. Thus a mirror imager would, through his or her interpretive methodology, deny the Soviets an authentic voice, for they have no independent position, but become merely a reflection of the attitudes and beliefs of the author who is supposed to be interpreting them. To make this accusation is to argue that the author misinterprets Soviet values, beliefs, and strategies by examining evidence uncritically from within his or her own perspective, twisting data to make it fit pre-determined assumptions. Each school believes that the other's strategic doctrine is flawed because it is based on the pseudo-analysis of mirror imaging. MAD advocates charge warfighters with mirror imaging when they posit a Soviet understanding of the escalation ladder and intra-war deterrence. Warfighters believe MAD advocates mirror image when they assume that the Soviets share their rejection of nuclear weapons as military tools. This dispute, however, is futile because both systems are based on mechanistic views of communication, using the Sender-Message-Receiver (SMR) model. The only feedback in the system comes from interpretations of evidence that are guided by circular understandings of evidence. The feedback is generated only by the original sender as it echoes its messages back from the receiver. Each side thus inevitably reproduced Soviet intentions within its own schema of interpretation and framework of assessment.

In an SMR communication system mirror imaging is unavoidable. All deterrence theorists recognize the importance of perceptions. What they do not account for is the inherent distinctions between Soviet perceptions and American authors' perceptions of Soviet perceptions. Deterrence theorists are not aware of the limits imposed by their own cultural horizons.[20] These limits would continue to exist even if the Soviets had been permitted an authentic voice. They certainly exist without standards of validity for evidence. Each school desires to improve its ability to communicate, and to refine its theory, by perfecting the means of obtaining information, which is held to be the product of developing better technical means of data acquisition and analysis. This belief traps theorists in a tragic frame.[21] Intrinsic limitations on the practice of textual interpretation are not recognized or understood. Each school senses in the other the limits that plague it, yet neither understands that these limits are unavoidable and that, in fact, they define the boundaries of the critical/interpretive enterprise.

With the individuals attempting to develop an effective communications system unable to recognize the constraints of textual analysis, audience analysis or message construction, how can risk manipulation possibly be communicated effectively? Burke has argued that the need is to develop a symbol system that permits conversation to continue.[22] Because both schools reject an authentic Soviet voice, relying on their own perceptions without understanding the way those perceptions are filtered through a critical lens, this most important conversation was not even permitted to begin.

The inability to develop a robust system of communication using the SMR model is demonstrated by the Prisoner's Dilemma game. The recurrent use of this game is another legacy of deterrence theory's origins in game theory. This game, like chicken, was repeatedly used as a metaphor for relations between the United States and the Soviet Union. It presents the social scientists' view of deterrence. Played by two people who are not in direct communication with one another, a series of plays determines the points for each side. When both sides take an action labelled by the controller of the game as "cooperative," both gain points. If one cooperates and the other does not, the uncooperative player gains more points than are gained when both sides are cooperative, and the cooperative player loses points. When both sides are uncooperative both sides loose points. The simplicity and elegance of the game make it a tempting model, but, because of the mechanistic model of communication it assumes, Prisoner's Dilemma is deeply flawed.

The point values are arbitrary and cannot account for real pressures faced by real decision makers. For example, both sides lose points when both choose an uncooperative play. But there is no assurance that a real decision maker in a real crisis would not judge such losses acceptable so long as the other side loses at least as much. Furthermore. not all losses will be assigned perfectly equivalent value by different opponents. Decision makers may believe, for example, that losses can be restrained to a particular area. Such losses might be judged acceptable, particularly if cooperation is judged to be so restrictive as to no longer be tolerable. It cannot be assumed that different players will weight even the same losses in equivalent fashion, nor can such evaluations be objectively determined. Nor is there any argument for such determinations in the game, where point values are simply assigned arbitrarily.

Given the random nature of assigning numerical values to entire segments of a civilization, the game radically decontextualizes communication. In the game players receive instructions from an omnipotent and neutral control. In the real world "players" are instructed by biased individuals whose experience with the game comes from playing it. Instruction occurs after normal acculturation and socialization into one culture's perspectives on the other, and is received from individuals who are not "neutral" but rather are wholly participants in their culture's historical and ideological perspective on the other side. One could not grow up in the United States without forming an opinion of the Soviet Union. Nor would that opinion be replaced in training by some "objective" way of knowing. Yet the game makes no allowances for preconceived bias about the other player. Nor is there an institutional history of plays. The game begins anew each time and can, in fact, be played by computers.[23] Yet U.S.-Soviet relations had a history that was known to any "player" and that was salient whenever the two nations dealt with one another. Americans still blame the Soviets for "violating" the Yalta agreements over Eastern Europe, and the Soviets never forgot the United States' part in the 1917 invasion of their country.

Finally, the game must be played in sequential moves. This points out a flaw in the use of any game as a metaphor for international relations. Interactions between states involve simultaneous moves of different value and risk. Like nuclear chicken, Prisoner's Dilemma reconceptualizes the frightening into the familiar. Games have easily understood and explicit rules, with clear penalties for their violation. Stakes that are pictured as arbitrary point values are easier to risk. Losses disappear when each game ends and the slate is wiped clean. Thus the ultimate nature of the stakes is repressed, as are communication difficulties, the lack of explicit and agreed upon rules, and the lack of an impartial arbiter with power to punish those who violate the rules.

The view of communication portrayed in Prisoner's Dilemma is completely decontextualized. Thus, the SMR model of communication is further entrenched in deterrence theory. Each play stands alone. The only context for a given play is the prior plays (since the game is generally composed of a series of plays between two players in one sequence). Yet, deterrence is meant to last an eternity. History, meaning, and interpretation cannot be ignored as they are in abstract games. Decontextualization is an attempt to insulate, by rationalizing the controlling discourse of nuclear weapons, and to subordinate traditional views of total war. Neutral language is believed to permit the stripping away of motives, leaving only pure rationality in the form of cost-benefit analysis.

Since deterrence is "only a game," the risks taken become nothing more than decontextualized tools. The attempt to decontextualize, and thus neutralize language and communication through the gaming model serves to diminish an understanding of the risks actually faced.

The Dialectic of Deterrence

Students of deterrence theory have emphasized substantive differences between MAD and warfighting. But when considered as theories of persuasion, they are identical in form and function. The two theories compete for dominance, yet they do so within an on-going dialectic. A critical perspective makes clear that the basis of that dialectic is that both doctrines are constrained by the SMR model of communication.

Consider, for example, the argument that technology "pushes" strategy.[24] Some analysts have argued that as technology produces new and different types of weapons, strategists simply accommodate their ideas to the new potentials offered by new weapons. This conception of the relationship between technology and strategy misses the most important element of the relationship. Technological developments may determine particular policies that must be addressed by theorists, but it is the logics of the theories that generate the argumentative positions that will be taken on those technologies. An engineering approach may provide a radical design breakthrough, but if it permits increased accuracy in warhead guidance systems, the responses of the theorists will be anything but new and radical.

Technology also demonstrates the dialectical nature of the relationship. For example, as technology provides missiles with greater accuracies and those missiles are deployed, the world less and less resembles the MAD ideal. Certainly MAD authors vehemently protest each breakthrough in accuracy as the decision to deploy missiles incorporating such advances is made. Yet some authors have suggested that it may ultimately be possible to reduce Circular Error Probable (CEP) to zero, to obtain perfect accuracy.[25] Although increased accuracy is sought by warfighters and rejected by MAD authors, *perfect* accuracy may change the basis upon which these arguments are structured. This technological development could conceivably turn the clock back, creating a situation where there is no advantage perceived from launching first. Technology has also increased the possibility of detecting submarines at sea, making them more and more vulnerable.[26] Less attention has been given the fact that quieting techniques are also being constantly improved.[27] These techniques may advance to the point where sonar cannot keep up, submarines cannot be detected against ambient sea noise, and become impossible to detect.[28]

It is generally assumed that such technological advances will further the trend towards development of a disarming first strike capability. But in perfecting that trend, these advances reassert the prominence of MAD. If submarines cannot be found, a secure second strike becomes absolutely invulnerable. Each side is able to ensure its capability to deter the other, through its ability to destroy the other's civilization. The system perpetuates itself, whichever school's precepts are reflected in the force structures of any given time. In discussing game theory, Freedman notes, "The policy imperative that flows from this is to explore means of co-operation to secure the stalemate at a lower level."[29] The opposite occurred. Deterrence perpetuated itself but at ever higher levels of tension, risk, and danger.

PROSPECTS FOR FURTHER RESEARCH

This study points towards significant areas for further research. The field of international relations and research into American foreign policy have suffered from their lack of exposure to theories of argumentation, textual criticism and interpretation, and communication. The critical enterprise, by the same token, has ignored an area that could enrich the theoretical underpinnings of criticism. Several programs of research are suggested by this study.

1. *Expansion and development of an understanding of American foreign policy in a nuclear age.* An overall understanding of American foreign policy from a communication standpoint suggests both limits and potentialities as yet unexplored. National actors communicate and persuade one another in discursive and nondiscursive ways. Yet the limits and the resources of symbolic action have not been considered in this context. American rhetoric contributes to the self-perceptions of those actors participating in state-to-state communication, but the function of international relations as persuasion provides a new perspective for research into the intrinsic limitations on the activities of government actors.

2. *Development of standards for testing strategic doctrine.* Because of the lack of standards for validity there is currently no way to move beyond conflicting assumptions in the deterrence debate. Those most concerned with communication with the Soviets were unable to advance their positions. Stasis occurred at the level of unproved belief, and argument went no further than that. This program might be considered as a way of ultimately asking the question: How can appropriate processes of communication be developed, validated, and secured in practice? While I have no desire to dictate a particular model of communication, some conclusions can be drawn from the current study. Most importantly, a

model of communication that does not take into account even the possibility that persuasion is a phenomena that occurs *between* participants is one that forces inherent contradictions and paradoxes. In the end, deterrence theory cannot move beyond its own assumptions without taking into account the complexities of symbolic action. As the world becomes increasingly multipolar, this project becomes all the more important, as deterrence will be applied to cultures and governments that have been subject to nowhere near the study given the Soviet Union.

The purpose of this study has not been to proclaim the good, but to unravel the bad as it pertains to communication of and about human motivations. To the extent that it has been successful in doing so, it demonstrates the importance of the critical stance.[30] Criticism can, and should, do more than express and justify aesthetic judgments. Many issues of public policy threaten us as a community. Criticism may not be able to resolve such urgent issues, but, if used, it can point out the limits of existing practice and clear the ground for the development of productive argument.

3. *Suggestion of potential alternative structures leading to a "peace process."* Deterrence theory structures an uneasy peace. It might, in fact, be better labelled a permanent state of unrequited war. A critical understanding of the communicative processes involved in sustaining such a system may suggest alternatives. Proposals not considered in this study, such as Osgood's theory of Graduated Reductions in Tension, partake of identical views of communication.[31] They suggest only refinements and modifications to the system of deterrence. A critical research perspective will be especially fruitful in the near future, as current doctrines are stretched to accommodate multilateral nuclearism and the Strategic Defense Initiative.

Critical perspectives may also provide a sounder understanding of the relationship between the public and technical spheres of discourse.[32] Declaratory policy and strategic doctrine are not the same thing. The need for public support exercises some constraints over technical understandings, at least at the margin. But public discourse has been unable to pierce the logics of the deterrence theories, and is therefore helpless to replace or repair them. How are actions justified to the public? How is support of the public given or coopted? Answers to such questions are central for it is not sufficient for academics to uncover alternatives to deterrence theories: Such alternatives must be empowered. There must be some way to make such alternatives workable and real.

4. *Consideration of game theoretic understanding of communication throughout the public sphere.* Game theory's vision of "hyperrational" modes of objectified language is not constrained to foreign policy. The gamut of institutions charged with protecting the public's interest in social activities adopt systems engineering and cost benefit. The protection of the

environment is only one example of an issue that concerns humans as members of communities where this is true. The critical enterprise needs to consider the consequences of such a vision of communication on policy, on communication, and on the publics that are to be protected and served. There have been many analyses of the impact of game theory and systems analysis on public policy, but few have considered the games from beyond the logic of the games themselves. Means for translating visions of communication into methods for competent deliberations for those asked to endure risks and their consequences must be considered.

NOTES

1. The only exception I have been able to find is the work of Michael MccGwire. In an appendix to his book, he provides a painstaking analysis of Soviet doctrine in which argumentative substance of a series of Soviet texts is crosschecked against other forms of evidence such as editorial board turnover, time necessary for censorship per issue, nuclear reactor production and distribution rates, and observable Soviet tactics in fleet exercises. Despite the detail of MccGwire's analysis, however, it is still subject to the other problems noted in this study. Soviet actions and statements are purely evidentiary. Thus even MccGwire is subject to the same criticisms regarding the model of communication selected. See Michael MccGwire, *Military Objectives in Soviet Foreign Policy* (Washington, D.C.: The Brookings Institution, 1987), 406–476.

2. See for example, "A Garthoff-Pipes Debate on Soviet Strategic Doctrine," *Strategic Review* 10, no. 4 (1982): 36–63.

3. It is for this reason that quotes are either answered with different quotes or with the argument that a mistake of some sort has been made. Authors do not even consider that multiple interpretations of a single piece of evidence are possible. If multiple interpretations exist it is because someone has mistranslated, taken evidence out of context, or made some other error. It is assumed that once mistakes have been eliminated the meaning of the evidence will be obvious.

4. Thus Pipes says, "It can also be nothing else but unfamiliarity with the sources that causes Ambasssador Garthoff to" ("Debate," 54) while Garthoff says, "If [Pipes] had read either my books or the original materials" ("Debate," 59).

5. Increasing numbers of theorists are realizing that this may be incorrect, in that our actions may be interpreted, particularly in a crisis, in ways other than our intention. But the assumptions are not changing. This is clear in that the solution proposed for misinterpretation is invariably to find some way to better understand our audience and more sharply refine our message. It is also clear that the problem is noted in regard to *signaling*—the use of the force structure in a given situation to send a particular message—not the use of the force structure *per se*.

6. Kenneth Burke, *Attitudes Towards History*, 3rd ed. (Berkeley: University of California Press, 1984), 308–314.

7. Thus "A 'successful' employees' strike is not one that destroys the em-

ployer financially, it may even be one that never takes place." Thomas Schelling, *The Strategy of Conflict*, 2nd ed. (Cambridge: Harvard University Press, 1980), 6.

8. Schelling, *Conflict*, 22. "If a man knocks at a door and says that he will stab himself on the porch unless given $10, he is more likely to get the $10 if his eyes are bloodshot."

9. See Ashton Carter, et al., *Managing Nuclear Operations* (Washington, D.C.: The Brookings Institution, 1987) for an in-depth treatment of command and control issues.

10. Schelling, *Conflict*, 187–204. For a discussion of the way Schelling's concept has been applied, see Lawrence Freedman, *The Evolution of Nuclear Strategy*, 2nd ed. (New York: St. Martin's Press for the International Institute for Strategic Studies, 1983), 219–224.

11. Freedman, *Evolution*, 188.

12. See Bruce Russett, *The Prisoners of Insecurity: Nuclear Deterrence, The Arms Race, and Arms Control* (New York: Freeman and Co., 1983), 119–130.

13. Freedman, *Evolution*, 182–183.

14. Carol Cohn, "Slick'ems, Glick'ems, Christmas Trees and Cookie Cutters: Nuclear Language and How We Learned to Pat the Bomb," *Bulletin of the Atomic Scientists* 43, no. 5 (1987): 17–24.

15. Philip Wander, "The Third Persona: An Ideological Turn in Rhetorical Theory," *Central States Speech Journal* 35 (Winter 1984): 197–216.

16. William Standenmeir, "Conflict Termination in the Nuclear Era," in Stephen Cimbala and Keith Dunn, eds., *Conflict Termination and Military Strategy: Coercion, Persuasion and War* (Boulder: Westview Press, 1987), 17.

17. Gregory Treverton, "Ending Major Coalition Wars," in Cimbala and Dunn, *Conflict Termination*, 90–91.

18. Freedman, *Evolution*, 180–181.

19. I assume that a "correct" model of communication would have to, at minimum, acknowledge communication as an interactive process. While I have no desire to dictate a particular model this seems to be a basic condition for understanding communication and one almost all communication scholars would agree on.

20. For a description of cultural horizons and their effect on criticism and critics see V. William Balthrop, "Argumentation and the Critical Stance: A Methodological Approach," in J. Robert Cox and Charles Willard, eds., *Advances in Argumentation Theory and Research* (Carbondale: Southern Illinois University Press, 1982), 238–258.

21. Burke, *Attitudes Towards History*, 92–105.

22. I believe this is part of what Burke means when he argues that a symbolic theory of motivations is "in principle" prior to other explanatory theories. See Kenneth Burke, *Permanence and Change*, 3rd ed. (Berkeley: University of California Press, 1984), vi–vii.

23. See Niall Fraser et al., "New Methods for Applying Game Theory to International Conflict," *International Studies Notes* 13, no. 1 (Winter 1987): 1.

24. See William Baugh, *The Politics of Nuclear Balance* (New York: Longman, 1984), 107–115.

25. This is certainly the goal of research in weapons development. See Thomas

Cochran et al., *Nuclear Weapons Data Book Volume 1: U.S. Nuclear Forces and Capabilities* (Cambridge, Mass.: Ballinger Publishing, 1984), 14–15.

26. Kevin Peppe, "Acoustic Showdown for the SSNs," *United States Naval Institute Proceedings* [hereinafter cited as *Proceedings*], 113, no. 1 (1987): 32–37. See also David Miller and Chris Miller, *Modern Naval Combat* (New York: Crescent Books, 1986): 188.

27. Daniel Nylen, "Melee Warfare," *Proceedings* 113, no. 10 (October 1987): 56.

28. Peppe, "Showdown," 32.

29. Freedman, *Evolution*, 189.

30. See Balthrop, "Critical Stance."

31. For example, Russett explains GRIT within the context of Prisoner's Dilemma since each side's activities are meant as explicitly communicative responses to those of the other side. Russett, *Insecurity*, 109–110.

32. I mean these terms as G. Thomas Goodnight uses them. See, for example, his article "Questions of Evacuation and Survival in a Nuclear Conflict: A Case Study in Public Argument and Rhetorical Criticism," in David Zarefsky et al., eds., *Argument in Transition: Proceedings of the Third Summer Conference on Argumentation* (Annandale, Va.: Speech Communication Association, October 15, 1983), 319–338.

Chapter Six

Deterrence Theory and the End of the Cold War: No Way Out

This study has focused primarily on texts from the mid–1980s. It would be only reasonable to ask at this point in what way conclusions drawn from an examination of that period would apply to a world in which the Berlin Wall is down, the nations of the former Warsaw Treaty Organization are applying for NATO membership, and the former president of the former Soviet Union visits the New York Stock Exchange. We live today in a time, after all, when the biggest problem facing those negotiating conventional arms reductions is trying to keep up with force reductions already planned and announced by participating nations. This chapter will make the argument that, in fact, understanding the Cold War analytical frameworks of MAD and warfighting is as essential today as it was ten years ago. For, as we search for conceptual tools capable of guiding us in the new "post post-war" era, it is to MAD and warfighting that analysts turn. If the argument made in previous chapters, that both schools of deterrence theory are fundamentally flawed at the level of underlying assumption, is true, then it is also the case that those flaws are being built into our analysis of the new international order. Haunted, in a sense, by the sins of the fathers, strategists will be unable to purge themselves of inadequate conceptual parameters without first reforming deterrence theory itself. There is no clearer evidence for the end of the Cold War than the fact that the Looking Glass, the Strategic Air Command's flying command center for nuclear war, has been taken off twenty-four-hour alert. For decades, every minute of every day, a command post was in the air, waiting. It did not land until its replacement was confirmed up and ready. Now that is all over.[1] Nonetheless, the new rapprochement in U.S.-Russian relations, and even the final collapse of the Soviet Union, did not make deterrence theory or its study irrelevant by any means. A worldview as dominant, as all pervasive, as deterrence has been for literally decades, does not go away or moderate easily. If anything the need to understand deterrence and its implications is greater than ever today, for without the supporting frame of U.S.-Soviet Cold War, it is less easy to see deterrence theory's influence on our thinking and our policy. Yet the continued impact of deterrence theory on our approach to the world has already been reflected in the responses to several events.

Initially, consider the response to the Iraqi invasion of Kuwait. Efforts to explain what may have motivated Iraq, even in the popular press, were drawn directly from the appeasement theory of war. Thus the question, "who lost Kuwait?" By not sending a strong enough "signal" of will to Iraq, we led them to miscalculate our willingness to go to war.

Transcripts of the Saddam-Glaspie meeting of 25 July suggests that Saddam must have believed he had obtained at least two "green lights" from Washington. One was that the US "takes no position" on the Iraq-Kuwait boundary dispute. The other was a statement that "many people in the US" approved Iraq's favourite price for a barrel of oil, $25. The final signals came in testimony by Jon Kelly before a House subcommittee on 31 July . . . [when he] again affirmed that no formal treaty with Kuwait obliged the US to use American forces to defend the oil state.[2]

Because U.S. representatives gave off the wrong signals, Iraq, like Nazi Germany at Munich, "miscalculated."[3] Indeed, U.S. analysts considering the causes of war in the Gulf could hardly have been more explicit in articulating the links between the situation in 1990 and the need to deter Hitler in 1939 or Stalin after the war.[4] Deterrence, in other words, failed, because the lessons of the Cold War were not carefully or effectively applied. Even without references to Communism, without a vision of the world constructed along East-West lines, the theory still defines the way we articulate and explain foreign policy successes and failures. Thus, "[c]ollective security systems can dissuade aggression only if all the member states pledge in advance to punish any aggressor state for its aggression regardless of its identity. Should dissuasion fail, the UN could attack the aggressor and *roll it back*."[5]

As the relaxation of tensions between the United States and the Soviets accelerated and the United States was able to turn more and more of its attention and resources to North-South issues, and the apparently inexhaustible range of conflict in the less developed parts of the world, the old frameworks remained dominant. Without a Soviet threat to distract us, this tendency will likely continue, informing debate and ultimately policy. Indeed, the president's protestations notwithstanding, American participation in the war in the Gulf did replay Vietnam in one important respect: We were at least to an extent fighting in order to demonstrate our willingness to fight.[6] And the death of the "Vietnam syndrome" is credibility in the bank, another way of saying that American deterrence credibility regarding Third World conflicts has returned.

The second indication that deterrence still reigns supreme is the range of responses made, not only to the changes in the Soviet Union immediately prior to its ultimate collapse, but to the apparent rightward turn in the Soviet Union evidenced in early 1991. What was needed was sound predictive methodologies. What we got were speculations of a return to "neo-Stalinism," an event viewed in some quarters more with relief than anything else: There is always a comfort to dealing with the devil you know. A turn to the right after the Soviet collapse would not be, could not be, however, a simple regression. The experience of reform, even failed reform, could not be forgotten. It became a part of the shared experience of all the Soviet peoples, lingering in the air like the stale odor of old cooking, and it will mean that whatever emerges out of the Gorbachev era will be new, even if it is a hard-line Communist government successful in an overthrow of Boris Yeltsin and other Commonwealth leaders. Reconstituting our approaches from a prior era would have been dangerous in any event, since old styles may not have been best against a hardline Soviet leadership whose every move would be informed and shaped by the events of the late 1980s.[7]

I will first articulate the ways in which deterrence theory, though often described as "sterile,"[8] still dictates the terms of debate. I will then explore the implications of using deterrence theory as a guideline for post–Cold War defense needs and arms control policy. Finally, I will argue that a deterrence-constrained view of the world, by virtue of its inability to accept *change*, freezes us into an unacceptable moment in history.

NEW THINKING AND REASONABLE SUFFICIENCY

With the coming to power of Mikhail Gorbachev, Soviet discussions of national security and defense were increasingly dominated by a loosely defined set of concepts which taken together constitute "New Thinking." Taken at face value, the Soviet position is as follows:[9] prior analyses of national security argued that Soviet armed force was adequate when it could be judged capable of dealing with all potential aggressors at the same time. This vision of security was more than unnecessary, it was counterproductive, for it generated a military machine so large and so capable that it frightened other nations into responding with their own military buildups. By dramatically increasing the forces against which the Soviet Union would have to fight, should deterrence fail, the net effect of total security was to actually *decrease* national security.[10] This was even more of a concern to the extent that the preparations for war were in fact making war more likely. The Soviets were "caught in a vicious cycle. . . . In preparing for the theoretical contingency of a war they could not afford to lose, the Soviets had in practice made world war more likely."[11]

A more appropriate, and more productive, perspective would instead be based on mutual security; a perspective which argues that any individual nation is most secure when its neighbors feel secure as well. For it is within such a structure that stability is to be found, and where the risk of actually going to war would be lowest.[12] This is best accomplished through the creation of a military force structure obviously capable of *non-offensive defense*. This is the condition which exists when a nation has clearly adequate force to defend its own territory, but clearly inadequate force for offensive (presumably aggressive) operations. Any other nation would be able to see that attack would be futile, while at the same time understanding there was little to fear.[13] (It hardly need be added that this is easier said than done, both because of the difficulty in declaring any individual weapon system either offensive or defensive and because of the potential inherent in the counteroffensive to serve as an effective defensive strategy.[14])

Before examining the implications of this announced change in the Soviet doctrinal debate for Western strategic analysis, I would like to point out that, if genuine, if more than a shift in Declaratory Policy, this in important ways serves to validate the conclusions of this study. Primarily, if this shift *was* motivated by a Soviet realization that their prior force structure sent the wrong message to other nations, then it would strongly suggest that the Soviets did in fact acknowledge a persuasive purpose to their force deployments. Thus the importance of the claim made in this study, that a deterrence structure that is incapable of accounting for such a motivation underlying Soviet arms is, to say the least, inadequate, is highlighted. At a minimum this points to the need to retain in potential a view of deterrence as *mutually* communicative.

Furthermore, as I will discuss below, the response of many analysts to these changes, that they are of little importance until manifested in actual force structures, confirms again the view of weapons themselves as nonverbal symbols for communication. Texts are of varying levels of importance, but it is still through forces, their numbers, structure, and characteristics, that we evaluate Soviet intentions and form desiderata for our own forces.

Finally, and most speculative, it is worth asking this question: If in fact Soviet forces were intended purely for use in a military situation, and not for communicative purposes, then how was it possible for the Soviets to take the risk of reformulating their force structure?

Those arguments aside for the moment, the Soviet Union in the form

of the successor Commonwealth, and primarily Russia, is still the primary military threat to the United States. Now, no less than before
Gorbachev, it is American national security—which in a nuclear age
must mean national survival—that is at stake. Changes in Soviet military
doctrine, and force structure, must be interpreted. Declaratory Policy
cannot be taken at face value. Additionally, even if one were predisposed
to presume that the Soviets would follow through on all changes announced, the *meaning* of those changes, like the meaning of *any* fact, is
not self-evident. It must be interpreted in order for it to be of any use
at all. In a socially constructed reality, it is the symbolic structures already
available to us which come into play when a new fact arises.[15]

As Balthrop explains, when something new is encountered, we employ pre-existing frameworks as interpretive schema. The way those
frameworks are employed, however, is variable.

> It is impossible to begin any investigation of an alien phenomenon without some
> framework of knowledge from which to proceed. That framework, however, may
> function in either a *dogmatic* or *pragmatic* way: Functioning dogmatically, existing
> constructs exert such influence on interpretations of experience that those ex-
> periences serve only to reaffirm and to reify existing views of reality. The
> framework, in other words, leads the interpreter to discover only what he or
> she is already capable of understanding. When existing constructs function
> pragmatically, however, they become a way "into" the event, a starting point
> from which a genuine dialogue between the interpreter's existing forms of un-
> derstanding the phenomenon itself may commence. Rather than confirming
> preexistent conceptualizations of reality, such a dialogue may well force those
> conceptualizations to adapt to create new explanations and perceptions of
> reality.[16]

In this instance the analytical structures available are those which grew
out of the Cold War: MAD and warfighting. Because of the structure of
deterrence theory, however, a pragmatic response is impossible. Neither
MAD nor warfighting is ultimately able to incorporate notions of change
in the environment at any level. For both, history ended long ago, with
a single, near-apocalyptic event which continues to shape humanity's
destiny and will do so into the forseeable future.

Interpretive Frames

Did the Soviet Union change? Is Russia any different from the Soviet
Union from a military perspective? Viewed from within the Cold War
analytical frameworks the answer to the first question was, quite simply,
no. The answer to the second is an extremely hesitant maybe. The debate
between MAD and warfighting has shifted, but it has not changed in
any fundamental way. Prior to Gorbachev, the debate was between those

who identified the Soviets as pragmatic and defensive, willing ultimately to accept the limitations imposed on superpower behavior by the mutual possession of devastating military force, and those who portrayed them as ideological and expansionistic, incapable of seeing a qualitative difference between nuclear and conventional weapons. Today the debate is between those who believe that the apparent changes in Soviet policy were in fact overt manifestations of a prior defensive orientation and those who instead see a desperate attempt to reconfigure and retool the Soviet economy in order to both permit participation in higher technology arms races and to use propaganda to slow Western arms development. Soviet activity, in other words, must still be interpreted, but the only interpretive frameworks available are still MAD and warfighting. Those frameworks, since they do not provide an authentic "voice" to the "other," can only be applied dogmatically.

For the MAD author, Gorbachev's New Thinking is a clearer and more forceful articulation of a position held by Soviet leaders for years. It is, they argue, directly descendent from the so-called "Tula Line," articulated by Leonid Brezhnev in 1977. In his speech in the city of Tula, Brezhnev argued that nuclear war could never be won and must never be fought, the implication being that prior Soviet commentary to the effect that world war between the world's two great systems, socialism and capitalism, was inevitable was no longer correct, and that therefore preparation for world war was unnecessary. Such preparation might well be counterproductive if preparation for world war made it more likely. "The basic framework of the new thinking is not new; many of the concepts currently articulated were introduced by the Brezhnev regime in the late 1970s and early 1980s [i]n his oft cited speech at Tula in January 1977."[17] The Tula declaration was important because the "discussion does not mean that the Soviets dismiss the possibility of strategic nuclear war involving preemptive counterforce strikes or abandon the desire to prevail in such a conflict. Rather, they debate the likely character and scope of such a conflict in order to define the military strategy and force posture with which to pursue their strategic objectives."[18] If the recent Soviet position reflects change, in other words, it is more a change in emphasis. The MAD author has maintained *all along* that the Soviets were rational, pragmatic, and defensive. The explicitness of the Soviet declaration of respect for the security of others is what is new. New accommodations in arms control negotiations,[19] or plans to unilaterally reduce weapons, nuclear or conventional,[20] reflect their willingness to finally break the Action Reaction Cycle, to stop imitating our expensive and useless weapons innovations. But that is not a *change* so much as an expression of what MAD authors and Soviet leaders have always known to be true: With both sides' cities permanently held hostage, adding more weapons effects nothing, a "recognition that increases in nuclear forces, particularly ballistic missiles, reached the point of diminishing returns."[21] As before Gorbachev, then, the theoretical structure generates an explanation for the evidence at hand consistent with that theoretical structure. And, once again, primary emphasis for the MAD author is placed on textual evidence in order to incorporate understandings of more quantitative sources of proof. They continue to emphasize the need to examine not only capability, but doctrine as well.[22] If few physical changes have been noticed, that may well be the result of honest confusion within the Soviet ranks. New Thinking, they argue, is still not only vague and poorly defined, but constantly in flux,[23] particularly with the arrival of newly relevant civilian analysts never heard from before.[24] Rather than condemning the slow pace of change in forces, it is more essential that we carefully follow the internal debates. For example, a MAD author would state:

[The Soviets are debating the use of the term nuclear war as opposed to the term nuclear missile catastrophe.] While this theorizing may seem very abstract to most American readers, it could be a very significant step toward substituting a form of minimum deterrence based on war-fighting capabilities. The contingency of *war* may justify hedging preparations for waging it; the contingency of *catastrophe* cannot, it can justify only measures to avert the possibility.[25]

A warfighter would merely complain that "[s]o far as can been seen, the 'new' Soviet military thinking has been tactical. It is primarily an acceptance, at least for the moment, of such new realities as independence in Eastern Europe: not so much a doctrinal reversal."[26] Or as another author noted, were "his [Gorabchev's] commitment to Western concepts in fact real, changes in the Soviet budget and military programs would be noticeable. But there has been nothing."[27]

For MAD analysts change is impossible because the single defining characteristic of the age is the nature of nuclear weapons. The laws of physics do not change. Evidence of a changing *audience* means little to these analysts since they always thought the Soviet audience to be knowable through the essential characteristic that they were constrained in the same way as the United States by the risks imposed by the very existence of nuclear weapons. What is pertinent to doctrine is the destructive potential of the weapons and our inability—on either side—to defend against them. There is no reason to believe that either of those conditions are going to change. Thus for the MAD analyst history froze, if not at Los Alamos,[28] then at that moment in time when both sides acquired a secure second strike, and nothing has, or can be, changed fundamentally since for "the essence of the matter is not quantitative, but qualitative."[29]

The warfighters, of course, are loathe to take Soviet doctrinal statements on face value, particularly when they indicate an acceptance of a need for cooperation and peaceful coexistance with the West. Their interpretation of New Thinking and reasonable sufficiency is less straightforward and more complex as a result. Warfighters still believe the Soviets to have been ideologically driven, aggressive, and expansionist right to the bitter end. But how can an aggressive Soviet Union be reconciled with a Soviet willingness to reduce force levels, particularly unilaterally?

The answer for the warfighter lies in the concept of *peredyshka*. While *glasnost* and *perestroika* have become household words in the West, it is peredyshka which occupies the warfighter. They translate the concept as breathing space or breathing spell, a "tactical retreat for the purpose of a later strategic offensive."[30] Their argument develops as follows: the Soviet economy was on the brink of collapse. While in itself hardly a controversial claim, the warfighters argue that the situation is in no small part due to the fact that the Soviet military buildup of the 1970s triggered the response of the early Reagan Administration: an enormous force buildup and modernization,[31] which the Soviets than felt bound to match. The warfighters believe, then, just as the MAD authors do, that the Soviets learned from this experience that offensive buildups and deployments on their part are provocative and therefore, at least in the short term, counterproductive. All that is accomplished by such actions is a stronger Western threat, and even greater demands for military resources. For the Soviet system to recover economically it was a breathing space, a period of international calm—in short, New Thinking—that was necessary.

New Thinking is driven not only by economic troubles in the civilian sector of the Soviet system (for warfighters still do not believe the Soviet leadership cared particularly about civilian hardships) but by the realization that the next round of the arms race will focus on high technology areas in which they were incapable of competing. Without a retooled and modernized economy, and Western aid,[32] they have little hope of producing the advances of microcircuitry, miniaturization, or computer technology that will be necessary.[33] But by shifting their emphasis from the military to the civilian sector of the economy, for at least a time, they could make themselves ready to compete. Thus the "agenda is not simply more butter and fewer guns . . . but, rather, fewer off-the-shelf guns now for the sake of more sophisticated guns (and computers!) later."[34] For, "looking down the road to the year 2000 and beyond, the Kremlin leadership may be alarmed. Follow-on weaponry will be dependent upon a modernized economy, a revitalized science and technology, and a more capable work force."[35] It was simultaneously necessary to slow the pace of Western military advancements.

Given current exigencies, the U.S.S.R. simply cannot compete across the broad spectrum of technological innovation which has characterized U.S. defense programs over this decade. To keep up it needs to blunt the edge of the competition—to slow its pace, as well as delimit its scope. And, as the experience of earlier detente periods has taught it, one of the most effective ways to get a handle on how the West responds to the threat is through manipulation of how the West perceives the threat.[36]

Because of this ability on the part of the Soviet Union to manipulate Western threat perceptions, their unilateral drawdowns of forces and accommodating negotiating postures, while essential to the goal of sustaining the development of a modern fighting force into the next century at the conventional level, have other dividends that, while of a short-term nature, are too substantial to ignore.

Seemingly removing the threat to Europe, while simultaneously negotiating deep cuts in strategic nuclear arsenals, the Soviets made it increasingly difficult to maintain NATO cohesion or for Western governments to maintain high levels of defense spending in the midst of increasingly strident calls for the realization of an economic "Peace Dividend."[37] Unilateral measures of reduction are therefore virtually forced upon the West, permitting the Soviets to make a virtue out of a necessity, undoing the buildup of the Reagan-Thatcher years without having to fire a single shot as "concerns over the bottom line . . . outweight [sic] concerns over the front line."[38] This is of concern since it means that "the Soviets are setting the terms of *our* national security debate and are well along in their effort to manage the superpower competition through management of Western threat perception."[39] This risks increasing tension between the members of the Western alliance,[40] makes the United States appear inflexible and aggressive,[41] and, perhaps most dangerous of all, delegitimates the deployment of nuclear weapons and their modernization.[42]

Kremlin leaders make major efforts to convince the outside world that fundamental changes are occurring in Soviet military policies. . . . But there is nothing new in these expressions. Gorbachev's predecessors implemented these slogans to change Western perceptions of Soviet military power. What is new is the skill of the public relations campaign to sell Gorbachev as the driving force behind glasnost and perestroika.[43]

There appears to be no question on the part of these authors that this manipulation is not only skillful but quite intentional.[44]

Furthermore, on the conventional level, force reductions carry their own intrinsic benefits. They permit a streamlined, more professional force, with the elimination of obsolete equipment. Here warfighters co-opt and employ all the arguments used by MAD authors to indict claims of Soviet military superiority made during the Reagan administration. In this context such arguments—that the Soviet forces are of low quality, that they tend to stockpile older models that would have been scrapped under the American system, and so forth—now become reasons why the size of Soviet force cuts are not meaningful and therefore are not reflective of a real change.[45]

The restructuring of Soviet forces along these lines, combined with Eastern Europe's new status as a defensive buffer zone for NATO,[46] probably destroys the Soviet capacity for offensive moves "in-place," the so-called "standing start." This does not mean, however, that they would be unable to initiate hostilities on the Central Front. If they were successful in obtaining a restructuring of NATO forces their chances of success in such a venture could in fact be greater *after* force reductions were completed. Not only would such reductions maximize the inherent advantage the Soviets have over the United States for a European conflict, with supply lines thousands of miles shorter,[47] any reductions could leave NATO's line of forward defense stretched so thin that puncturing those lines would be far easier than before.[48] Traditional notions of the advantages which inhere in the defense are thus upended.[49]

Thus for the warfighter as for the MAD author the theoretical framework with which they work still functions in the same way. Whether increasing or decreasing, Soviet forces must be *explained*; motives must still be imputed to hardware. Or, in the words of one analyst, the "landing gear of the MiG-29 or the treads of the T-80 tank will not speak for themselves . . . specs will not explain Soviet intentions."[50] The theories therefore generate an explanation for the available evidence which is internally consistent, which focuses on hardware over texts, and which cannot be disconfirmed.

Again for the warfighter as for the MAD advocate change is impossible. The single defining characteristic of the age is the nature of the Soviet Union.

To bring about fundamental change in the factor underlying Soviet national strategy would require reversing many of the ingrained attitudes of Slavic culture, the accepted lessons from the experience of Russian history, and the imperatives of Marxist-Leninist ideology—all of which create the national mindset that shapes Soviet national goals. Even in this time of great turmoil, it is unlikely that more than a thousand years of culture and history will be overcome or seventy years of propagated ideology will be undone.[51]

Periodically, and temporarily, they give the *appearance* of change, but it is always a calculated performance, always designed for Soviet advantage, and always revealed in the end to be a sham, despite the apparently unending willingness of some in the West to be naively taken in. Warfighters lay out ever stricter litmus tests, hurdles the Soviets must pass in order to prove that *this* time is different.[52] Yet each time such a test is passed interpretation again takes place which explains it as temporary, calculated, targeted at Western publics.[53] There is no action which cannot be interpreted as suspicious within this context.[54] Change is, in short, inauthentic. Standards for assessing and evaluating apparent changes are fluid and indeterminate, flowing with each sign of change so as to demonstrate anew Soviet disingeniousness. For the warfighter history froze in 1917, with the birth of a nation ideologically driven to see through world revolution and the death of capitalism: "[F]or the liberals the threat is nuclear technology, not the Russians; for the conservatives the threat is the Russians, not the technology."[55] Everything else since is merely a part of that overarching drama, a struggle to the death between two systems where the stakes are infinite.[56]

Based on mechanistic models of communication neither MAD nor warfighting is able to incorporate conceptions of a changing context. When there is no understanding of communication as an interactive phenomena the image of the other is of necessity frozen in time. Thus while others may herald the most radical changes in international relations in forty-five years, deterrence theorists are able to see nothing more than minor adjustments in a self-perpetuating status quo.

Policy Choices

As a result of the inability to incorporate notions of change, there has been the gradual development of a consensus between advocates of MAD and warfighting on specific policies rarely, if ever, seen before. For different reasons the conclusions arrived at regarding the structure of U.S.-Soviet relations in a post–Gorbachev world are shockingly similar. The differences in interpretation of New Thinking, it should be remembered, are differences primarily over the nature of adjustments in the *conventional* force balance. It is in the relationship between conventional and nuclear arms, and the way those weapons interact for deterrent purposes, that the two sides come together.

This convergence is seen most clearly in the response to initiatives in strategic and tactical nuclear arms control. The policy prescriptions offered by the two sides to the debate are here far more in concert than in opposition. Consider initially the response to the Intermediate Nuclear Forces (INF) Treaty of 1987.

That treaty eliminated precisely the weapons, the Pershing IIs and GLCMs, over which advocates of MAD and warfighting had most violently disagreed in the European context. Nonetheless, the treaty was substantially more important from a symbolic perspective, as a sign of improving U.S.-Soviet relations and a newly accommodationist Soviet posture, than it was from a "purely" military perspective.[57] After all, "the issues involved are complex and technical, the desire to remove the nuclear threat to mankind is legitimate and strong, and the INF agreement seems superficially to be very favorable to the West. Yet the INF treaty has only a small quantitative effect on the nuclear threat; its main significance is political and strategic, not military."[58] To deterrence theorists, its real importance lay in the question of what was to *follow* the INF. Key barriers to arms control, especially in the area of verification,[59] were now down. Great damage was done to the ability of Western governments to employ standard rhetorics of a "Soviet threat" to ensure continuing support for arms buildups.[60] It now appeared possible to proceed with negotiations over "Triple Zero," functionally denuclearizing Europe.

Deterrence theorists rejected such an option as with a single voice. The dispute between MAD and warfighting authors was over the reasoning behind the need to retain nuclear weapons in Europe and some vestige of Flexible Response, but not over the goal itself.

For the warfighter Soviet willingness to negotiate an INF Treaty and an eagerness to go farther was no surprise. They have argued for some time that it would be the preferred Soviet strategy to attack Western Europe with conventional weapons only, while simultaneously denying NATO the opportunity to escalate the war to the nuclear level (either by winning before the alliance could take the decision to go nuclear or by destroying the nuclear weapons and support facilities before such a decision could be made and before decisive victory on the continent). This physical denuclearization of the conflict would presumably be one of the Soviet military's primary goals should war break out in Europe: They would seek the physical destruction of the ability to escalate prior to the political decision's being made. Given that view, how much easier it would be for the Soviets if NATO denuclearized itself before fighting began, either through a series of arms control agreements or through unilateral moves imposed by publics unwilling to support the continued deployment of nuclear weapons on their national territories. "The historical bottom line under the INF Treaty is that Gorbachev has achieved what his predecessors failed to achieve: a long stride toward the denuclearization of NATO Europe."[61] The goal of the warfighter remains deterrence by denial, but nuclear weapons are essential to communicating to the Soviet Union NATO's ability to follow through. Nuclear weapons, in other words, convey a critical component of the overall deterrent message, and the specifics of weapons characteristics are here less important than is the fact that some of the weapons deployed continue to be nuclear as opposed to conventional.

While the MAD author disagrees on the issue of Soviet motivation, he or she clearly agrees on the need to retain a specifically European nuclear capability. Nuclear weapons deployed on European soil serve as explicit symbols of the risks embodied in any clash of arms, at any level, between nuclear powers.[62] The goal is still deterrence by punishment but even with a cooperative adversary eager to reduce tensions the reminder is necessary as insurance against that day of crisis when someone somewhere may be tempted, out of panic, desperation, or—most likely of all—miscalculation to take the risk.

Thus for both sets of theorists the inability to acknowledge change directly affects beliefs about appropriate message construction. For the warfighter even a Soviet renunciation of the ability to begin a war without obvious and lengthy mobilization does not undermine the need to retain at all times a persuasive threat to escalate any conflict. And for the MAD advocate a hedge must be retained against inadvertent or accidental escalation, even under circumstances where other channels of communication are beginning to open up: words are still not as trustworthy as the nonverbal. Nothing changes the risks imposed by Soviet expansionism on the one hand and by the dynamics of nuclear weapons on the other. The system itself is fraught with peril, and reductions in tensions matter little so long as tension remains. Yet as long as the Soviets continue a commitment to Communist ideology (and they always will, whatever Soviet propaganda says) and so long as they retain nuclear weapons (which they must, since we will, which we must, since they will[63]) tension will remain.

A similar convergence occurs over proposals for deep cuts in strategic nuclear weapons such as the Strategic Arms Reductions Treaty (START). Although it is still the case that the two schools disagree over normative force structures along the lines described previously, and therefore disagree over the particulars of negotiating postures, there are substantial points of agreement. As with the need for nuclear weapons in Europe, policy is advocated for reasons as radically different as the schools of thought themselves. Nonetheless, it is still the case that there are points of agreement.

There are three broad areas where this is true. The first is the need to alter the ratio of warheads to Strategic Nuclear Delivery Vehicles (SNDVs), or launch platforms. As of this writing, it appears that the START Treaty will be structured in such a way as to reduce the number of warheads per missile.[64] The question is whether or not that is a good idea. For the MAD advocate the answer is definitely yes. Reducing MIRVing (the placement of Multiple Independent Reentry Vehicles on a single missile) reduces incentives to launch by making both sides' retaliatory forces less vulnerable and, more importantly, by eliminating benefits that might otherwise accrue from launching first. When forces are heavily MIRVed, one side might be tempted to attack in a crisis for Damage Limitation purposes, since each warhead launched could neutralize up to ten enemy warheads. With fewer warheads per missile, the exchange ratio shifts in favor of waiting.[65]

To the warfighter, reducing the warheads per missile involves a cost, a calculated risk, since there would be fewer American warheads available for Escalation Dominance.[66] What makes that risk worthwhile, however, or at least worth exploring, is that it would simultaneously reduce precisely those elements of the Soviet arsenal posing the largest threat to American ICBMs. Thus in this instance as well, the rationales for support of policy differ dramatically, based as they are on different argument structures, but the ultimate answer is the same.

The second level of agreement regarding deep cuts concerns the ultimate size of the nuclear arsenals. Whether or not the Soviet willingness to engage in verifiable nuclear arms control was motivated by benign intent or not, they did appear willing. But as many authors have noted, it would be foolish to enter negotiations without a clear picture of where we would like to end up. Simply put, "[w]e have to know where we want to go before we decide how to get there."[67] That determination must be based on "a sound strategy for deterring the Soviets and on some general strategic force planning criteria for measuring our ability to meet that strategy."[68] The urgency with which this claim is made no doubt has something to do with the horror with which strategic analysts of all stripes reacted to the near deal reportedly discussed between Reagan and Gorbachev in their meeting at Reykjavik, Iceland. That deal would, if consummated, have led to the elimination of ballistic missiles on both sides, and was discussed without prior warning to advisors.[69]

The response of strategic theorists to potential START outcomes is similar to their reaction to that near deal. Both sides agree that stability—whether defined as secure second-strike ability or as Escalation Dominance—can be retained with far fewer warheads than are currently deployed. They further agree that the system can take reductions down to between three and six thousand warheads. Most importantly, they further agree that additional reductions below that level would be destabilizing. Below two to three thousand neither side believes that adequate coverage of target sets could be maintained.

For the warfighter, reductions in Soviet arsenals reduces the target set concomitantly. That is still a threshold issue, nonetheless. In other words, below a certain point, it would be impossible to retain dominance over the Soviets, cover all necessary Other Military Targets, and still have the ability to threaten escalation to industrial and other post recovery targets.[70] For the MAD author a certain number of warheads is necessary to guarantee enough redundancy to ensure that under all circumstances a secure second-strike capability is clearly and obviously available.[71]

The notion of redundancy is central to the third area of agreement. Although for different reasons, both sides have previously defended a triad-basing system. Here both sets of theorists agree that the START Treaty must be structured in such a way as to protect the traditional triad structure.[72] And, in this instance, they even agree on the rationale.

The argument is as follows.[73] In order for the Soviets to destroy hardened American ICBM silos the primary requirement is accuracy. They would therefore need to use their own ICBMs, with a flight time of approximately thirty minutes and a warning time of between fifteen and twenty. For the Soviets to destroy American alert bombers and submarine pens the primary requirement would be speed, since the whole point of attacking these facilities is to prevent the bombers from launching and the submarines from being flushed. They would therefore presumably employ SLBMs launched from submarines off the American coast, flight time of approximately fifteen minutes, warning time of five to seven minutes.

This presents the Soviets with an inescapable tactical dilemma. They have two choices: they can either launch ICBMs and SLBMs simultaneously or launch so that they impact simultaneously, a fifteen-minute gap between launches. If they launch at the same time, there would in all probability be inadequate time for the United States to get the bulk of the bombers and submarines off. But their destruction, providing incontestable proof that an attack upon the United States was indeed under way, would provide fifteen or more minutes of warning, more than enough time to launch the ICBMs. The Soviets would therefore face total destruction whether that is defined in the terms of MAD or of warfighting.

Their alternative is little more attractive. If they launch so that their weapons land simultaneously there would be a twenty-minute gap in which the United States would have warning of attack, since the Soviet ICBMs would have been launched but not the Soviet SLBMs. This would provide more than enough time for the launch of the bombers and submarines since even an American president reluctant to launch without confirmed proof of attack would be willing to take the obvious, practical, and defensive step of getting the bombers and submarines, which can always be recalled, out of harm's way. Thus again the Soviets face destruction.

The triad, by virtue of incorporating different characteristics into the American arsenal, imposes different and mutually exclusive demands upon a Soviet Union intent upon attack. So long as all three weapons platforms are retained, in other words, it is impossible for the Soviets to launch a disarming first strike. It is not just redundancy but redundancy based on distinct weapons characteristics that ensures deterrence.

From the perspective of deterrence theorists of all stripes there is, in other words, no way out of the situation we find ourselves in. The goal of START is not, cannot be, disarmament.[74] Stability cannot be ensured without nuclear arsenals in place and ready. Nuclear weapons cannot be "uninvented." START will not "alter the basic nuclear strategies of either side," but will only "moderate the strategic competition and make it more predictable."[75] We are fated "not to inevitable general war but, at a minimum, to policies of balanced power and deterrence."[76] Thus deterrence theorists point out their own permanent relevance, for "many aspects of traditional U.S. and Western analysis of nuclear issues would remain relevant, though transformed in their implementation by changes in the world context."[77] Meanwhile, "complete nuclear disarmament should be consigned firmly to the fantasy, or nightmare, file."[78]

The nuclear era and the Cold War were born at about the same time, but the end of the Cold War will not mean the end of nuclear weapons. No amount of international reconciliation and no amount of arms control will erase the knowledge of how to build such weapons and, while revolutionary reductions may well be possible, there is little real prospect of total nuclear disarmament. So nuclear weapons will continue to exist and will require management and analysis. In principle, nuclear management should be easier in a world of reduced confrontation, but such a world is also likely to be more complex than the simple divisions of the Cold War—and it cannot be entirely free of the spectre of a revived Cold War.[79]

Were both sides to disarm the system would become far too brittle, too vulnerable to "breakout."[80]

Thus for both sides the deterrent structures imposed by nuclear forces are forever. As Carol Cohn has argued, there is no construct for "peace" in the strategic lexicon of deterrence.[81] Perpetual stability is the best we can do. And there is no acknowledgment in the literature of a future in which this condition can be shrugged off. For the United States and the Soviet Union, and now for Russia, giving up nuclear weapons would be like giving up breathing.

Similarly, as we move towards a unified Europe, and a democratic nonaligned Eastern Europe, with the debate now being primarily over which institutional structures are likely to be most efficient, negotiations over conventional forces in Europe merely strengthen our need to have nuclear weapons on the continent.[82] Coupling, whether Europeans want it or not, remains an absolute necessity.

Thus we come full circle. Stretched to the fullest intellectual limits deterrence theory fails: it cannot adjust to the realities of a new age. Both schools are pushed to logical extremes which, although utterly reasonable from within the parameters of deterrence theory, make little sense when considered from outside of those perspectives. These extremes take different shape, as one would expect, for MAD and warfighting.

But as the dominance of nuclear deterrence appears to fade from the international scene, the grasp of deterrence theorists tightens. Before examining the "end game" for MAD and for warfighting, I would like to point out that, ironically, where authors in the 1980s worried about and warned of the "conventionalization" of nuclear weapons, in actual fact MAD and warfighting authors are currently joined together in the nuclearization of conventional weapons. Despite the emphasis on the interaction between nuclear and conventional deterrence there is a substantial focus on conventional weapons independently. And it is in that literature that the concepts and constructs developed in order to deal with nuclear weapons have expanded to the point where they now dominate the discussion of conventional-only deterrence. Thus the complaint in the literature, and the establishment of a new goal: "The literature lacks, however, a systematic assessment of the nature of stability at the conventional level that NATO is seeking. The literature has not defined a criteria for determining . . . 'stability'. . . ."[83] For, just as when discussing nuclear weapons, an "unstable political relationship can destabilize an otherwise stable military relationship. Similarly an unstable military relationship can provide the opportunity for conflict if political relationships become stable."[84] And, just as in the nuclear sphere, the weapons themselves carry the burden of communication and of assuring a healthy relationship between nations.

For many authors the goal of conventional arms control ought be defined in the same way as it is for nuclear arms control. That means that, as with nuclear arms, motivations are measured by military force. No matter how the political relationship is progressing, there will need to be tremendous sensitivity to what capabilities are available to either side, and the status of the military balance alone could prove dangerously destabilizing and provocative. "[H]opes of reducing tensions will prove illusory if either side perceives the military balance has tilted against it."[85] As with nuclear weapons, the evaluation must involve more than simply the numbers of weapon systems owned by each side, but their quality, their missions, the way they would interact with the forces of the opponent on the battlefield.[86]

On the military level, we argue that stability derives from minimizing incentives for preemptive attack. To many, parity or balance of military forces is the dominant measure of stability, owing in part to the traditions of nuclear arms control and the natural inclination to focus on numbers of weapons systems as the currency of arms control agreements. Parity does indeed serve important political purposes and provides a useful and visible measure of the military effect of an arms control agreement. Nonetheless . . . [w]hat matters is whether the military relationship is such that it offers incentives to either side to initiate conflict, either because the likelihood of success is good or because the risks of failure are acceptable.[87]

The new concern with conventional deterrence, encouraged no doubt by the attention given to New Thinking, provides a new arena for deterrence theorists.[88] The binding, defining terms of debate become those of the nuclear debate. The greatest concern for security in Europe after conventional arms control is comparative ability for *reconstitution*. How quickly can the two sides, should the need arise, mobilize and return to full (i.e. offensively capable) force levels? Can NATO be protected from the Soviet Union's intrinsic geographic advantage, with supply lines thousands of miles shorter than those of NATO? Can forces be in place to deal with time urgent targets quickly enough?

Yet, these changes, even if all faithfully implemented, would still leave Moscow with an ability to launch an offensive against NATO within two and three weeks from the day of the outbreak of conflict, while reducing precisely those NATO assets (air and naval power) that can be used to slow down Soviet mobilization and secure the arrival of U.S. reinforcements. Thus, the net impact of the present Soviet conventional arms control proposals is highly advantageous to the Soviet Union. Consequently, despite oft-repeated Western speculations about the Soviet military's opposition to Gorbachev's arms control schemes, harmony appears to reign between Soviet security requirements, as defined by the military, and Soviet political and foreign policy imperatives, as enunciated by Gorbachev.[89]

What is this but a translation of the debate over prompt Hard Target Kill capability into the terms of the conventional debate? Both sides, further, explicitly acknowledge that new high technology weapons will permit conventional weapons to "take over" targets from the nuclear arsenal.[90] But because the targets will be the same, the effect on deterrence will be the same and, in the end, nuclear discourse invades and occupies the conventional debate. Now not only is nuclear disarmament rejected, it is almost irrelevant to the doctrinal debate, as the system remains the same, whether the forces are nuclear or not.

The intellectual stagnation of deterrence theory is reflected, as well, in the logical extremes to which deterrence theory is pushed. For the warfighter this extremism is reflected in the recent discovery of War Termination as a disciplinary offshoot all its own, worthy of independent articulation and defense.[91] War Termination is the ability to quickly "turn off" a war, specifically a nuclear war, before the natural termination that would occur as a result of both sides fighting until exhausted. While any nuclear war of any size or duration would produce unprecedented levels of destruction, an all-out nuclear war would, say advocates of War Termination, surely be the worst of all possible outcomes.

While surely the urgency of War Termination would never be as apparent as after a nuclear war had begun, it is an unfortunate truth, contend these authors, that there would be no worse time to consider effective War Termination procedures. Their argument is that procedures, battle plans, even force structures must be in place before the war. For unless "the expectation that war termination is important finds its way into the organizational routines and standard operating procedures in peacetime, war termination capabilities will not be available in wartime."[92] For, of course, a "question to be asked is whether it is at all wise to plan on having effective strategic warning, or even timely, unambiguous tactical warning."[93] Some have gone so far as to suggest menus of cease fire arrangements, in place and negotiated now.[94] If a war were to start without appropriate attention having been given to War Termination in advance, the only alternative is a level of destruction that would be absolutely devastating.[95]

If these arguments are correct, then it logically follows that so long as the risk of nuclear war is greater than zero, simple prudence would dictate that steps be taken to facilitate War Termination should the worst happen. And since the risk is always greater than zero, obviously War Termination activities would make a wise investment, since "we cannot allow both our security and our survival to rest exclusively upon the hope that war between the United States and the U.S.S.R. will never occur."[96]

Here is the devil's dilemma: If the new technologies make strategic conflict five times more likely and five times more negotiable, how do we vote?... The choice, if it comes to that, between making wars less likely and less negotiable or more likely and more negotiable, pivots on the internalized (and implicit) models of the behavior of humans: If war is avoidable, and human behavior in war is irrational, making wars less likely—even at the expense of making them less negotiable—is to be preferred. But if, by the nature of humans, war is inevitable, making those wars more negotiable and less destructive will be preferred. Those models of human behavior are deeply ingrained, seldom argued, and almost impossible to change. They have to do with the perfectability of humans: they are at the very center of human faith.[97]

What this eminently reasonable argument disguises, however, is that the notion of "pre-war" preparation for War Termination involves a radical shift in presumption. Says one author,

[W]e have rounded our logical circle again. If we care morally about nothing but preventing a nuclear war in the first place, we can safely close our minds to all talk of limited nuclear wars. If we morally must identify not only with the victims of the first day of a thermonuclear war but with the possible victims of the fifth or fifteenth day, we will be much more torn, and we will have to wander down some of the very paths of analysis and speculation that indeed can be so treacherous.[98]

What is so amazing about such statements is that they take the failure of deterrence for granted, for while it is obviously true that all victims of such a war are equally deserving of attention, it is presumably also true that if war prevention were feasible it ought receive the greatest priority, particularly if War Termination cut against the possibility of war prevention, even on the margin. Yet for the War Terminator, as Ikle explained it simply above, "we cannot allow both our security and our survival to rest exclusively upon the hope that war between the United States and the U.S.S.R. will never occur."

Deterrence theory, either school, builds on, is centered on, a presumption against any action increasing the probability of nuclear war. Warfighters and MAD authors may disagree on which actions those are, but they certainly agree on the goal. War Termination procedures involve taking a number of steps that could increase the risk of war.[99] However, presumption, in a deterrence dominated world, is in favor of avoiding nuclear war even if that might mean such a war, if it came, would ultimately be more difficult to stop.

How can reasonable people be willing to accept an increased risk of war when they themselves concede that even an exceedingly limited war would be a disaster? War Termination authors defend this evaluation on the basis of two arguments. The first is simply an assessment that any risk of war is intolerable so long as War Termination procedures are absent. It is here that these authors signal the exhaustion of deterrence with their own resignation. Because any risk requires War Termination, probability becomes irrelevant in evaluating policy options. All risks are treated as equivalent. So long as any risk exists then conceptually nuclear war might as well be inevitable. Once that move is made, any efforts designed to maximize deterrence and reduce the risk of war becomes obviously secondary. When the requirements of deterrence and those of War Termination come into conflict War Termination has to win. For these authors deterrence has reached the end of the line. Unable to guarantee an elimination of risk in a world where the continued existence of nuclear weapons is presumed, deterrence is simply rejected. If there will always be a risk of nuclear war then we might as well shift our energies and attention to a useful direction that might actually produce results, since war avoidance will never completely succeed, and start planning to make war as painless as possible.

The second reason why increasing the risk of war is irrelevant is more prosaic, and more familiar. Like the warfighters whose positions they often share, War Terminators place the onus on the Soviets. If and when a nuclear war begins the Soviets will fight to win. "In Soviet doctrine, no quarter is to be given. There are to be no negotiations."[100] This attitude will be somewhat of a problem for War Termination efforts since the "Soviet goal of total victory in a nuclear war precludes the possibility of war termination short of its attainment."[101] After all, the Soviets "regard a nuclear war with the United States as the ultimate test of their world revolutionary war movement. Accordingly, it is to be approached with a revolutionary or religious zeal."[102] If War Termination is to be something other than surrender, the United States must be able to fight to win as well. And since a nuclear war, unlike prior conflicts, will be strictly "come as you are" the best way to prepare for War Termination is to do everything possible to maintain force superiority at all levels at all times.[103] The emphasis on Escalation Control and Escalation Dominance promotes advocacy of force structures virtually indistinguishable from those advocated by the more ordinary garden variety warfighter.

[The rules for Termination preparation:] 1. Be militarily stronger than the enemy. . . . 2. Be more resolute in prospective defense than the enemy anticipates being in pursuit of gain. . . . 3. Do not assault the enemy's political and military leadership, the means of communication to his armed forces, or his assets for attack assessment—or, assault only some targets in these categories, and those very carefully. . . . 4. Do not strike Soviet home territory with nuclear weapons. . . . 5. Do not insist upon conditions for war termination that the Soviet Union must refuse—or, at least, wage a great deal of war to resist. . . . 6. Be militarily stronger than the enemy. Just on the off-chance that any reader might believe that the author was not really very serious about rule 1.[104]

Our ability to bring nuclear war to an end without intolerable political concessions would be predicated on retaining better options at any given time than those available to the Soviet Union. It is just not good enough to ensure that deterrence cannot fail or that, if it does, nothing the United States could do would make a difference. The side capable of withstanding the worst of the effects of a nuclear war will have superior means to effect the termination of such a conflict on terms more satisfactory to itself. In this respect, profound differences exist between the approaches taken by the Soviet Union and the United States and its allies to the vexing problems of strategic war termination.[105]

Note that for this author even a guarantee of *successful* deterrence is not enough to end our dilemma or our need to prepare for War Termination. After all, it "is obvious that our ability to bring nuclear war to an end without intolerable political concessions is predicated on having available, at any given time, better options than the Soviets."[106] And yet, U.S. "acquisitions policy" for weapons development and procurement has simply "not provided the requisite forces for flexible targeting and escalation control in some instances."[107] Certainly the "ideal shopping list" matches that of the warfighter—"accurate weapons that are survivable [so they do not need to be used too quickly] and highly flexible [to permit retargetting]."[108] It is important to remember that the criteria by which a nuclear arsenal is judged is far more difficult to meet if the standard develops out of a War Termination scenario, since it then becomes not preferable, but vital, that the United States be assured of retaining superiority *after* the first salvo.[109]

Thus these authors sound on the surface like other warfighters, saying things like "the key to success in de-escalation has to be an escalation control . . . or an escalation dominance"[110] but then pushing past those arguments, taking them to a previously unheard of logical extreme, where the same author also says, for example, "one may need to escalate rapidly if one is later to be in a position to de-escalate on politically acceptable terms."[111] Hence where the warfighter talks the language of capability and perception, the War Terminator talks the language of action. This is believed a necessary hedge since the starting point is the assumption that if the Soviets believed

they could attack with relative impunity, it could be considered criminal for the Soviet leadership not to seize the opportunity. . . . The more serious the crisis, the more plausible would be a Soviet first strike, and the greater would be the preparations required for deterrence. Thus, U.S. deterrent forces should be designed to deter in a severe crisis, not just during peacetime.[112]

The difference, again, is that whatever deterrence value would be gained through such deployments, manifested in effective manipulation of the probability of war, is purely additive.[113]

The primary critique of policies designed to affect the "course and outcome" of a nuclear war from deterrence advocates would be that such activities and deployments make war thinkable by making it appear limitable. But that argument is made meaningless, since the likelihood of nuclear war is not in any way affected by *American* perceptions. These authors are not particularly concerned one way or the other about affecting U.S. sensibilities other than to structure forces so as to permit the NCA to fight to win when the time comes. They themselves are not positive nuclear war can be limited,[114] but since it is treated as not just a real threat but as a potent and constant one, the hope of limiting it when it comes is the only game in town.

War Termination takes the conventionalization of nuclear war beyond anything Robert Jervis ever dreamed of. Obviously limited nuclear war must be assumed. If nuclear war cannot be controlled, for any of the reasons normally given—the fragility of command and control, the likelihood that national officials would seek revenge under the stress, the physical problems attendant to accurate and coordinated strikes—then it is not even worth discussing War Termination.[115] Furthermore, War

Termination revives the appeasement theory of war, central to the war-fighter's conception of deterrence, and applies them to the way a war way would be *fought*. "Wars will be won by military action, but they will be lost by political will and control."[116]

With deterrence rejected as at best inconsequential, War Termination, if accepted, implies the need for constant vigorous development, deployment, and modernization of nuclear forces. Nothing the Soviets do changes that requirement except in so far that their force levels dictate what levels we need to maintain superiority. War Terminators quickly concede that any discussion of methods for terminating a nuclear war is completely dependent on the boundary conditions set by the scenario chosen.[117] There is, however, no way to predict in advance which scenario we will actually need to be prepared for. The only possible answer then, is to prepare for *all* of them, including ones we have yet to conceive of. "Just because theorists can conceive of particular processes, or series of options, and give them names, it does not follow that those processes or options necessarily have, or might have, any reality beyond the realm of theory."[118] "There is no certainty that our present concepts of strategic conflict are valid."[119] Or, to phrase it somewhat more eloquently, the "point is that the course of, and problems in, terminating a Soviet-American war might not be highly variable with reference to the very rich menu of outbreak scenarios that can be imagined."[120] Thus are we trapped, not just with nuclear weapons, but with a perpetual quest for preparedness for controlling the uncontrollable since at some level, the scenario itself becomes meaningless.[121]

The more troubling implication, should this conceptual move gain credibility, is the way War Termination objectifies society itself. Since no value has meaning once a society is destroyed, the ability to preserve society in a post-attack world must be the predominant value in society if the War Terminator's risk assessment is correct. This is reminiscent of articulations about social priorities made first by the nuclear freeze movement.[122] All other values in conflict with the demands of War Termination must give way. The goal, the purpose of society, is to preserve itself even through a nuclear war. All of civilization is thus effectively objectified. It serves a purely instrumental value, as does every component of civilization considered alone: it can only be evaluated based on its ability to serve the purpose of preserving itself, even during a nuclear war. Because the Soviets might begin a war with acts of sabotage, efforts at installing a "revolutionary" government, even attacks by Spetznaz forces disguised as sports teams, absolute vigilance is perpetually necessary.[123] Certainly societal resources must be channeled into constant reshaping and modernization of strategic nuclear forces. Everything and every action is to be evaluated based solely on its ability to contribute to or detract from War Termination efforts. Thus all elements of society are robbed of intrinsic value. Furthermore, any actions designed to break us out of the system, to open up and legitimize channels and means of communication other than the weapons systems themselves, are rejected out of hand. It is, for these authors, too plausible that any particular program or interaction is a sham cleverly constructed by the Soviets either to throw us off guard, infiltrate us, or lull us into a false sense of security.

War Termination strives to move beyond deterrence, asking the question: Are our forces and our warfighting options designed to maximize our ability to "turn it off" quickly should deterrence fail? Whether the possibility of War Termination is a chimera or not is not the point here. The question I would rather address is what the focus on War Termination says about strategic doctrine.

It is first and foremost a sign of exhaustion. The entire enterprise is based on the presumption that nuclear arsenals will exist and on the implicit fear that so long as they do exist someone somewhere will probably use them. It says in short that deterrence theory is an elaborate set of constructs for dealing with the tiger we have by the tail, but that sooner or later it is inevitable that we will fall off that tiger. The only question with any relevance in such a circumstance is what you should do then.

Arguments to the effect that structures designed to make War Termination more likely may simultaneously make nuclear war itself more likely are not compelling from within this perspective. Unlike the classic warfighter the War Terminator has already given up. Burke argues that human beings are "rotten with perfection,"[124] which might be best translated from his terminology as "overripe with fulfillment." Symbol systems carry us forward with their own momentum, even when the destination is disastrous.[125] Burke would recognize the War Terminators as purveyors of the "ultimate negative" believing that eventually we will have to see what we have wrought.[126]

It is ironic that to the War Terminator society has a primary purpose: the creation of a structure designed to save it. Society is a vehicle for societal survival, not through peace and cooperation, but through preparation for the war that must never come, that no one wants, but that will come nonetheless, as inexorable as the tides.

For MAD authors the logical extreme is reflected in the obsession with returning to a day when force structures truly reflected the dictates of MAD. Historical studies make clear that, despite Declaratory Policy to the contrary, the United States was never content with mere finite deterrence. As warfighters have argued for years, technology has passed MAD by, accuracy and MIRVing taking us, apparently, past the point of no return. But now, via the START Treaty and re-

ductions imposed by changes in the very structure of Europe, a return is possible. "Whatever the validity of these claims [that
counterforce was necessary] in the past, however, recent developments in international politics and strategic nuclear deterrence have
rendered them all anachronistic."[127]

And it is not only reductions which offer us a way back to a world
with the potential for MAD dominance: political structures which are
most fertile for MAD are supported. The danger is that an essentially
conservative orientation is entrenched, where even changes that offer
the potential for breaking us out of the deterrence cycle altogether should
probably be rejected as if to say the destination may be a desirable one,
but the journey is just too dangerous. John Mearsheimer was soundly
attacked for his nostalgic defense of the Cold War,[128] but he was only
giving full voice to that which remains implicit for most authors. His
defense of bilateralism makes perfect sense from this perspective, for it
is a bilateral system for which MAD was originally designed. His policy
prescription—to arm the Germans—makes sense as well. If the system
is no longer bilateral, then it must be made to accommodate MAD, not
vice versa. How are new players, whose entry carries dangerous potential for instability, to be co-opted? The same way the United States and
the Soviet Union have been co-opted for all these years: by making them
direct participants in, and their people hostages to, the balance of terror.

Goodnight has argued that conservative movements are marked by a
desire to return to an idealized past, a moment where choice was made,
and paradise lost.[129] For deterrence theorists, as I have argued, such a
return is impossible, redemption beyond reach. Nuclear weapons cannot
be uninvented on the one hand; the Soviets cannot be other than Communist ideologues on the other.[130]

But it is possible within both frameworks to return to a better time.
For the warfighter that ability is made manifest in our capacity to return
to a moment when wars were not society ending. For the MAD advocate
we must return to a moment when a completely stable balance of terror
reigned supreme and unchallenged.

Both schools of thought are thus revealed as fundamentally conservative in nature, unadmitting of change in the world, wanting to return
to a time when the world was easier to deal with. Thus we head into a
New World Order instructed by perspectives not just unwilling but
ultimately incapable of altering the fundamental state of affairs. Stagnant
and unchanging, they can neither incorporate nor promote change. So
long as deterrence theory remains in its current configuration, policy,
whether dictated by a MAD or a warfighting point of view of the world,
will leave us in a nuclear framework for all time to come. Theory is
incapable of anything else.

IMPLICATIONS

Even the most ardent deterrence theorist would admit today that "the rationale for a Soviet attack on the West can hardly be conceived."[131] But as long as defense policy is guided by the dictates of deterrence theory, in either form, the fact that we cannot conceive of a motivation for attack is insufficient. We cannot *guarantee* that there will be no war; the level of risk is perpetually greater than zero, no matter how warm relations between the United States and the Soviet Union, or, for that matter, the Commonwealth of Independent States might be.[132] As long as that is the case, policy continues to be guided by worst case analysis.

The problem is that worst case analysis can lead to self-fulfilling prophecies regarding international relations.[133] The reliance on worst case analysis, assessment hinged on understanding intent and motivation *via* hardware and capabilities, is that there is no real place for discourse. Even as summits, meetings, negotiations, and other forms of discursive communication are increased, they are dominated by a perspective that believes these activities to be side shows. It is still the case that words can lie, or be misunderstood, while weapons are there for the counting and interpretation. "Deterrence, at its core, presumes the aggressive intent of an adversary. A deterrence mindset inherently tends to prejudice attempts to dispel misconceptions and, even more important, to prejudice efforts to reduce tensions and to resolve real conflicts of interest."[134] But without any weight given to new and serious channels for communication, the image of the other, and of our requirements, remain frozen. Nonverbal means of communication privileged in a situation where national survival was at stake, remain privileged even when no one can think of a reason to consider the other a threat: they *might* be one, or become one one day.[135] Any level of plausibility must be considered at the level of serious risk. The context within which the weapons are placed becomes completely ignored and indeed irrelevant.

The result is that even those willing to embrace the apparent changes in the Soviet Union hold as their greatest ambition the possibility that the level of armaments and tension at which the balance of power is maintained might be lowered.[136] Deterrence theory operates within a closed system. As long as the Soviets, and now the Russian successor state, retain weapons capabilities, particularly nuclear capabilities, deterrence continues to look only to what weapons they own. Elements of the relationship proceeding beyond that narrow and limited context are either ignored or dismissed. Because of its flawed nature at the level of underlying assumption, deterrence cannot accommodate a changed and changing scene: it is not designed to do anything other than assess military force. The result, insofar as defense policy is guided by the needs of deterrence, is a hopeless structure of belief and thought which is incapable of offering anything other than modified visions of the status quo. For the deterrence theorist there is indeed, no way out.

NOTES

1. See James Wirtz, "Ground Alert for Looking Glass: SAC's New Emphasis on Strategic Warning," *Defense Analysis* 7, no. 1 (1991): 104.

After nearly 30 years of continuous airborne alert, the SAC Airborne Command Post, better known as "Looking Glass," no longer flies day and night over the American midwest. Instead, the EC–135, commanded by an Air Force general and capable of controlling land-based strategic forces if ground-based communication and command facilities are destroyed, will now be maintained on "quick-reaction ground alert."

2. John Cooley, "Pre-War Gulf Diplomacy," *Survival* 32, no. 2 (March/April 1991): 127–128. Glaspie was, of course, then U.S. Ambassador to Iraq April Glaspie.

3. Shahram Chubin, "Post-War Gulf Security," *Survival* 32, no. 2 (March/April 1991): 144.

4. Typical is Norman Friedman who argues in *Desert Victory: The War for Kuwait* (Annapolis: Naval Institute Press, 1991), one of the first scholarly assessments of the Gulf War, that the Ba'athist party's original "manifesto recalls earlier Nazi rhetoric in its emphasis on a Leader who would embody the mystical spirit of the Arab nation (that is, in a combination of blood and culture)" (15), that "Saddam played Beria to his older cousin's Stalin," (17) and that the Republican Guard "recalls the creation of the Waffen SS" (20).

5. Robert Art, "A Defensible Defense: America's Grand Strategy after the Cold War," *International Security* 15, no. 4 (Spring 1991): 45 [My emphasis]. Furthermore, had "Kuwait agreed to some American military presence before August 2, 1990, Saddam Hussein would probably not have attacked, knowing beyond a doubt that if he did, he would have killed American troops and thereby directly engaged and enraged the United States" (52). Thus the theory of the tripwire is alive and well.

6. See Art, "Defensible Defense."

7. The concern is reflected to some extent in what is known about changes in U.S. targeting policy. See Charles Glaser, "Nuclear Policy without an Adversary," *International Security* 16, no. 4 (Spring 1992): 45–46.

8. "Until the rise of Mikhail Gorbachev thoroughly shook up Western evaluations of Soviet strategic intentions, US analysts of the Soviet military were locked in a sterile debate over whether the Soviet Union had realistic plans for nuclear combat." William C. Green, "Assessing Soviet Military Literature: Attempts to Broker the Western Debate," in Green and Theodore Karasik, eds., *Gorbachev and His Generals: The Reform of Soviet Military Doctrine* (Boulder: Westview Press, 1990), 13. Another author called the disputes over deterrence "a debate that perhaps should have been ended some two decades ago." George Questor, "Cultural Barriers to an Acceptance of Deterrence," in Roman Kolkowicz, ed., *The Logic of Nuclear Terror* (Boston: Allen and Unwin, 1987), 86.

9. I use the present tense intentionally for several reasons. First, as of this writing it appears as if the Commonwealth of Independent States has, to the

extent that it inherited the personnel and particularly the leadership of the old Soviet military, inherited its doctrinal positions as well. Second, the collapse of the Soviet Union happened so quickly after the onset of New Thinking that the Western debate had barely begun. It continues now within the new context, so that authors are currently grappling with both the meaning of New Thinking as it appeared in the late 1980s and with what that doctrinal shift implies for the military of the Commonwealth. Finally, for Western authors, as I discuss below, the coup in many ways served as a warning that the shape of what was the Soviet Union is not settled and will not be for some time. The coup serves as the exemplar event justifying continued study of Soviet/Commonwealth military doctrine. Since intentions stem from governments, and Western analysts are not yet assured that the Commonwealth government will survive, the focus must still be largely on the hardware available and the doctrine espoused by the professional military, especially since they are often identified as a likely group of candidates for the next coup.

10. "Thus, Soviet strategists have concluded that the attempt to achieve total security has paradoxically resulted in a weakening rather than a strengthening, of the U.S.S.R. vis-à-vis its potential enemies." Marshall Brement, "Reflections on Soviet New Thinking on Security Questions," *Naval War College Review* 42, no. 4 (Autumn 1989): 10.

11. Michael MccGwire, "The Soviet Navy and World War," in Philip Gillette and Willard Frank, Jr., eds., *The Sources of Soviet Naval Conduct* (Lexington: Lexington Books, 1990), 217. See also Andrew Goldberg, "Rethinking Nuclear Arms Reductions," in *Coping with Gorbachev's Soviet Union*, Significant Issue Series 10, no. 9 (Washington, D.C.: CSIS, 1988), 14; Brement, "Reflections on New Thinking," 10; Ilana Kass, "Gorbachev's Strategy: Is Our Perspective in Need of Restructuring?" *Comparative Strategy* 8, no. 2 (1989): 187; and Paula Dobriansky and David Rivkin, Jr., "Changes in Soviet Military Thinking: How Do They Add Up and What Do They Mean for Western Security?" in Green and Karasik, *Gorbachev and His Generals*, 173.

12. "Briefly, the new thinking includes a devaluation of the role of technology in security; a reaffirmation of war and peace as problems solvable only through political, rather than military means . . . ; A definition of security as attainable only by mutual rather than individual efforts; and an attempt to use the mechanisms of international organization to secure peace." Thomas Nichols and Theodore Karasik, "The Impact of 'Reasonable Sufficiency' on the Soviet Ministry of Defense," *Naval War College Review* 42, no. 4 (Autumn 1989): 22–23.

13. For an excellent explanation of the subtle distinctions between various Soviet schools of thought on this criteria for force sizing and structure see MccGwire, "Soviet Navy," 220.

14. Thus, American authors are skeptical not only because authors are generally skeptical of the Soviets when they write from within the warfighting perspective, but even in instances where they are for the most part sympathetic to the Soviets. In other words, some believe as I will explain below that this move is a purely propagandistic one, while others believe the Soviets to be genuine, but attempting to do the impossible. For examples of critiques of the possibility of a non-offensive defense see Schuyler Foerster, et al., *Defining Stability: Conventional Arms Control in a Changing Europe* (Boulder: Westview Press,

1989), especially 57, and Dobriansky and Rivkin, "Changes in Soviet Military Thinking."

15. Symbolic interactionism does not preclude notions of cultural change— it could not, and remain a valid description of the way human beings live—it merely acknowledges that change comes on a foundation laid by what has come before, in a fashion akin to what the archeologist sees in the layering of civilizations. For a description of the way change is understood within the perspective see Stephen Littlejohn, "Symbolic Interactionism as an Approach to the Study of Human Communication," *Quarterly Journal of Speech* 63, no. 1 (February 1977): 85–174. For a more detailed articulation, see Peter Berger and Thomas Luckmann, *The Social Construction of Reality* (New York: Anchor Books/Doubleday, 1967).

16. V. William Balthrop, "Argumentation and the Critical Stance: A Methodological Approach," in J. Robert Cox and Charles Willard, eds., *Critical Advances in Argumentation* (Carbondale, IL: Southern Illinois University Press, 1987), 242.

17. Daniel Goure, "Soviet Doctrine and Nuclear Forces into the Twenty-first Century," in Green and Karasik, *Gorbachev and His Generals*, 86. The same author argues that the "concept of sufficiency is also not new . . . the debate within the Soviet leadership is over the criterion for judging military sufficiency" (87), although he does concede that there are differences between what was conceptualized during Brezhnev's era and during Gorbachev's. It should also be noted that Goure believes that the Soviet debate is now deeply fragmented.

18. Goure, "Soviet Doctrine," 91.

19. For example the sudden shift in Soviet negotiating positions in the INF Treaty to permit On Site Inspections and the principle of asymmetrical reductions. See Cori Dauber, "Negotiating from Strength: Arms Control and the Rhetoric of Denial," *Political Communication and Persuasion* 7, no. 2 (1990): 97–114.

20. The West was taken by surprise when, on December 7, 1988, Gorbachev promised a huge unilateral drawdown of conventional forces in Europe while speaking before the United Nations in New York. Similarly the Soviets unilaterally retired some of their short range nuclear weapons deployed in the European theater.

21. Goure, "Soviet Doctrine," 81.

22. See, for example, Raymond Garthoff, "The Tightening Frame: Mutual Security and the Future of Strategic Arms Limitation," in Derek Leebaert and Timothy Dickinson, eds., *Soviet Strategy and New Military Thinking* (New York: Cambridge University Press, 1992), 57–78.

23. Andrew Goldberg, "The Present Turbulence in Soviet Military Doctrine," *The Washington Quarterly* 11, no. 3 (Summer 1988): 166; Raymond Garthoff, "New Thinking in Soviet Military Doctrine," *The Washington Quarterly* 11, no. 3 (Summer 1988): 146.

24. Goldberg, "Present Turbulence," 166; Garthoff, "New Thinking," 146.

25. Raymond Garthoff, *Deterrence and the Revolution in Soviet Military Doctrine* (Washington, DC: The Brookings Institution, 1990), 113. [Emphasis in original.]

26. Derek Leebaert, "The Stakes of Power," in Leebaert and Dickinson, eds., *New Military Thinking*, 7. This obviously ignores the role the Soviet Union played

in the reversal of Communism in Eastern Europe, through their willingness to signal their intent to stay out of other nations' internal affairs.

27. Jean Quatras, "New Soviet Thinking Is Not Good News," *The Washington Quarterly* 11, no. 3 (Summer 1988): 177.

28. With the advent of nuclear weapons the world was changed forever, and it is illusion to believe we can recapture the moment. "We are neither in 1914 nor in 1939." Stanley Hoffman, "Back to the Future Part II: International Relations Theory and Post-Cold War Europe," *International Security* 15, no. 2 (Fall 1990): 192. Admittedly, some warfighters also concede the point. For example, "the prenuclear world is lost beyond retrieval." Colin Gray, "Nuclear Strategy: What Is True, What Is False, What Is Arguable," *Comparative Strategy* 9, no. 1 (1990): 1.

29. Garthoff, *Deterrence and the Revolution*, 13.

30. Kass, "Gorbachev's Strategy," 185. Also a "respite rather than a true transformation." Patrick Cronin, "Prestroika and Soviet Military Personnel," in Green and Karasik, *Gorbachev and His Generals*, 127.

31. The defense buildup carried out under the Reagan administration was the largest ever in peacetime.

32. "Gorbachev may hope for a repeat of the 'detente' period of the 1970s when Soviet scientists roamed the United States visiting defense plants and research institutes.... Since detente in the 1970s helped to make possible the Soviet military buildup during that decade, why should it not again work in the late 1980s and 1990s?" William F. Scott, "Soviet Military Doctrine: Continuity and Change?" in Green and Karasik, *Gorbachev and His Generals*, 10.

33. Marshall Bremant notes:

The Soviet General Staff realizes that to keep the U.S.S.R. in the military forefront—and this is almost certainly the aim of Gorbachev as well—the leadership will have to make enormous investment in microelectronics, automated decision support systems, lasers, enhanced munitions lethality, telecommunications, and other high technologies. In order to do so, savings will have to be found elsewhere.... The East's proposal in the Conventional Force Negotiations last spring to cut Soviet tanks from 41,500 to 14,000 almost certainly was motivated in part by this need.

Brement, "Reflections on New Thinking," 11. See also Sergei Zamascikov, "Gorbachev and the Soviet Military," *Comparative Strategy* 7, no. 3 (1988): 242 and 247.

34. Kass, "Gorbachev's Strategy," 185.

35. Scott, "Soviet Military Doctrine," 9. In short if "its leaders believe that the economic potentials of warring states are the first law of war, priority must be given to improving the economy" (8).

36. Kass, "Gorbachev's Strategy," 185.

37. For authors arguing that without a present threat there will be no public support for necessary defense expenditures see Bruce McKenzie, "Arms Control: A Naval Perspective," *Naval War College Review* 42, no. 1 (Winter 1990): 87; Ronald Kurth, "Soviet Change and Assessing Naval Conduct," in Gillette and Frank, *Sources of Soviet Naval Conduct*, xiv; Scott Truver, "The U.S. Navy: Global Commitments, Greater Uncertainty, Fewer Dollars," *Naval Forces* 11, no. 2 (1990): 9; Brement, "Reflections on New Thinking," 19; Charles Larson, "National Inter-

ests and Naval Forces in the 1990s," *Naval War College Review*, 45, no. 1 (Winter 1990): 10.

38. Kass, "Gorbachev's Strategy," 186.

39. Kass, "Gorbachev's Strategy," 182–183.

40. Some evidence of tension over who is to pay for what is already evident. Kass, "Gorbachev's Strategy,' 186.

41. Arguing for defense increases makes us look intransigent. See Jan Lodal, "An Arms Control Agenda," *Foreign Policy*, no. 72 (Fall 1988): 159; William Carpenter, "The U.S. Navy Beyond the Year 2000: A Strategic Forecast," *Comparative Strategy* 7, no. 3 (1988): 279. And as one author noted (Brement, "Reflections on New Thinking," 6) "this country cannot afford to convey the impression that when the chips are down, we somehow prefer maintaining leadership of an alliance based on fear to a fundamental transformation of our relationship with the only nation that can destroy our homeland." In fact our caution just makes Gorbachev look even better, as even softline authors would agree. (Brement, "Reflections on New Thinking," 6.) See Steven Kull, "Dateline Moscow: Burying Lenin," *Foreign Policy* 78 (Spring 1990): 191.

42. See Robert Wood, "Strategic Choices, Geopolitics, and Resource Constraints," *The Washington Quarterly* 12, no.1 3 (Summer 1989): 150.

43. Scott, "Soviet Military Doctrine," 1.

44. Scott, "Soviet Military Doctrine," 6. Garrett argues (*Tenuous Balance*, 2) that Gorbachev's announced military reductions "will dramatically diminish Soviet coercive power in Europe by reducing the apparent threat. However, it will also reduce political support in the West for armaments while not greatly diminishing future Soviet bargaining power."

45. During the immense arms buildup of the early 1980s, the Reagan administration justified enormous defense expenditures by comparing U.S. and Soviet arsenals in order to prove that the United States was behind militarily. The basis for those comparisons was critiqued by the left on several grounds: Soviet weapons were obsolete, in many instances warehoused, they were less technologically sophisticated than American counterparts, and so forth. (See Chapter 2 for a more detailed analysis.) When the Soviets began to talk about unilateral drawdowns, however, those who had rejected these critiques suddenly adopted them, claiming that it would be all too easy for the Soviets to symbolically eliminate large numbers of weapons without really affecting their ability to fight in any meaningful way. See Dauber, "Negotiating from Strength."

46. Since the new democracies stand in between the Soviet Union and the NATO alliance members Soviet troops would have to move through their territory, presumably without permission.

47. See John Galvin, "The NATO Alliance: A Framework for Security," *The Washington Quarterly* 12, no. 1 (Winter 1989): 88; Wood, "Strategic Choices," 150–151 and 147.

48. This is particularly a concern given the reductions in nuclear forces which have been negotiated and which make NATO much more reliant on the strength of conventional deterrence. See Lodal, "Arms Control Agenda," 162.

49. Apparently the legendary "3:1" force ratio necessary for a successful attack is a threshold issue, which a defender below a certain depth or strength cannot benefit from.

50. Thomas Nichols, "Conclusions: The Unresolved Agenda," in Green and Karasik, *Gorbachev and His Generals*, 202.

51. William Manthorpe, Jr., "A Background for Understanding Soviet Strategy," in Gillette and Frank, *Sources of Soviet Naval Conduct*, 14. Note that the claim made here would hold true as worded for the Russian successor state.

52. Thus one author wrote that 'he [Gorbachev] should publicly set as his ultimate goal the following 17 points" and proceeded with a list including cutting men in uniform, freezing ICBM production, withdrawing from various locations, and ranging from these changes in deployments all the way to increasing student exchanges. Brement, "Reflections on New Thinking", 16–17. See also Zbigniew Brzezinski, "Ending the Cold War," *The Washington Quarterly* 12, no. 4 (Autumn 1989): 33. "The Berlin Wall and free elections are not just slogans; they are the substance of the political contests. The Cold War will thus have a terminal date when the wall is firmly scheduled for dismantling (even if that action is not taken instantly) and when some (even if not immediately all) of the East European states firmly schedule free elections."

53. This is in no small part driven by official rhetorics in the United States. See Dauber, "Negotiating From Strength."

54. If the Soviets, for example, reduce the readiness of their military forces, that may be a sign that they are preparing to attack—and therefore need to mislead us. (Robert Pfaltzgraff, Jr., "Summary and Conclusions," in Stephen Cimbala and Joseph Douglass, Jr., eds., *Ending a Nuclear War: Are the Superpowers Prepared?* [New York: Pergamon Brassey's International Defense Publishers, Inc., 1988], 181). This logic is unimpeachible, since nothing is ever taken as disproof.

55. David Tarr, "Avoiding a Nuclear War by Other Means," in Stephen Cimbala, ed., *Strategic War Termination* (New York: Praeger, 1986), 36.

56. Even the failed Soviet coup was not adequate. For several years these authors had taken the position that Gorbachev would primarily achieve a reinvigoration of the Soviet right and his own ousting. See Brement, "Reflections on New Thinking," 14; Walter Slocombe, "Strategic Stability in a Restructured World," *Survival* 32, no. 4 (July/August 1990): 301; Garrett, *Tenuous Balance*, 6; Thomas Nichols and Theodore Karasik, "The Impact of 'Reasonable Sufficiency' on the Soviet Ministry of Defense," *Naval War College Review* 42, no. 4 (Autumn 1989): 33; Ronald Kurth, "Soviet Change in a Changing World," *Naval War College Review* 43, no. 1 (Winter 1990): 3; Patrick Cronin, "Perestroika and Soviet Military Personnel," in Green and Karasik, *Gorbachev and His Generals*, 125. The coup, within this context, merely reinforces the notion that even if Gorbachev was sincere, we must remain vigilant, since presumably the old guard still remains and may again rally. Again note that this is a claim that remains true regarding Russia.

57. Which may say something about the arms race, since the weapons, as abstractions, are of vital importance up until the moment they are gone, when everyone notes how little use they would have been in an actual exchange. For an assessment of the symbolic impact of INF and the various subsidiary agreements it spawned, see Cori Dauber, "Ritual Justifications and Arms Negotiations," unpublished manuscript, University of North Carolina, Chapel Hill, NC, 1991.

58. Lodal, "Arms Agenda," 157.

59. Although the relative importance of On Site Inspection from a technical point of view is arguable, it is incredibly important for political acceptance of arms control in this country (see Dauber, "Negotiating From Strength,") and Soviet acceptance of it was a radical shift compared to their former posture. See Garthoff, "New Thinking," 149.

60. This was evidenced by the politically necessitated decision to permanently postpone the modernization and update for the short range Lance systems stationed in Germany.

61. Walter Hahn, "The INF Treaty, the Alliance, and the Failure of Strategic Realism," *Comparative Strategy* 7, no. 4 (1988): 350. See, for example, Lodal, "Arms Agenda," 158; Graham Rys-Jones, "Greeks Bearing Gifts: Impact of the INF Treaty on European Security," *Naval War College Review* 62, no. 1 (Winter 1989): 62; Dobriansky and Rivkin, "Changes in Soviet Military Thinking," 174.

62. The Aspen Strategy Group and the European Strategy Group, *After the INF Treaty: Conventional Forces and Arms Control in European Security* (Boston: The Aspen Institute for Humanistic Studies in cooperation with the University Press of America, 1988), Executive Summary, xiii–xiv; Hahn, "The INF Treaty," 350.

63. One author wrote recently,

I also assume that Russia believes that the end of the Cold War has not eliminated its need for a nuclear deterrent. Mirroring U.S. concerns, Russia will almost certainly conclude that its security policy should recognize the possibility of renewed adversarial relations with the West. In this case, assuming that the United States and other Western powers retain nuclear weapons, Russia will want to maintain a nuclear deterrent. . . . My working assumption is that Russia will want to retain at least an assured destruction capability if the United States has such a capability.

Glaser, "Without an Adversary," 37. But of course he advocates retention of just such a capability on the grounds that Russia will likely retain such a capability.

64. Robert Einhorn, "Revising the START Process," *Survival* 32, no. 6 (November/December 1990): 497.

65. See Lodal, "Arms Agenda," 165; Dobriansky and Rivkin, "Changes in Soviet Military Thinking," 176, and Max Kampelman, "START: Completing the Task," *The Washington Quarterly* 12, no. 3 (Summer 1989): 8.

66. Slocombe, "Strategic Stability," 308; Roman Kolkowicz, "Intellectuals and the Nuclear Deterrence System," in Kolkowicz, *The Logic of Nuclear Terror*, 37.

67. Brement, "Reflections on New Thinking," 19.

68. Thomas Troyano, "U.S. Strategic Forces Under a START Agreement," *Comparative Strategy* 8, no. 2 (1989): 227. This is true since "before any decisions can be made regarding our force posture, we must determine what the requirement is for ensuring deterrence under START" (233). See also Arnold Kanter, "The Relationship Between Arms Control and Modernization," in Eric Arnett, et al., eds., *U.S. Strategic Forces: Modernization Under Arms Control and Budget Constraints: Proceedings from a Congressional Seminar* (Washington, DC: AAAS Program on Science, Arms Control, and National Security, June 1, 1989), 11. The problem is that when such claims are made, they continue to assume that arms control itself cannot bear the traffic of increasing communication. Nego-

tiations are instruments designed to get to a particular strategic end, rather than open dialogues, since true communication only occurs via the weapons remaining when the treaty is signed. For example, one author states that what "is required is an in-depth understanding of what types of targets we will need to destroy under a START environment to deter the Soviets and a re-examination of our assumptions regarding the size of the target lists, the priorities of, and levels of damage required against certain functions and the various issues associated with weapon allocation. This will in turn help define the specific characteristics and capabilities required from our force posture." Troyano, "U.S. Strategic Forces," 234.

69. See Michael Mandelbaum and Strobe Talbott, *Reagan and Gorbachev* (New York: Council on Foreign Relations Books, February 1987).

70. See Gray, "Soviet Nuclear Strategy," 41–43.

71. See Michael May, George Bing, and John Steinbruner, *Strategic Arms Reductions* (Washington, DC: The Brookings Institution, 1988), 7; John Steinbruner, "The Purpose and Effect of Deep Strategic Force Reductions," in Committee on International Security and Arms Control of the National Academy of Science, ed., *Reykjavik and Beyond: Deep Reductions in Strategic Nuclear Arsenals and the Future Direction of Arms Control* (Washington, DC: National Academy Press, 1988), 1–10. The author assumes that a target set of between 1,500 and 2,000 "aim points" would be more than sufficient. In fact even in the post–Soviet World, the criteria MAD authors would apply to arms control agreements continue to be "the U.S. ability to deter premeditated attacks; crisis stability, which measures both countries' incentives to strike preemptively in a crisis; arms race stability, which measures the U.S. ability to maintain necessary military capabilities in the face of a Russian arms buildup; and the damage the United States would suffer if war occurs." Glaser, "Without an Adversary," 40.

72. There is, however, disagreement over whether or not it would be in the United States' interests to encourage the Soviets to deploy a larger portion of their strategic arsenal on submarines than is currently the case. See Harold Feiverson and Frank Von Hippel, "Beyond START: How to Make Much Deeper Cuts," *International Security* 15, no. 1 (Summer 1990): 165; Lodal, "Arms Agenda," 166; R. James Woolsey, "U.S. Strategic Force Decisions for the 1990s," *The Washington Quarterly* 12, no. 1 (Winter 1989): 73; Kampelman, "Completing the Task," 8.

73. See, for example, Russell Dougherty, "The Value of ICBM Modernization," *International Security* 12, no. 2 (Fall 1987): 165; Robert Gray, "The Bush Administration and Mobile ICBM," *Survival* 31, no. 5 (September/October 1989): 418; Fred Chernoff, "START or Finish? The Future of Strategic Arms Control and Profound Force Reductions," *Defense Analysis* 6, no. 3 (September 1990): 241; and Donald Rice, "The Manned Bomber and Strategic Deterrence," *International Security* 15, no. 1 (Summer 1990). 108.

74. For an explanation of the similarity between post–START arsenals and those of the early 1980s see Walter Slocombe, "Force Posture Consequences of the START Treaty," *Survival* 30, no. 5 (September/October 1988), and Gray, "Bush and Mobile ICBM," 418.

75. Kampelman, "Completing the Task," 12.

76. Wood, "Strategic Choices," 146. See also Einhorn, "Revising Start," 503, and Lodal, "Arms Agenda," 172.

77. Slocombe, "Strategic Stability," 303.

78. Gray, "Nuclear Strategy," 16.

79. Slocombe, "Strategic Stability," 299. After all "Russian political seasons can change faster than a U.S. deterrent can be modernized." Woolsey, "Strategic Force Decisions," 69.

80. According to Walter Slocombe

[a] third requirement of stability is that the nuclear relationship and the effectiveness of deterrence should be invulnerable, not just to direct military attack by the other side's current forces, but to changes in those forces accomplished by clandestine build-ups, by the open build-ups so large or so technologically leveraged that they exhaust the other side's financial or technological ability to compete, or by quick—and quickly exploited—technological breakthroughs that render previously survivable forces vulnerable.

Slocombe, "Strategic Stability," 307.

81. See Carol Cohn, "Slick'ems, Glick'ems, and Christmas Trees," *Bulletin of the Atomic Scientists* 43, no. 5 (1987): 17–24.

82. For the warfighter's perspective, see Slocombe, "Strategic Stability," 303; Gary Guertner, "Flexible Options in NATO Military Strategy: Deterrent or Escalation Trap?" *Comparative Strategy* 8, no. 3 (1989): 345; Dobriansky and Rivkin, "Changes in Soviet Military Thinking," 176; Rys-Jones, "Greeks Bearing Gifts," 60; Carpenter, "U.S. Navy," 289; Hahn, "INF Treaty," 349; Lodal, "Arms Agenda," 153. For the MAD perspective, see Kaiser, "From Nuclear Deterrence," 487; Aspen Strategy Group, *After the INF Treaty*, xvi.

83. Michael Moodie, "Conventional Arms Control: An Analytical Survey of Recent Literature," *The Washington Quarterly* 12, no. 1 (Winter 1989): 194. Similarly "we are facing the possibility of a postnuclear world in strategy. Yet traditions and habits of mind are hard to break and future Soviet military posture will likely be the result of tension between continuities and changes." "Preface," Gillette and Frank, *Sources of Soviet Naval Conduct*, xv.

84. Foerster, *Defining Stability*, 4.

85. Rys-Jones, "Greeks Bearing Gifts," 58.

86. Dobriansky and Rivkin, "Changes in Soviet Military Thinking," 178; Foerster, *Defining Stability*, 55–57.

87. Foerster, *Defining Stability*, 6.

88. There has always been a serious and extensive literature on conventional-only deterrence. It may be that what has changed is the number of authors previously occupied with nuclear scenarios who are now considering a broader scope of scenarios. See Moodie, "Conventional Arms Control, 190.

89. Dobriansky and Rivkin, "Changes in Soviet Military Thinking," 179. See also Foerster, *Defining Stability*, 33; and Slocombe, "Strategic Stability," 301, for related discussions. Some authors have suggested that because a successful Soviet attack depends on a slow Western response, it is critical that the Soviets mislead the West—which may explain their sudden interest in arms control proposals. See Garrett, *Tenuous Balance*, 22.

90. Stephen Cimbala, *First Strike Stability: Deterrence After Containment* (Westport, Conn.: Greenwood Press, 1990), 7.

91. The Maritime Strategy discussed in Chapter 4 had an independent War Termination justification. Nevertheless, War Termination *qua* War Termination has until recently been largely ignored. The bulk of the material available is to be found in four fairly recent books, three collections of essays edited by Stephen Cimbala, and a book by Cimbala. Despite the paucity of material, some of the most prolific and respected warfighters are represented in the collections. Virtually every author participating, moreover, complained that War Termination had to receive much more attention in the future. Thus the comment that the "literature on war termination strategy, theory, and processes is extremely limited" (Barry Schneider, "War Termination for Strategic Nuclear Conflicts," in Stephen Cimbala, ed., *Strategic War Termination* [New York: Praeger, 1986], 129). Authors complain that it is not discussed in the service academies, noting that things "are not much better in the world of think tanks and academia" (Schneider, "War Termination," 120). Indeed, "war termination has been a neglected element in both mainstream and alternative deterrence theories" (Stephen Cimbala, "Strategic War Termination: The Missing Element," in Cimbala, ed., *Ending a Nuclear War*, 163). In fact, "The problem of war termination is a neglected stepchild both in policy and in theory" (Colin Gray, "Global Protracted War: Conduct and Termination," in Cimbala, ed., *Strategic War Termination*, 80). Thus, "war termination as a general field has not received adequate examination from either the academic or the policy-making communities" (Robert Mandel, "Adversaries' Expectations and Desires About War Termination," in Cimbala, ed., *Strategic War Termination*, 174). It should be noted, however, that War Termination possibilities are beginning to be explored by other authors as additive impacts to their own ideas on force structure, which does indicate these ideas are gaining some legitimacy. For example, see Michael Mazarr, "Beyond Counterforce," *Comparative Strategy* 9, no. 2 (1990): 158.

92. Pfaltzgraff, et al., "Summary and Conclusions," in Cimbala and Douglass, ed., *Ending a Nuclear War*, 174.

93. William Van Cleave, "U.S. Strategic Nuclear Forces and War Termination," in Cimbala and Douglass, ed., *Ending a Nuclear War*, 81.

94. Robert Leahy, "The Mechanics of War Termination," in Cimbala and Douglass, ed., *Ending a Nuclear War*, 121. The same author advocates communication protocols in place now (119) and even designated successors to the NCA (92).

95. "Indeed, the pre-war failure to plan force structure, employment strategies, and diplomatic activities with an eye to concluding conflicts rapidly and on advantageous terms nearly guarantees that any superpower nuclear war will be uncontrollable." Schneider, "War Termination," 121. Note that to the War Terminator we do not even exist in a state of "strategic stability" as opposed to "peace" but should instead consider ourselves as in a pre-war period.

96. Fred Ikle, "Foreword," in Cimbala and Douglass, eds., *Ending a Nuclear War*, ix.

97. Carl Builder, "The Impact of New Weapons Technologies," in Cimbala, ed., *Strategic War Termination*, 170–171. Of course, to put the issue of War Termination onto the table is therefore to signal a choice. Said another author,

This is where force requirements for war termination and for deterrence begin to diverge. From the standpoint of deterrence, beyond a certain retaliatory capability, any further accumulation of warheads makes no sense. From the standpoint of war termination objectives, redundancy is necessary because it increases options and does not force on us a particular course of action, allowing at the same time for some losses without jeopardizing our ability to continue in a limited fashion.

Leon Sloss and Paolo Stoppa-Liebl, "War Termination: Targeting Objectives and Problems," in Cimbala, ed., *Strategic War Termination*, 118.

98. George Questor, "The Difficult Logic of Terminating a Nuclear War," in Cimbala, ed., *Strategic War Termination*, 58.

99. As an example, we should be prepared to act promptly at the first sign of warning. Leon Sloss, "Flexible Targeting, Escalation Control, and U.S. Options," in Cimbala and Douglass, eds., *Ending a Nuclear War*, 7.

100. Joseph Douglass, Jr., "Nuclear War Termination: Soviet Style," in Cimbala and Douglass, eds., *Ending a Nuclear War*, 36. Of course this author also claims that there are Soviet agents in place throughout the United States, especially in industry and banking (perhaps explaining the S&L crisis), waiting to provide an important negotiating "edge" to the Soviet Union in the event of nuclear war.

101. Leon Goure, "The Soviet Union and Post-Attack Recovery," in Cimbala and Douglass, eds., *Ending a Nuclear War*, 10.

102. Douglass, "Termination Soviet Style," 29.

103. While at first glance, these protestations that the Soviets are preparing to fight to win would appear to eliminate the viability of War Termination strategies, since such strategies involve cooperative efforts (Colin Gray, "Strategic De-Escalation," in Cimbala and Douglass, eds., *Ending a Nuclear War*, 75) and mean that "the enemy must be persuaded to change his mind" (Pfaltzgraff, Cimbala, and Douglass, "Summary and Conclusions," 174), these worries do not overly concern War Terminators. Much as MAD authors presume the Soviets understand the wisdom of maintaining a mutual balance of terror, these authors presume that once the war began Soviet attitudes would change. And luckily "Soviet concepts of warfare in distinct stages would appear to provide for brief periods during which a meaningful exchange of signals could take place." In other words, since the Soviet Strategic Rocket Forces evolved out of the artillery ranks (a reason some authors believe Soviet military personnel are inclined to view nuclear weapons as "just" bigger artillery shells) they are also conditioned to think "in terms of salvos." Uri Ra'anan, "Soviet Political-Diplomatic Signalling and War Termination," in Cimbala and Douglass, eds., *Ending a Nuclear War*, 141). Essentially, the communicative function of the weapons is now believed to remain operative even when they are functioning *as* weapons. See Sloss, "Flexible Targeting," 2. The reciprocal nature of War Termination, in other words, is conceded. Mandel, "Adversaries' Expectations," 184.

104. Gray, "Strategic De-Escalation," 73–74.

105. Pfaltzgraff, Cimbala, and Douglass, "Summary and Conclusions," 185.

106. Sloss, "Flexible Targeting," 9.

107. Stephen Cimbala, "Countercommand Attacks and War Termination," in Cimbala, ed., *Strategic War Termination*, 142. And, of course, says the same author, if "one want to talk about strategic forces that provide capabilities for prompt, selected, and controlled targeting, there is no equivalent to a modernized ICBM force" (142).

108. Sloss and Stoppa-Liebl, "War Termination," 106.

109. Sloss and Stoppa-Liebl, "War Termination," 116. Thus "the U.S. should be capable of ensuring that it would always be able to charge a price for its defeat so high that victory would be impossible by any responsible Soviet definition of the conditions for that achievement" (Gray, "Global Protracted War," 83). Ironically, this means, as these authors freely admit, modelling U.S. practice after what they see as Soviet doctrinal requirements. Cimbala, "Strategic War Termination," 163. And it is clear that, for these authors, the U.S. arsenal has a way to go despite "the impressive intellectual progress made in U.S. strategic doctrine over the past fifteen years." Van Cleave, "U.S. Forces and War Termination," 82. (In other words, despite the increasing dominance of the war-fighting perspective.)

110. Gray, "Strategic De-Escalation," 71.

111. Gray, "Strategic De-Escalation," 66.

112. Douglass, "Soviet Style," 40.

113. See Douglass, "Soviet Style," 19; Cimbala, "Strategic War Termination," 158; and Gray, "Strategic De-Escalation," 68.

114. One author articulated the distinction this way: "We are by no means confident of this assumption, but we differ with those who are confident that nuclear war cannot be limited." Sloss and Stoppa-Liebl, "War Termination," 100.

115. And these authors tend to be fairly explicit about this. See, for example, Sloss and Stoppa-Liebl, "War Termination," 100 and 101.

116. Builder, "New Technologies," 169. This is the danger in War Termination policies, that "one side will take the other's haste for peace as a sign that this should be exploited, that a war should be launched again as soon as the aggressor has had a chance to catch his breath." Questor, "Difficult Logic," 65. See also Sloss, "Flexible Targeting," 3–6.

117. See William Martel, "Exchange Calculus of Strategic Nuclear War, " in Cimbala, ed., Strategic War Termination, 3; Sloss, "Flexible Targeting," 2; Builder, "New Technologies," 157 and Gray, "Strategic De-Escalation," 66.

118. Gray, "Strategic De-Escalation," 63–64.

119. Builder, "New Technologies," 157.

120. Gray, "Global Protracted War," 76.

121. Douglass, "Soviet Style," 19.

122. The freeze movement made the argument in the context of liberal social activism, taking the position that movements designed to enhance the quality of life by improving social justice, or educational curricula, or even children's health, were of little import in a situation where the continuation of human life and society was at risk.

123. See Douglass, "Soviet Style," 32 and 33.

124. Kenneth Burke, "Definition of Man," in Language as Symbolic Action (Berkeley: University of California Press, 1966); 16–20.

125. As an example, the symbolic logic of scapegoating employed by National Socialism carried with it the potential for identifying certain groups within society as "sub-human," that is to say, animal. Once that move is made the logic carries Germany virtually inexorably to the death camps, for if one is dealing with

"vermin" who are not really people but only human in appearance, then genocide becomes fairly easy to justify.

126. See Burke, "Definition of Man," 20–24.

127. Mazarr, "Beyond Counterforce," 152.

128. His article, "Back to the Future: Instability in Europe After the Cold War," appeared in the Summer 1990 issue of *International Security* (15, no. 1: 5–56), but the journal wound up giving space to substantial commentary and unusually harsh criticism over the next two issues. Said one respondent, "One simply can't deal with international politics at the level of theoretical abstraction and dogmatism exhibited here. The paper has all the elegance of a mathematical theorem, and just about as much relevance to reality." Hoffman, "Back to the Future II," *International Security* 15, no. 2 (1990): 191.

129. See G. Thomas Goodnight, "The Liberal and Conservative Presumptions: On Political Philosophy and the Foundation of Public Argument," in Jack Rhodes, ed., *Proceedings of the Summer Conference on Argumentation* (Backlick, Va.: Speech Communication Association, January 1980), 304–337.

130. And this risk, of course, remains even now, given the number of communist ideologues still "at large" within the Commonwealth's various nations.

131. Kaiser, "From Nuclear Deterrence," 485.

132. See Jonathon Howe, "NATO and the Gulf Crisis," *Survival* 32, no. 3 (May/June 1991): 247; Mearsheimer, "Back to the Future," 33; James Schear and Joseph Nye, Jr., "Addressing Europe's Conventional Instabilities," *The Washington Quarterly* 11, no. 3 (Summer 1988): 46.

133. See Laurence Martin, "The Influence of Soviet Military Doctrine on Western Strategy," in Gregory Flynn, ed., *Soviet Military Doctrine and Western Policy* (New York: Routledge, 1989), 406, or Richard Ned Lebow and Janice Gross Stein, "Beyond Deterrence," *Journal of Social Issues* 43, no. 4 (1987): 40.

134. Garthoff, *Deterrence and the Revolution in Doctrine*, 24.

135. See Donald Hicks, "ICBM Modernization: Consider the Alternatives," *International Security* 12, no. 2 (Fall 1987): 175.

136. Mearsheimer, "Back to the Future," 52.

Selected Bibliography

Adams, Ruth, and Susan Cullen, eds. *The Final Epidemic*. Chicago: Educational Foundation for Nuclear Science, 1981.

Aldridge, Robert. *The Counterforce Syndrome: A Guide to US Nuclear Weapons and Strategic Doctrine*. Washington, DC: Institute for Policy Studies, 1979.

Arkin, William. *Research Guide to Current Military and Strategic Affairs*. Washington, D.C.: Institute for Policy Studies, 1981.

Arkin, William, and Richard Fieldhouse. *Nuclear Battlefields*. Lexington, Mass.: Ballinger, 1985.

Art, Robert. "A Defensible Defense: America's Grand Strategy After the Cold War." *International Security* 15, no. 4 (Spring 1991): 5–53.

Aspaturian, Vernon. "U.S. Perceptions of Soviet Behavior: Contending Approaches or Analytical Continuum?" In *Containment, Soviet Behavior, and Grand Strategy*, ed. Robert Osgood, 19–28. Berkeley: University of California Press, 1981.

Ball, Desmond. *Can Nuclear War Be Controlled*? Adelphi Paper no. 169. London: International Institute for Strategic Studies, 1985.

———. *Targeting for Strategic Deterrence*. Adelphi Paper no. 185. London: International Institute for Strategic Studies, 1985.

Balthrop, V. William. "Argumentation and the Critical Stance: A Methodological Approach." In *Advances in Argumentation Theory and Research*, eds. J. Robert Cox and Charles Willard, 238–258. Carbondale: Southern Illinois University Press, 1982.

Baugh, William. *The Politics of Nuclear Balance*. New York: Longman, 1984.

Berg, Per, and Gunilla Heroff. "Deep Strike: New Technologies for Conventional Interdiction." In *SIPRI Yearbook 1984*, ed. Stockholm Institute for Peace Research. Philadelphia: Taylor and Francis, 1984.

Betts, Richard. "Conventional Deterrence: Predictive Uncertainty and Policy Confidence." *World Politics* 7, no. 2 (1986): 153–179.

Blair, Bruce. "Alerting in Crisis and Conventional War." In *Managing Nuclear Operations*, eds. Ashton Carter, John Steinbruner, and Charles Zracket, 75–120. Washington, D.C.: The Brookings Institution, 1987.

———. *Strategic Command and Control: Redefining the Nuclear Threat*. Washington, D.C.: The Brookings Institution, 1985.

Booth, Ken. *Strategy and Ethnocentrism*. New York: Holmes and Meier, 1979.

Bracken, Paul. *The Command and Control of Nuclear Forces*. New Haven: Yale University Press, 1983.

Breemer, J. "U.S. Maritime Strategy: A Re-Appraisal." *Naval Forces International Forum for Maritime Power* [hereinafter cited as Naval Forces] 8, no. 2 (1987): 64–77.

Brement, Marshall. "Reflections on Soviet New Thinking on Security Questions." *Naval War College Review* 42, no. 4 (Autumn 1989): 5–21.

Brooks, Linton. "Naval Power and National Security: The Case for the Maritime Strategy." *International Security* 11, no. 2 (1986): 58–88.

———. "Conflict Termination Through Maritime Leverage." In *Conflict Termination and Military Strategy: Coercion, Persuasion and War*, eds. Stephen Cimbala and Keith Dunn, 161–174. Boulder: Westview Press, 1987.

Bundy, McGeorge, George Kennan, Robert McNamara and Gerald Smith. "Nuclear Weapons and the Atlantic Alliance." In *The Nuclear Controversy: A Foreign Affairs Reader*, ed. William Bundy, 23–38. New York: New American Library, 1985.

———. "The Unimpressive Record of Atomic Diplomacy." In *The Nuclear Crisis Reader*, ed. Gwyn Prins. New York: Vintage Books, 1984.

———, et al. "Back From the Brink." *The Atlantic Monthly* (August 1987): 35–45.

Burke, Kenneth. *A Grammar of Motives*, 2nd ed. Berkeley: University of California Press, 1969.

———. *Permanence and Change*, 3rd ed. Berkeley: University of California Press, 1984.

Caravelli, John. "The Role of Surprise and Preemption in Soviet Military Strategy." *International Security Review* 6, no. 2 (Summer 1981): 209–233.

Carter, Ashton, et al. *Managing Nuclear Operations*. Washington, D.C.: The Brookings Institution, 1987.

Cartwright, John, and Julian Critchley. *Cruise, Pershing and SS–20: The Search for Consensus: Nuclear Weapons in Europe*. New York: Brassey's Defense Publishers, 1985.

Chant, Christopher, and Ian Hogg. *Nuclear War in the 1980s?* New York: Harper and Row, 1983.

Charles, Daniel. *Nuclear Planning in NATO: Pitfalls of First Use*. Cambridge: Ballinger Publishing, 1987.

Cimbala, Stephen, ed. *Strategic War Termination*. New York: Praeger, 1986.

Cimbala, Stephen, and Joseph Douglass, eds. *Ending a Nuclear War: Are the Superpowers Prepared?* New York: Pergamon Brassey's International Defense Publishers, 1988.

Cochran, Thomas, et al. *Nuclear Weapons Data Book Volume 1: US Nuclear Forces and Capabilities*. Cambridge, Mass.: Ballinger Publishing, 1984.

Cohen, Donald. *The ABCs of Armaggedon*. New York: Pharos Books, 1988.

Cohn, Carol. "Slick'ems, Glick'ems, Christmas Trees and Cookie Cutters: Nuclear Language and How We Learned to Pat the Bomb." *Bulletin of the Atomic Scientists* 43, no. 5 (1987): 17–24.

Cordesman, Anthony. "Europe's Armies and Extended Deterrence: When Is Enough Enough?" In *Adapting NATO's Deterrent Posture*, eds. Richard Lugar and Robert Hunter. Significant Issue Series no. 7, 27–60. Washington, D.C.: Center for Strategic and International Studies, 1985.

Cotter, Donald. "Peacetime Operations: Safety and Security." In *Managing Nuclear Operations*, eds. Ashton Carter, et al., 17–74. Washington, D.C.: The Brookings Institution, 1987.

Dagleish, Douglas, and Larry Schweikart. "Trident and the Triad." *U.S. Naval Institute Proceedings* [hereinafter Proceedings] 112, no. 6 (June 1986): 73–81.

Dawisha, Karen. "Soviet Ideology and Western Europe." In *Soviet Strategy Towards Western Europe*, eds. Edwina Moreton and Gerald Segal, 26–35. Boston: George Allen and Unwin, 1984.

Dean, Jonathan. *Watershed in Europe*. Lexington, Mass.: Lexington Books for the Union of Concerned Scientists, 1987.

Drury, F. "Naval Strike Warfare and the Outer Air Battle." *Naval Forces* 4, no. 7 (1986): 44–53.

Epstein, Joshua. *The 1988 Defense Budget*. Washington, D.C.: The Brookings Institution, 1987.

———. *The 1990 Defense Budget*. Washington, D.C.: The Brookings Institution, 1989.

Epstein, Joshua, Kim Holmes, John Mearsheimer, and Barry Posen. "Policy Focus: The European Conventional Balance." *International Security* 12, no. 4 (Spring 1988): 152–202.

Ermath, Fritz. "Contrasts in American and Soviet Strategic Thought." In *Soviet Military Thinking*, ed. Derek Leebert, 50–69. Boston: George Allan and Unwin, 1981.

Friedman, Norman. *Desert Victory: The War for Kuwait*. Annapolis: Naval Institute Press, 1991.

Fitzgerald, Mary. "Marshal Ogarkov on the Modern Theater Operation." *Naval War College Review* 34, no. 4 (1986): 6–25.

Flynn, Gregory, ed. *Soviet Military Doctrine and Western Policy*. New York: Routledge, 1989.

Flynn, Nigel. *The Nuclear Duel*. New York: Arco, 1985.

Foster, Richard. "On Prolonged Nuclear War." *International Security Review* 6, no. 4 (Winter 1981–1982): 497–518.

Fraser, Nigel, et al. "New Methods for Applying Game Theory to International Conflict." *International Studies Notes* 3, no. 1 (Winter 1987): 9–18.

Freedman, Lawrence. *The Evolution of Nuclear Strategy*. New York: St. Martin's Press for the International Institute for Strategic Studies, 1983.

———. "Flexible Response and the Concept of Escalation." In *RUSI and Brassey's Defense Yearbook*, ed. Royal United Service Institute, 89–115. Washington, D.C.: Brassey's Defense Publishers, 1986.

Frei, Daniel. *Perceived Images: U.S. and Soviet Assumptions and Perceptions in Disarmament*. Totowa, N.J.: Rowan and Allen, in cooperation with the United Nations Institute for Disarmament Research, 1986.

"A Garthoff-Pipes Debate on Soviet Strategic Doctrine." *Strategic Review* 10, no. 4 (1982): 36–63.

Garthoff, Raymond. "Letter to the Editor." *Comparative Strategy* 2, no. 4 (1980): 365–366.

———. "New Thinking in Soviet Military Doctrine." *The Washington Quarterly* 11, no. 3 (Summer 1988): 131–158.

———. *Deterrence and the Revolution in Soviet Military Doctrine.* Washington, D.C.: The Brookings Institution, 1990.

Gati, Charles. "The Stalinist Legacy in Soviet Foreign Policy." In *Soviet Foreign Policy in a Changing World*, eds. Robbin Laird and Erik Hoffman, 16–28. New York: Aldine, 1986.

Gervasi, Tom. *The Myth of Soviet Military Superiority.* New York: Harper and Row, 1986.

Gillette, Philip, and Willard Frank, Jr., eds. *The Sources of Soviet Naval Conduct.* Lexington, Mass.: Lexington Books, 1990.

Glaser, Charles. "Nuclear Policy Without an Adversary." *International Security* 16, no. 4 (Spring 1992): 34–78.

Goodnight, G. Thomas. "Questions of Evacuation and Survival in a Nuclear Conflict: A Case Study in Public Argument and Rhetorical Criticism." In *Argument in Transition: Proceedings of the Third Summer Conference on Argumentation*, eds. David Zarefsky et al. Annandale, Va.: Speech Communication Association, October 15, 1983.

Gray, Colin. "Letter to the Editor." *Comparative Strategy* 2, no. 4 (1980): 366–368.

———. "What Deters? The Ability to Wage Nuclear War." In *American Defense Policy*, 5th ed., eds. John Reichart and Steven Sturm, 176–187. Baltimore: Johns Hopkins University Press, 1982.

———. "Warfighting for Deterrence." *Journal of Strategic Studies* 7, no. 11 (1984): 5–27.

———. "Maritime Strategy." *Proceedings of the United States Naval Institute* 112, no. 2 (1986): 34–42.

———. *Maritime Strategy, Geopolitics and the Defense of the West.* New York: Ramapo Press for the National Strategy Information Center, 1986.

———. "Strategic Forces." In *American Defense Annual 1986–1987*, ed. Joseph Kruzel, 67–88. Lexington, Mass.: Lexington Books, 1986.

———. *Nuclear Strategy and National Style.* Lanham, Md.: Hamilton Press, 1986.

———. "The Maritime Strategy 1988: Bad Strategy or Global Deterrent?" *Proceedings of the United States Naval Institute* 114, no. 2 (February 1988): 52–59.

———. "Nuclear Strategy: What Is True, What Is False, What Is Arguable." *Comparative Strategy* 9, no. 1 (1990): 1–32.

Gray, Colin, and Jeffrey Barlow. "Inexcusable Restraint: The Decline of American Military Power in the 1970's." *International Security* 109, no. 2 (1986): 27–69.

Green, William, and Theodore Karasik, eds. *Gorbachev and His Generals: The Reform of Soviet Military Doctrine.* Boulder, Co.: Westview Press, 1990.

Gueritz, E. F. "NATO Strategy and Extended Deterrence: The Changing Role of Sea-Based Forces." In *NATO's Maritime Strategy: Issues and Developments. Special Report 1987: The Atlantic Alliance and Western Security: The Maritime*

Dimension, Vol. II, ed. Institute for Foreign Policy Analysis. Washington, D.C.: Pergamon Brassey's International Defense Publishers, 1987.

Hampson, Fen Oster. "NATO's Conventional Doctrine: The Limits of Technological Improvement." *International Journal* 41 (Winter 1985–1986): 159–188.

Haynes, Fred. "Emerging Technologies and Deep Attack Concepts." In *Adapting NATO's Deterrent Posture*, eds. Richard Lugar and Robert Hunter. Significant Issue Series, no. 7, 60–68. Washington, D.C.: Center for Strategic and International Studies, 1985.

Holloway, David. "Soviet Policy and the Arms Race." In *Nuclear Crisis Reader*, ed. Gwyn Prins. New York: Vintage Books, September 1984.

————. *The Soviet Union and the Arms Race*, 2nd ed. New Haven: Yale University Press, 1984.

Jervis, Robert. "What Deters? The Ability to Inflict Assured Destruction." In *American Defense Policy*, 5th ed., eds. John Reichart and Steven Sturm, 161–170. Baltimore: Johns Hopkins University Press, 1982.

————. "Deterrence and Perception." *International Security* 7, no. 3 (Winter 1982–1983): 3–29.

————. *The Illogic of American Nuclear Strategy*. Ithaca, N.Y.: Cornell University Press, 1984.

Journal of the American Forensic Association 24, no. 3 (Winter 1988): entire issue.

Kahn, Herman. *Thinking About the Unthinkable in the 1980's*. New York: Simon and Schuster, 1984.

Kaldor, Mary. "Beyond the Blocs: Defending Europe the Political Way." *World Policy Journal* 1, no. 1 (Fall 1983): 1–21.

Kaplan, Fred. *Dubious Spector: A Skeptical Look at the Soviet Threat*, 4th ed. Washington, D.C.: Institute for Policy Studies, 1984.

Kass, Illana. "Gorbachev's Strategy: Is Our Perspective in Need of Restructuring?" *Comparative Strategy* 8, no. 2 (1989): 181–190.

Kaufmann, William. *A Thoroughly Efficient Navy*. Washington, D.C.: The Brookings Institution, 1987.

Kennedy, William. "The U.S. Defense Organization." In *The Modern US War Machine*, ed. Ray Bond. New York: Crown, 1987.

Kolkowicz, Roman, ed. *The Logic of Nuclear Terror*. Boston: Allen and Unwin, 1987.

Krepon, Michael. *Arms Control: Verification and Compliance*. Foreign Policy Headline Series, no. 270. New York: September/October 1984.

Laird, Robbin, and Dale Herspring. *The Soviet Union and the Strategic Arms Race*. Boulder: Westview Press, 1984.

————. "The Soviet Union and Strategic Arms." In *Soviet Foreign Policy in a Changing World*, eds. Laird and Erik Hoffman, 369–386. New York: Aldine, 1986.

Lambeth, Benjamen. "What Deters? An Assessment of the Soviet View." In *American Defense Policy*, 5th ed., eds. John Reichart and Steven Sturm, 188–197. Baltimore: Johns Hopkins University Press, 1982.

————. "Contemporary Soviet Military Policy." In *The Soviet Calculus of Nuclear War*, ed. Roman Kolkowicz and Ellen Propper Mickiewicz. Lexington, Mass.: Lexington Books, 1986: 25–48.

———. "Theater Forces." In *American Defense Annual 1987–88*, ed. Joseph Kruzel, 89–112. Lexington: Lexington Books, 1987.

Leaning, Jennifer, and Langley Keys, eds. *The Counterfeit Ark: Crisis Relocation for Nuclear War*. Cambridge: Ballinger, 1984.

Leebaert, Derek, and Timothy Dickenson, eds. *Soviet Strategy and New Military Thinking*. New York: Cambridge University Press, 1992.

Levgold, Robert. "The Nature of Soviet Power." In *Soviet Foreign Policy in a Changing World*, eds. Robbin Laird and Erik Hoffman, 29–48. New York: Aldine, 1986.

Levy, Jack. "Misperception and the Causes of War: Theoretical Linkages and Analytical Problems." *World Politics* 36, no. 1 (October 1983): 76–99.

Lind, William. "The Maritime Strategy 1988: Bad Strategy or Global Deterrent?" *Proceedings of the United States Naval Institute* 114, no. 2 (February 1988): 52–59.

Littlejohn, Stephen. "Symbolic Interactionism as an Approach to the Study of Human Communication." *Quarterly Journal of Speech* 63, no. 1 (1977): 84–91.

Lodal, Jan. "An Arms Control Agenda." *Foreign Policy* no. 72 (Fall 1988): 152–172.

Luttwak, Edward. *The Grand Strategy of the Soviet Union*. New York: St. Martin's Press, 1983.

———. *On the Meaning of Victory*. New York: Simon and Schuster, 1986.

Mandelbaum, Michael. *The Nuclear Revolution*. Cambridge: Cambridge University Press, 1981.

MccGwire, Michael. *Military Objectives in Soviet Foreign Policy*. Washington, D.C.: The Brookings Institution, 1987.

McNamara, Robert. *Blundering Into Disaster: Surviving the First Century of the Nuclear Age*. New York: Pantheon Books, 1986.

Mearsheimer, John. "Nuclear Weapons and Deterrence in Europe." *International Security* 9, no. 3 (Winter 1983–1984): 19–46.

———. "A Strategic Misstep: The Maritime Strategy and Deterrence in Europe." *International Security* 11, no. 3 (1986): 3–57.

———. "Back to the Future: Instability in Europe after the Cold War. *International Security* 15, no. 1 (Summer 1990): 5–56.

Miller, Mark. "Soviet Strategic Thought: The End of an Era?" *International Security Review* 5, no. 4 (Winter 1980–1981): 477–510.

Neild, Robert. "What Political Signals Should Our Armed Forces Send?" In *Nuclear Crisis Reader*, ed. Gwyn Prins. New York: Vintage Books, September 1984.

Nichols, Thomas, and Theodore Karasik. "The Impact of 'Reasonable Sufficiency' on the Soviet Ministry of Defense." *Naval War College Review* 42, no. 4 (Autumn 1989): 22–36.

O'Rourke, Ronald. "U.S. Strategic Sealift: Sustaining the Sea Battle." *Naval Forces* 7, no. 3 (1986): 30–39.

Osgood, Charles. "Psycho-Social Dynamics and Prospects for Mankind." In *Disarmament: The Human Factor*, eds. Ervin Laszlo and Donald Keys, 73–91. New York: Pergamon Press, 1981.

Payne, John. *The American Threat: National Security and Foreign Policy*. College Station, Tx.: Lytton Publishing Co., 1981.

Payne, Keith. *Nuclear Deterrence in U.S.-Soviet Relations*. Boulder: Westview Press, 1982.

Peppe, Kevin. "Acoustic Showdown for the SSNs." *Proceedings of the United States Naval Institute* 113, no. 1 (1987).

Posen, Barry. "Measuring the European Conventional Balance." *International Security* 9, no. 3 (Winter 1984–1985): 47–88.

Potter, William. "Perception and Misperception in U.S.-Soviet Relations." *Problems of Communism* 29, no. 2 (March-April 1980): 68–71.

Quatras, Jean. "New Soviet Thinking Is Not Good News." *The Washington Quarterly* 11, no. 3 (Summer 1988): 171–184.

Russett, Bruce. *The Prisoners of Insecurity*. New York: Freeman, 1983.

Sagan, Scott. "Nuclear Alerts and Crisis Management." *International Security* 9, no. 4 (1985): 99–139.

Schelling, Thomas. *The Strategy of Conflict*, 2nd ed. Cambridge: Harvard University Press, 1980.

Schwartz, David. "A Historical Perspective." In *Alliance Security: NATO and the No First Use Question*, eds. John Steinbrunner and Leon Sigal, 5–21. Washington, D.C.: The Brookings Institution, 1983.

Sigal, Leon. *Nuclear Forces in Europe*. Washington, D.C.: The Brookings Institution, 1984.

Simes, Dmitri, "Gorbachev: A New Foreign Policy?" *Foreign Affairs* 65, no. 3 (1987).

Sloan, Ann. "Soviet Positions on Strategic Arms Control and Arms Policy: A Perspective Outside the Military Establishment." In *The Soviet Calculus of Nuclear War*, eds. Roman Kolkowicz and Ellen Mickiewicz, 115–142. Lexington, Mass.: Lexington Books, 1986.

Slocombe, Walter. "The Future of Extended Nuclear Deterrence." In *Adapting NATO's Deterrent Posture*, eds. Richard Lugar and Robert Hunter. Significant Issue Series no. 7, 12–26. Washington, DC: Center for Strategic and International Studies, 1985.

Smith, Steve. "Theory and Policy Analysis: Dealing with the Soviet Threat." In *Clash in the North: Polar Summitry and NATO's Northern Flank*, ed., Walter Goldstein. Washington, DC: Pergamon Brassey's International Defense Publishers, 1988.

Standemaier, William. "Conflict Termination in the Nuclear Era." In *Conflict Termination and Military Strategy: Coercion, Persuasion and War*, eds. Stephen Cimbala and Keith Dunn, 15–32. Boulder: Westview Press, 1987.

Steele, Jonathan. *Soviet Power: The Kremlin's Foreign Policy, Brezhnev to Chernenko*. New York: Simon and Schuster, 1983.

Talbott, Strobe. *Deadly Gambits*. New York: Vintage Books, September 1985.

Train, Harry. "Seapower and Projection Forces." In *American Defense Annual 1986–1987*, ed. Joseph Kruzel, 121–138. Lexington, Mass.: Lexington Books, 1986.

United States Naval Institute. *The Maritime Strategy*. Supplement to the United States Naval Institute Proceedings, January 1984.

Van Der Meer, Frans-Banke. "Impact of Emerging Technologies and Military

Doctrines on Crisis Stability, Arms Control and Disarmament, and Detente." In *Emerging Technologies and Military Doctrine: A Political Assessment*,
eds. Frank Barnaby and Marlies Ter Borg, 251–266. New York: St. Martin's
Press, 1986.

Vermaat, J. A., and Hans Bax. "The Soviet Concept of Peace." *Strategic Review*
11, no. 4 (Fall 1983): 64–70.

Von Tol, Robert. "Soviet Naval Exercises." *Naval Forces* 7, no. 6 (1986).

Watzlawick, Paul. *How Real Is Real?* New York: Vintage Books, February 1977.

"Weapons in Space: Volume II Implications for Security." *Daedalus* 114, no. 3
(Summer 1985).

Weinland, Robert. "The Soviet Naval Buildup in the High North: A Reassessment." In *The Military Buildup in the High North*, eds. Sverre Jarnell and
Kare Nyblom. Boston: University Press of America, 1986.

Williams, David. " 'Drama' and 'Nuclear War' as Representative Anecdotes of
Burke's Theories of Ontology and Epistemology." Paper presented at the
Speech Communication Association Annual Convention, Chicago, Il.,
November 14, 1986.

Wood, Robert. "Strategic Choices, Geopolitics, and Resource Constraints." *The
Washington Quarterly* 12, no. 3 (Summer 1989): 139–156.

Wood, Robert, and John Hanley, Jr. "The Maritime Role in the North Atlantic."
In *The U.S. Navy: View From the Mid–1980's*, ed. James George. Boulder:
Westview Press in Cooperation with the Center for Naval Analysis, 1985.

Zarefsky, David. "Foreign Policy as Persuasion: Lyndon Johnson and Vietnam."
Paper presented at the Speech Communication Association Annual Convention, Washington, D.C.: November 11, 1983.

Index

ABOUT THE AUTHOR

CORI ELIZABETH DAUBER is Assistant Professor of Speech Communication and Director of Forensics at the University of North Carolina at Chapel Hill, where she is a member of the Curriculum on Peace, War, and Defense. She has worked primarily in the area of argument studies and the rhetoric of defense, and has published articles in *Defense Analysis*, *Political Communication and Persuasion*, and the *Journal of the American Forensic Association*.